The Split Time

SUNY series in Theology and Continental Thought

Douglas L. Donkel, editor

The Split Time

Economic Philosophy for Human Flourishing in African Perspective

Nimi Wariboko

Published by State University of New York Press, Albany

Printed in the United States of America

For information, contact State University of New York Press, Albany, NY
www.sunypress.edu

Library of Congress Cataloging-in-Publication Data

Names: Wariboko, Nimi, author.
Title: The split time : economic philosophy for human flourishing in African perspective / Nimi Wariboko.
Description: Albany : State University of New York Press, [2022] | Series: SUNY series in Theology and Continental Thought | Includes bibliographical references and index.
Identifiers: ISBN 9781438489797 (hardcover : alk. paper) | ISBN 9781438489803 (ebook)
Further information is available at the Library of Congress.

10 9 8 7 6 5 4 3 2 1

To Justice A. G. Karibi-Whyte
(1932–2020)

Contents

Acknowledgments

Good luck. May you find what you are looking for in this book, even if it is not there. This is what creativity is about. Be creative in your engagement with this book. Creativity is born neither in your thoughts nor in the book in front of you. It will happen in the interstitial space between your thought and the book. So, leave yourself and leap into the gap between you and the book. In inhabiting the split, you will broaden (contract) yourself; this is to say you will create a conceptual space within you—in the manner of *tzimtzum*—to conjure up and manifest ideas, which are new visitors to our planet. Congratulations: you are a new creator and a great imitator of God. I acknowledge you as a worthy creator within the nothingness, the sacred void that is inside of you.

You as a thinker have mastered the domain of this book and have made the creative leap and fished out innovative ideas, but one thing remains to be done. You need other experts, creators, readers, to acknowledge that your newfound ideas constitute domain-changing creativity. Now you get the point I am after in this acknowledgment. I am because you are. You are because we are, others are. Acknowledgments are always *co-knowledging*, the co-sensing of the creative leap, the co-sharing of the sensation of being. Acknowledgment is the retroactive realization that I as the writer had the boldness to jump into the creative abyss knowing (awkwardly knowing) that you (a stranger, an other) would hold the rope that encircles my waist and you would pull me out if I got lost or run out of air while in it. The rope is still in your hands; pull me out now. Contra Roland Barthes, this author is not dead. He desires to sit by his reader and share a cup of coffee with her. The year 2020 is not the time to drink or eat alone. Let us hold each other a little closer, let us tend the ropes of our relationality more tenderly, and let us, as one family, conspire (breath together) against whatever evil that thwarts our co-flourishing.

Before this book in your hands brought you and me together, I was conspiring with others to get you into our circles. These are Robert Neville and Abimbola Adunni Adelakun, who read the first draft (or portions) of this book and made helpful comments so it would be good enough to ginger you into taking that creative leap. I wish to thank Miroslav Volf and the Yale Center for Faith and Culture (Yale University), who invited me in October 2018 to give a lecture in a workshop on desire, temporality, religion, and human flourishing. That lecture is now chapter 1 of this book, and it was what set me on the course of writing this book. Thanks to Anwuli Ojogwu of Lagos, who copyedited this lecture in the summer of 2018. Nancy de Flon did the copyediting of the whole manuscript.

Thanks to James Peltz, associate director and editor-in-chief at State University of New York Press, who worked with me at various stages of this book. Other staff of SUNY, Diane Ganeles, Eileen Nizer, James Harbeck, Alicia Brady, and Kate R. Seburyamo did wonderful work in bringing this book to the public. I also wish to thank Douglas L. Donkel, editor of the SUNY Series in Theology and Continental Thought, for his support.

Finally, let me thank Rowman & Littlefield for permission to reuse a revised portion (pp. 181–206) of my book *The Principle of Excellence: A Framework for Social Ethics* (2009). Thanks to Springer Nature for permission to reuse portions of my chapter 9, "Between Community and My Mother: A Theory of Agonistic Communitarianism," in *The Palgrave Handbook of African Social Ethics*, edited by Nimi Wariboko and Toyin Falola (2020), pp. 147–163.

Preface

The quest for economic development is arguably the most frustrating and tragic dimension of human existence in Africa. Through the exploration of the notions of destiny, temporality, and desire, I bring together three fundamental aspects of human life to rethink or theorize practical solutions to the problem. The basic aspects of economic life are the *agential* (accounts of human agency, telos), the *circumstantial* (material/social context), and the *affective* (to feel appropriately what matters to a people as an economy/the feeling of human flourishing). In this book I hope to create an evaluative perspective, an economic-philosophical framework in which the circumstantial, the affective, and the agential come together to fire social imagination about economic policies and development projects that can elevate the levels of human flourishing on the continent.

There are long-neglected resources within African philosophy to guide economic policymakers toward creating an African economy that can sustain human flourishing. How can an African government craft an economy that can positively respond to the existential desire of its citizens as it relates to human flourishing? In this book I examine the place and temporal structure of desire in African accounts of human flourishing. I then turn to the implications of the accounts of desire and the temporal structure of human existence for an ethics of economic development in Africa.

The primary task of this book is to construct an economic philosophy from a tradition of thought that is indigenous to Nigeria. As I do not have the ability or sufficient time for an in-depth study of the philosophies of many indigenous groups for this book, I have chosen to focus on the Kalabari-Ijo people. They are located in the Niger Delta in southern Nigeria. Nigeria is a country of over 200 million people in the throes of poverty, economic misery, and corruption, but with great potential for economic development. What are some of the resources within Kalabari philosophy to guide economic policymakers toward creating a Nigerian economy that can sustain human flourishing? How can the Nigerian government craft an economy that can positively respond to the existential desire of Nigerians as it relates to human flourishing?

The resources within Kalabari philosophy that I found most useful for the task at hand are the notions of destiny (*fiyeteboye*, slightly recast as a materialist social theory), time (*saki*), and human flourishing (*ibi-eri, lolo*), three important ideas the combination of which is leavened by a form of desire (*tari*) that circulates around the gap between the existential ideal of *fiyeteboye* (prenatal wishes) and concrete levels of achieved human flourishing or actualization of individual potentialities. Economic policy must be driven by decisions to close this unbridgeable gap.

Desire functions to forestall existential deviation. In the Kalabari philosophy of desire, the space for the motion between existential ideal and achieved human flourishing is always conceptualized as a force of being, the power of an incomplete being-in-the-world. This form of desire is not defined by its circulatory motion around (transcendental, eternal) lack, but operates as an opening through which a person might realize her ideal, step back into it, or reconstruct it to actualize her potentialities or critically comprehend her becoming and identity. Desire as a force of being, as the power of an incomplete being-in-the-world, draws its form and content from women's and men's lived experiences and lived endurances.

Desire here is not merely an affective activity; it is responsiveness to concerns that are conducive to well-being. It is about accountability to things that *matter* to the person. Desire is not some kind of heteronomous weight, a form of alien gravity that determines a person's behavior but is shared autonomy in a "kind of friendship." By desire the individual is open to destiny (*fiyeteboye*), to the existing gaps in actualization of destiny. And desire is the form in which heaven, which anchors prenatal wishes, is opened to the person's lived experiences and lived endurances. In the exercise of shared autonomy and shared doxastic and axiological commitments to her well-being, the individual renders herself rationally beholden to her self-represented *fiyeteboye*.

What does this kind of human desire entail for human flourishing or economic development? Desire is the immanent present/not-yet relation between people and their creativity, between potentiality and actualization, between form and content in the movements of economic development.

Besides, every economy is a *plural agency* constituted and driven not only by the desires of individuals as to the concerns that are conducive to their well-being, but also by the desires of the relationship of *us-ness* that unites and preserves their joint autonomy.

Desire is an opening that every movement toward actualization of potentialities creates between actuality and the not-yet. Desire in this sense has its form as future (coming) events that cast their shadows before them.[1] This is a form initiated by infinite longing, self-actualization. The substance of the shadow is the coming into presence of creativity, the dense actuality of being, a mode of being for human flourishing. This coming into availability, this movement into concentrated actuality, does not happen in some transcendental realm beyond the human world but in the realm of intelligibility, in the phenomenal, embodied human world. Nonetheless, it may be directed toward an eternal being who is (perhaps) fully actualized in a beyond-human realm or directed toward a community telos informed by some belief in an ultimate concern.[2]

The movement of the matter (as form and substance) of desire is not containable. It is an opening like the horizon that forever shifts as one gets close to it. Thus, this form of desire does not try to fill a preexisting lack (*proper lack* or *hole*) or void; it creates the space, the opening it attempts to step into.[3] There is no "there" to constitute a(n eternal or transcendental) site or *para-site*, subsidiary site of "lack" for desire to circulate around. Desire has to create this immanent new space, the new site that it attempts to occupy and fill. The creation of and movement into the new space are simultaneous, in the same way the universe expands by creating its own space and expanding into it. The expanding actualization of potentialities—represented by upward shifts in human flourishing—is in the grip of this form of desire, bending the arc of survival and sustenance toward the not-yet. I consider increasing levels of human flourishing as the visible stand-in and the *name* of the dynamics of desire in an economy. The shifts in the frontiers of human flourishing that mark the concrete expansion (development) of an economy, that reveal an economy's self-revolutionizing force, and that point to the ongoing partial realization of desire are not only the path toward the truth of the desire (as informed, rooted, and routed by *fiyeteboye*) but also part of the truth.

This truth, which I do not claim to be timeless, is pressed into the service of awakening Nigerians. Nigeria is asleep. Nigerians are eating, drinking, defecating, copulating, snoring, dreaming, and praying. And they are approaching the hour of their common awakening. Now is the acceptable time; their emancipation is nearer than when they first dreamed it in 1960. Let those of us that are awaiting their awakening and expecting their *coming* make provision for their action, the capacity to radically alter their inherited dehumanizing systems and cast away the chains that easily beset them. This book offers resources to the persons stirring from their sleep and for stirring the masses toward an emancipatory development paradigm by drawing from indigenous economic philosophy. *The Split Time: Economic Philosophy for Human Flourishing in African Perspective* is written as a response to the question: What kind of economic philosophy does Nigeria need to step on to the stage of sustained human flourishing? This book carefully works out a response in all its transdisciplinary complexities to demonstrate the profound contributions African philosophy can make toward (re)constructing a philosophy of economic development for a humane world. In undertaking this exercise, I have to expand slightly some indigenous ideas. Every time we as Africans must tackle twenty-first-century economic problems by drawing from the past, our indigenous philosophies or received wisdom must be slightly expanded. "Everything up to and including the very nature of pre-capitalist [indigenous communities], so well explained by [our ancestors and their collective philosophies], must here be thought out again."[4]

Introduction

Destiny, Temporality, and Economic Development

The order of destiny is the destiny of order in economic development. To be precise, the order of destiny in Kalabari can inform the destiny of order in Africa's economic development. This is the order of destiny in Kalabari: creative beginning . . . disruption . . . new beginning.[5] This homologizes with the creation . . . destruction . . . creation cycle of economic development (capitalist transformation) that economists, including Joseph Schumpeter, taught us. The order in either the "order of destiny" or in the "destiny of order" is split. Time traverses it and prevents it from being self-identical. Time decenters or destabilizes it and thus its coherency is supported by or intertwined with fantasy. Economic development, like destiny in African (Kalabari) religion, is a mixture of reality and fantasy. Destiny and economic development (human flourishing, human good living) are bound up with our basic "investment in survival" or the temporal dynamics of survival.[6] And our finitude—what can be lost or gained in our time-bound lives—is the foundation of the order we desire or the disorder we fear. Time (this is always split in its sense as a movement of successions—an unstable present that is penetrated by the memory of the past and driven by the anticipation of the future) impinges on the experience of destiny or development not from an outside, but rather from within. Split time constitutes the experience of either form of order from within.

The goal of this book is to introduce readers to the economic philosophic dimensions inherent in ideas, notions, terms, theories, and practices associated with African (traditional) religions (ATR).[7] Once we are able properly to articulate such dimensions, we will proceed to investigate their potential contributions to the crafting of an endogenous paradigm of development for African nations. In particular, this book asks this question: Can indigenous notions in African religion make a contribution to current economic philosophy? And it answers "Yes." It argues that there are notions in African religion that may not only make contributions to economic philosophy but may also inform the processes of enacting a paradigm of economic development in Africa that is oriented toward human flourishing. We explore the possibility of these contributions through the lens of the notion of destiny in the traditional religion of the Kalabari people of the Niger Delta region in Nigeria. The notion of destiny in Kalabari is concerned with the prenatal wishes of an unborn soul that will guide its life course on earth. The wishes not only represent the "first decision" of a subject, but also (supposedly) condition her decision and contingent actions. There is an (often) immanent split between the first decision and subsequent ones or actions. The split is caused by time (temporal successions) that attends all forms of subjectivity. Temporal successions also transform destiny from a pre-given state of conditions (opportunities) into an unstable project.

At the very core of the transformation of traditional or modern society stand some mechanisms that structure destiny and economic development (or capitalist transformation of an economy). These are the production of value and the logic of fantasy. Karl Marx himself argues that human needs have two sides: bodily needs ("use-value") and fantasmatic needs.[8] There is a psychic investment of consumers in the appeal of commodities. This is an investment that is undergirded by the feeling that one's satisfaction is always incomplete; no one specific commodity will ever fulfill desire. Desire becomes drive in the Lacanian sense of the word. There is jouissance obtained from circling around the fantasmatic object or dimension of the object. Destiny also has a "use-value" and a fantasmatic supplement. Destiny functions in two ways. First, destiny as a prearranged path of life (ostensibly) generates "use-value" (purpose) for a life as a lived experience. Second, when people in the traditional community are dealing with hard reality, they use destiny as a "real" prop to support their fantasizing about their nonexistent Reality. Life in the traditional Kalabari world—at least, its symbolic representation—is framed and sustained by destiny as its fantasmatic supplement. Time as a negativity in the heart of life or existence forces it to generate its own supplement, spectral double. Both destiny and economic development are sustained by (or need) fantasy—but not odd fancies.

Every induction of citizens into the processes and promises of economic development involves some sort of "seduction" whereby their commitment to a nation's push for the (capitalist) transformation is always, in part, sustained by a fantasmatic supplement, a future enjoyment of possibilities undergirded by fantasy.[9] The fantasmatic supplement is needed because economic development is decentering, traumatic, or lacking—the lack of satisfaction of desire, the absence of the ultimate guarantee of eudaimonia, the lack of its completion in a community's lifetime. Time always renders economic development incomplete. Time as pure difference ensures the nonidentity of every destiny with itself. Destiny is an attempt to fixate logical, conceptual, or fantasmatic objects on an empirical life "and to conceal the gap that separates the two realities," to hide the gap between eternity (heaven) and temporality (earth), transcendence and immanence, to bridge essence (the ideal) and existence (the real).[10] Similarly, economic development is an endeavor to bridge the gap between empirical conditions of poverty (underdevelopment, inadequate prosperity) and an envisioned site of a higher level of human flourishing. The gap that separates destiny from itself is the same gap that renders economic development always incomplete: time. Time is not even identical with itself. It also has a double character. The presence is always wracked by the traces of the past and the anticipations of the future.

Destiny is structured as economic development. Destiny in Kalabari is an unconscious. The unconscious is economics. This does not mean that economics is unconscious or that we can reduce economic development to unconscious complexes. It means three things. First, the notion of destiny informs us about how to think of the complexes of information and decision-making in the task of economic development. Second, the subjects (citizen-believers) of destiny (the unconscious) are formally included in the labor of economic development. Third, destiny is a logic of fantasy (imagination). It is fantasy that undergirds the perceived conjunction of prenatal wishes and their earthly value. The two are, in reality, separated by temporality, and each of them is undermined by the same. Prenatal wishes point to a relationship between heaven and actualization of human potentialities on earth, making heavenly sanction (approval) both the sign of human flourishing and a subject to whom the sign can be attributed. Existential (earth-bound) value, however, concerns the actualization of the subjects' potentialities, which is subject to temporality that is without heavenly sanction. Time (temporality) is the sign under which both the human subject and her flourishing happens. The logic of time and its movement does not take orders from words "spoken" before birth. As I will demonstrate throughout this book, time works to split destiny, to make it non–self-identical once it reaches earth. The conjunction of prenatal wishes (pre-spoken words without temporality) and its existential value (temporality without pre-spoken words) is sutured by fantasy.

This book attempts to ground an African philosophy of economic development in the African notion of destiny that is always destabilized, disrupted, and transformed from a state into a movement. Drawing from the Kalabari notion of destiny that can be changed, that can be renegotiated with God (deity, heaven)—making destiny as not ahistorical—it offers a notion of human flourishing that is driven by immanent desires. Not to put a fine point on it, this is to say that this book examines the production of destiny by time and not by eternity or divinity. It thereby proposes a conception of human flourishing in terms of the immanent movement of disruptions that constitutes economic development. Though the belief of destiny was developed in a religious setting, it is quite amenable as a philosophical notion to enable us to understand the logic of value and the logic of fantasy that undergird the capitalist transformation of economies or the economic development process.

Among other contributions, this book demonstrates the importance of the economic significance of African religious concepts and the critical roles they can play in forging an African economic philosophy of development. I engage the terms and practices on a philosophic register while seeking economic and social solutions to the impediments confronting Africa's economic development. I also raise a call for a more engaged study of the religious underpinnings of Africa's economic development at a time when economic policy-making is dominated by a "technical mindset" that disdains indigenous knowledge systems.

Our efforts to bring the indigenous religious notion of destiny into the modernist discourse of economic development contribute to the demythologization of destiny in African religion. The interpretation of destiny undertaken in this book amounts to a rejection or a downplaying of the cosmological division of two-tiered world, eternal and temporal—at least when it comes to the analysis of human flourishing in the purview of the economic transformation of nations. Our interpretation also moves the focus from souls to subjects when trying to understand the economic philosophical implications of the notion of destiny. Subjects (interpreted under the aegis of materialist theory) rather than souls (agents in premodern cosmologies) are the key agent in our phenomenological world of modern economies. In this very move we also hope to demystify neoclassical development economic thinking.[11] ATR's notion of destiny next to development economic thinking questions the tendency of most economic experts to ignore how indigenous notions can inform the ethos of economic development in Africa. As we shall demonstrate throughout this book, the Kalabari notion of destiny is a veritable tool to deciphering a people's perceptions of their world or decision-making orientation. This notion at its heart shows how human beings generate information about their environment when there is uncertainty and things are not going as normally expected, and how they procced to make decisions or take concrete actions based on the changing perceptions of their dynamic world.

Economic development is an outcome of decisions and unplanned human actions. The notion of (or belief about) destiny in Kalabari traditional religion embeds in itself a theory of how perceptions of the world inform how human beings (agents) act or make decisions. If properly harnessed, this theory can enrich our understanding of economic development. Decisions or human actions are a process that extends over time and depends on three main types of orientation toward information or assumptions about how economic actors perceive the world. First, we can postulate that though we cannot absolutely know the future we can today predict the form it would take tomorrow. It is believed that we can know the set of random variables and the range of values they can take tomorrow. Decision makers start with a range of probability distributions that they continually update in the light of experience. The world is perceived as a world of risk (uncertainty). Second, others perceive the world not as that of risk and uncertainty. Decision makers are ignorant of the future. The agent may know some of the variables and not others. She believes some variables can suddenly emerge, and thus probability judgment based on the updating of information in the light of experience is not useful. The key orientation that drives decision-making is not risk or uncertainty, but ignorance. This calls for alertness. Finally, the third approach holds that the question is not about whether the future can be known, estimated, or discovered. The agent is bent toward searching for and discovering opportunities that might aid his or her flourishing. It is about creating the future, starting from the assumption that it does not exist and is indeterminate at any moment of decision-making. "The agent's task is not to estimate or discover, but to create. He must therefore exercise imagination. The agent is aware of the flimsiness of his conjectures about the future and the vulnerability of his plans to the independent imagination of other agents."[12] These three perceptions of the world or decision-making orientation are discernible in the notion of destiny in Kalabari traditional religion, which projects human beings as uncertain about their environments and posits that their perceptions of it change over time. Hence, it is expected that their decisions will change over time. This is not the usual way scholars interpret the notion of destiny; it is usually presented as a static concept. The Kalabari notion of destiny has three types of process that "focus attention on quite different devices that might be used by agents as a means of increasing their information about their environment or reducing their exposure to uncertainty."[13] Of course, this articulation of the three processes is based on my interpretation.

There are three types of process in the Kalabari notion of destiny. First there is *fiyeteboye*. Before a soul is born it goes before God to decide what its life course on earth will be—the vicissitudes of her particular life. This is the stock interpretation of destiny. But there is a difference here. The soul, on reaching earth, cannot remember its prenatal wishes. Thus, her conscious self does not know what she wished. Destiny is a form of unconscious. The problem is that of ignorance, and over time the person learns to know some components of her life course and not others. She discovers things about herself that she did not know before. Assuming things are not working well for her, she can go to a diviner to renegotiate with God and revoke her prenatal destiny. (This is a key difference between the Kalabari notion of destiny and those of many other communities in Africa. Destinies are revocable![14]) The process of the revocation of destiny is called *bibibari*. The person chooses a new destiny, and thus the form that her future will take is known in advance. There is risk and uncertainty in the sense that the variables that condition her life and the range of their values operate by means of probability distribution. The process of *bibibari* might not deliver the level of human flourishing the agent needs. There is the third process of *after-bibibari*. The person uses her imaginative vision to create the future she wants. In processes of *fiyeteboye* and *bibibari,* the agent assumes that a determinate future exists, and it could be known or unknown. Yet, in the process of *bibibari*, the agent has started to use her imaginative vision to craft an alternative world or plan of well-being for herself, believing that the future is indeterminable or nonexistent. *After-bibibari* is just one more device of managing her exposure to uncertainty and supplementing the information she has about her environment by her imagination. There is a crucial difference between *after-bibibari* and *bibibari. Bibibari* is beholden to the imaginary of transformation as in moving from an old fixed order to a new fixed order, from one determinate future to a new and improved determinate future. *After-bibibari* seems to usher in a new interpretation of destiny. Rather than basing the expectation of her life on her past prenatal wishes or the renegotiation of them as a transformation of the past into a site for a new and improved fixed formation, she now bases it on her imagination. She puts forward an account of destiny that is constantly changing, that has a fluid character. Destiny as a "solid" has entered into a liquid phase. Destiny is now something that stimulates her own imagination of her flourishing.

What is discernible in the notion and practice of destiny in Kalabari are three approaches to the world: *fiyeteboye* is characterized by ignorance and alertness, *bibibari* by risk and estimation, and *after-bibibari* by indeterminacy and creativity.[15] In this book, I will deploy the Kalabari notion of destiny to articulate a vision of economic development and human flourishing. Our study will focus on the approach of *after-bibibari* to think of economic development as a disruptive process that creates something new. What kind of theo-economic and social-ethical influences should be brought to bear on citizens, Nigerians, as they exercise their imagination? We are not going to assume that economic development is a thing, a well-defined optimal or pregiven state that exists out there, and that reaching it is ultimately what economic advancement or human flourishing is all about (*fiyeteboye* information-decision process). It is also not about following the *bibibari*-type. This model assumes that the information about Nigeria's logic and dynamic of economic development is either known or unknown and what citizens need to do is to discover and react to new economic and technological opportunities over time. The *after-bibibari* approach holds that all actions and decisions must be taken in the "light of imagined future conditions and hence emphasizes creativity and uncertainty."[16] The task before us now is to show how the creativity and imagination in the Kalabari dynamic notion of destiny can be harnessed as the fundamental framework of economic development in Africa. The notion—as I am interpreting it here—is an acknowledgment of structural uncertainty and complexities in the lived world and how best to cope with them rather than downplaying them. Earlier interpretations of the Kalabari notion of destiny have tended to downplay its dynamism and emphasized its false fixity as unchanging fate. With this approach, they missed the potential contributions it can make to our understanding of how a people should orient themselves to the uncertainty concerning economic development. The flawed line of reasoning also missed the important insight that the Kalabari notion of destiny is about individual innate potentialities that can only be actualized in a relationship with a person's community. To think of destiny in relation to economic development is to think of how a society can create the social imagination and capabilities that can enable persons to be all that they can be and contribute to the betterment of their community. This is a dynamic process and never a done deal.

It is always about the continuous production of subjectivity that is the primary step in the pursuit of economic development. This is the production that goes into every other production of economic transformations. What is the connection between belief in destiny and *bibibari* and the constitution of subjects for economic development? *Fiyeteboye-bibibari* speaks to four key components of economic subjectivity: desire, change, choice, and fantasy. The *fiyeteboye-bibibari* syntagma speaks to the constitution of subjectivity by producing a *desire* that plays off on the gap between the ideal good (consumption, human flourishing) and the real one. As a procedure of subjectivation the gap moves a person to subject herself to practices and virtues that will enable her to attain her ideal (pre-given) level of human flourishing. When the pre-given is not attainable, she *changes* the course of her patterned actions (after a period of self-probing and self-interpretation) and makes a new *choice* of an ideal level of flourishing, satisfaction of desire. Desire, change, and choice are all supported by fantasy. This fantasy is never a metastatic vision whereby a person denies reality and believes that mundane conditions will be divinely transfigured to create a new world for her. Fantasy is an imaginary that articulates the other three key components (desire, change, and choice) to forge an (new) order of meaning. Indeed, economic development requires the human capability that Mr. Thomas Gradgrind deprecates in Charles Dickens's *Hard Times* as "fancy." But according to Martha Nussbaum, such fancy leads to certain postures of mind, creating the "ability to imagine nonexistent possibilities, to see one thing as another and one thing in another, to endow a perceived form with a complex life."[17] By enabling citizens to imagine possibilities, thinking about worlds that do not yet exist, the public policymakers become an aid to acknowledging the present economic condition and its limitations and to making choices in it more reflectively.

The human being is never passive before destiny and is not belittled because of its operation in her; instead, her subjectivity is forged and enhanced. She plays an integral part in the process of her destiny, a life course that cannot be brought to completion without her intervention. Her destiny's operation and its alteration require her contribution. Since she (that is, her life course) was created in the image of her prenatal words, her first duty on earth is to create, to sculpt her life. Her unique capacity as a creator is not abolished here on earth—she is to perfect her life and her worlds through her creative acts. Her life course requires her contributions for its completion. She is a true partner in the act and course of her destiny. This, in my opinion, is the primary and most important philosophical import of the *fiyeteboye-bibibari-after-bibibari* syntagma.

To grasp the import of this syntagma is to realize that for the Kalabari "life is painting a picture not doing a sum."[18] Kalabari approach destiny not content to show what has happened or what is fixed to happen, but to show themselves, as Aristotle might say, "things such as might happen." Destiny is directed at human possibilities. So is economic development, properly or broadly conceived.

Destiny—the *fiyeteboye-bibibari-after-bibibari* triumvirate—is a form of life: a person recognizes that her life is under a transimmanent word (telos) and she periodically evaluates her actions to know whether they conform to or deviate from the telos. This orientation to create an order that bestows meaning on her existence can exercise a constitutive function in the performance of economic development. The "inner form" of this orientation as creativity is conducive to the creative-destructive impulse of economic transformation. The subject of this orientation is a divided subject—the Kalabari person is split from her unconscious prenatal wishes. In this sense, the person does not know what she "wanted" and her prenatal phenomenal "I" does (may) not want what she desires in her post-natal phenomenal "I."

Destiny and Split Subjectivity: "I Propose Where I Am Not"

Destiny is about an unborn soul in the eternal realm working out its life course before coming into the world. The life course is the undergirding power and driver of the purpose of the soul's earthly sojourn. Destiny is about the purpose of life and is the great qualifier or conditioner of human existence. A person's existence is about standing out and standing in pre-defined purpose. Destiny could be regarded as "I propose, therefore I am." The coming of the soul to earth splits the "I propose" from the "I am." Thought and being are disconnected by time, by temporality. Destiny becomes "I proposed where I am not, therefore I am where I did not propose. I am not whenever the ontological 'I propose' is not self-identical with me."[19] The "I" that proposed is not identical with the "I" that is; the "therefore I am" is not the content of the "I propose." The "I" is split, non-identical with itself. This is the repressed truth of the African (Kalabari) notion of destiny that tries to conceal the non-identity of thinking (enunciation in heaven) and being (subject of the enunciated on earth). It posits identity as harmonious when it is actually split.[20] Where the person is *is* not what the person proposed to "purpose" his life and where he is *is* not what he purposed to propose. The split is between the frozen image of the self that was proposed before earthly existence, to pursue as the telos of existence, and the real self in existence, which is at odds with this frozen image. The identity between being and thinking (the metaphysical image of the self as thought, that which precedes subjectivity) is split. The thought or destiny as the signifier is unable to fully signify itself on earth, and therefore all earthly existence or subjectivity is ontologically cracked. Or thought cannot fully support substantial being. We (propose) purpose where we are not and are not where we propose (purpose). The subject is not located where the thought originated in reference to the gaze of the other, the divine other. It is elsewhere, in the phenomenal self. The split is even inherent in the original proposition: "I propose therefore I am." The "I" that proposed in the eternal realm is not equivalent to the "I" that exists. The "I" that proposed constituted the symbolic "I" through its agency. As per meaning of destiny the substantive, positive contents of the symbolic "I" come from the metaphysical "I." This split is masked by the illusion that there is one "I," a single (instead of double-natured), harmonious "I" in both of them. But the "I" is traversed, cut by time. It is cut by time not only in the sense of temporality being an external relation between the two "I's," but also by the internal inconsistency of time, which constitutes the unstable, decentering, and groundless link between them.[21] Time is a cut. It makes a difference between two components, the "I's." It is also the foundation of differentiation in each of the components. Time makes each one of them—whether signifier or signified—as difference in itself. This is to say, time makes each component not to be self-identical.

In the scholarly discussion of destiny in African religion, the role of time is often ignored. At the minimum, intellectuals ignore or downplay how temporality corrupts, disrupts, or changes destiny and even leads to the forgetting of destiny. In this book we want to ensure that time is integral to our understanding of destiny. As we shall demonstrate later, the split in the subject is a function of the split in time. In order properly to understand destiny and its place in the conceptualization of human flourishing we must make time the prime mover and distinctive feature of our analysis in this book. The book examines the production of destiny by time (that is, split time) and not by eternity or divinity. The method of this book is a unification of African religious thought, continental philosophy, and economic theory for an understanding of the relations between destiny, desire, temporality, and human flourishing.

Organization of Chapters

The goal of this section of any book's introduction is twofold. First, to address each of the particular chapters of the book. Second, to relate each of them to the unifying structure (process) of the book. In this organizing structure each preceding chapter should seamlessly call forth its subsequent chapter. This is to say, each chapter should flow into the next in a logical manner of either how the subject is unfolding or some questions, issues, and unexplored paths of the underlying argument in a chapter demand to be treated in the one following it. When all these are done well the reader can see (sense) the overarching plan for the book. If the parts of the introduction before "organization of chapters" have adequately laid out the main arguments of the book in their outline form, explained their structural integrity, carefully aided the reader to avoid any misunderstanding, and informed the reader about the methodology of the book, then this last section is likely to imprint the overarching plan for the book in the reader's mind. This is what I intend to do here.[22]

Chapter 1 ("Religion, Temporality and Desire") presents the whole book's arguments *in nuce*. For in this chapter all of the fullness of the book is exemplified or dwells in the form of a swatch to its cloth. This chapter foreshadows key arguments of the chapters that come after it. In it we find the basic arguments of the book that relate to the human creative act, ontological principle, destiny, desire, human flourishing, and temporality. It begins with an analysis of the temporal structure of the process of economic growth, a condition necessary for raising the levels of human flourishing. It investigates what holds together the three temporal modes of any economy. I name this "thing" as the *human creative act*. The creative act is the ultimate reality of the economy. It is the context in which creative things, the creativity of the various sectors, and the temporal modes of the overall economy are relevant to one another. I ground this conception of temporality of economy in African religious notions of God, divine creativity, and personhood (subjectivity). Desire, temporality, and human flourishing are rooted in one ontological principle: the *togetherness* of the three temporal modes of the human creative act that is itself undergirded by an *ontological creative act.*

This chapter moves on to demonstrate the connection or interface between economic development and destiny. Economic development not only elevates the order of human flourishing, but also is a transformation of humanity itself. Broadly and properly understood, economic development is a magnificent unfolding of human potentialities—a continuous actualization of human flourishing—in a particular context. This perspective on economic development easily fits the Kalabari notion of destiny. Destiny is not the truth of one's existence on which one can settle down forever, but a short-run series of completeness in the long run of incompleteness of actualization of human potentialities. The truth of destiny and the truth of economic development, as this chapter demonstrates, are connected by the forces of desire and temporality. The chapter offers an analysis of human flourishing in the tensions between temporality and desire, between destiny and economic development.

On the whole, this chapter sets out the logic and experience of the Kalabari people in the movements and counter-movements of destiny, desire, temporality, and economic development. This is all about their participation in their ongoing drama of actualization of potentialities, the increase and transformation of the order of human flourishing. This participation is always broken, penetrated, or decentered by the finitude that attend all human existence. And the participation is bound up with or animated by their primary "investment in survival."

The chapters that follow move from the broad, panoramic perspective of the drama to individual scenes, so to speak. Thus, chapter 2 takes up destiny and desire, chapter 3 looks at temporality and desire, chapter 4 dwells on economy and destiny in the light of a theory of agonistic communalism, and chapter 5 addresses economic development in the light of actualization of human potentialities. The lines of meaning in chapter 1 wind their way throughout the other chapters. The entire argument of the book is prefigured in chapter 1. The soul of the book is chapter 1 and the other chapters constitute its body. The nature and excellence of the soul is gradually grasped as we comprehend the excellence of the body. At the end, the soul emerges or re-emerges as the culmination, compactness, or community substance of the advances of the other chapters. Thus, there is an integral relation between the first chapter and the rest of the chapters. It is only in the glare or shelter of the soul of the first chapter that the other chapters unfold the potentialities of their arguments; and without the ordering and deepening of the whole book by the truths of the other chapters the soul loses its courage to be.

Chapter 2 ("Destiny and Desire: An Ontology of Human Flourishing") formulates a theory of destiny in Kalabari as a preparatory step toward demonstrating what insights it can possibly shed on economic development or to inform the economist's search for standards of evaluating development policies. Destiny is neither a fixed course that must be inexorably followed nor an iron cage that confines or constricts human life. Rather, destiny is a sermon on the prenatal sentence (*fiyeteboye*) as its text.[23] This text is not something that is out there to be discovered or read. It is unknown and forgotten.[24] The text, indeed, is the Kalabari person's engagement with the whole of her existence. It is her participation in being and human culture, community. The text is the experiencing of herself as a consciousness striving for human flourishing in the tension of existence. *Fiyeteboye* (a metonymic sentence) seen as a text that precludes the person, its writer, from essentially knowing it is a term that speaks to human beings "falling" into existence, the innocence of essence, potentiality falling into existence, which it cannot leave alone—as Paul Tillich might put it. To put it differently, for *fiyeteboye* as text, existence is its own essence. The text—rather, the substance of the text—is the subject. Its truth is the real only as the deeds of the subject.[25] Kalabari people say "*tombo tombo so*," meaning "let a person (human being) become a person (human being)." A person is both her own subject and predicate. A person is a person as she actualizes her potentiality. This is given as an imperative. The indicative of being a human demands the imperative of personhood. Destiny is practically a notion of subjectivation that carries the idea that a person becomes what actually he or she is essentially and therefore potentially in the contingency of time. Becoming a true person is thus a moral imperative. It is deemed immoral not to do and actualize what one is essentially and potentially capable of doing. This idea also applies to groups and communities, as each of them has its *fiyeteboye*. Ethics of development or societal transformation is in a sense internal to the subjectivation process founded on Kalabari philosophic notion of destiny.

Let me now give a few insights into the arguments of chapters 2 to 5 as they relate to economic development. The insight of chapter 2 is that if we want to comprehend the destiny of economic development we must understand the destiny of the human beings that work for its actualization. This is to say, we must investigate how they interpret their anthropology and its weightiness in stimulating and sustaining increasing levels of human flourishing, which is always unfinishable. And if we have a notion of the highest actualization of human destiny or potentiality, as understood by the people, we must craft the standards for evaluating the effectiveness of economic policies (paradigms) for maximum actualization of human potentiality.

I seek to draw out the standards or principles of interpretation from the Kalabari materials available to me. I do not approach this study with *a priori* methodological tools or categories of thought. Rather, I have approached the doctrines and practices in Kalabari religion and the experiences of the people not only as "documents" that show how Kalabari make sense of their encounters with reality, but also as "texts" that offer their *secrets* in an open-ended inquiry. What I mean by *secrets* here is not some esoteric or hidden patterns that can only be seen by a select few, but the evocative centers of their materials. I believe that there are some sites of concentration of meanings in these materials that give coherence to Kalabari people's existence and self-interpretation.[26] In this way, the theoretical formulations of this chapter—and, indeed, of the whole book—were born and borne by the materials.

Chapter 3 ("Temporality and Desire") makes the argument that time, temporality, crafts a lack, a gap within the human being, a shocking space around which desire circulates. Time does this by virtue of the fact that it simultaneously gives us and withdraws experience; it renders and protects human beings from surprises, always playing on experience and novelty. "It is experience that best affords us protection from surprises, and the production of shock always implies a gap in experience. To experience something means divesting it of novelty, neutralizing its shock potential."[27] Time as the fragile, fleeting, and slippery para-site of event and structure simultaneously situates the human being in the past place of experience and withdraws her in the non-place that promises the new, novelty of the future. Time is always approaching and withdrawing approach. This tango of the experienceable and the unexperienceable places a gap, a shocking split, an abiding lack at the center of existence that desire "longs" to suture. The interplay of the experienceable and the unexperienceable engenders lost and hope and our investments of converting them to reasons for survival are our primary engagement with temporal dynamics.

Time is disjoined within itself. Its being (the present or its presence) is always what it is not (past) and what it is yet to become (the future). This is time's basic split or essential negativity. It never grasps itself as a harmonious whole, as an entirety, or even as self-identical. This is all so because it has gaps within it. This negative character structures human existence; striving for survival is about inhabiting these gaps, making provision for the gaps, putting themselves between the past and the future. Human beings are always struggling not only to relate to the world as it *is*, but also *as it can be* given a particular vision of unexplored possibilities. In this venture of mediating the worlds of "is" and "as," they insert themselves between the past and future of the time spectrum. From here they push toward a new horizon of possibilities. Suspended between (or subtracted from) the "no more" (or no longer acceptable) and the "not-yet," they face two antagonists like Franz Kafka's parable of the *He*.[28]

Kafka's *He* has the dream of jumping out of the struggle. But this is not possible for any group of human beings or nation. The "place of time" is their unavoidable site of struggle against the dark forces of past and future. No nation can afford to elude this battle if it wants to create a flourishing economy. At a deeper level the parable is about human beings stepping into the continuum of time to create a gap between the past and future where they can change the meaning of the past and stop or redirect its perceived evil trajectory in order to help life better flourish.

Making provision for the future is what an economy is all about. Indeed, the key character of the economy is the provision for the future.[29] What kind of ethical, philosophical framework should guide the making of provision for the future for the purpose of human flourishing? The task here is to think of economic development as a *praxis*, in which society posits human potentiality—destiny—as the point of departure and character of the economy. In economic development as praxis, economic growth is not merely a means to the end of fattening the stock market or posing with a big gross domestic product, but a social process in which means and end coincide. Economic development is a communal process (common-good project), a means that contains its proprietary end within itself. The people are both the means and end of their economic development; economic development is doing what is right and just for the community. This is about the actualization of human potentiality as the concrete activity and essence of making provision for the future, so every member of the community can be the best that he or she can be given their gifts, endowment, and communal support.

At the minimum, economic development should involve the creation of possibilities for community and participation by all its members so that their potentialities can be drawn out for the common good. An economic development paradigm should be adjudged good because it allows citizens to develop their potentialities in the pursuit of ever-greater common good. How well an economy does this will depend on how it allows individuals to develop their unique traits, capabilities, and potentialities and on how well these individual endowments are related to each other in the pursuit of the common good. A properly, ethically organized economy is the one that is adept at combining these two opposite tendencies or processes: a movement toward uniqueness counterbalanced by movement toward union. We will craft a notion of agonistic communitarianism to articulate this delicate balance. This will enable us to explore the emancipatory possibilities of communitarianism. The concept of agonistic communitarianism is developed in chapter 4 ("Economy and Destiny: A Theory of Agonistic Communitarianism) in relation to the basic questions concerning human flourishing, economic development, and temporality. Chapter 5 ("Pursuit of Excellence and Economic Development") interprets the notion of excellence (*arete*) as the actualization of human potentialities, which is one form of overcoming obstacles to economic development, a way of removing "unfreedoms" that thwart humanourishing, as Amartya Sen might argue.[30]

Chapters 4 and 5 constitute the part of the book where I discuss the vision of the economy that is informed by our study of split time, destiny, desire, and human flourishing. Specifically, these two chapters examine the relationship between economic ethics and the principal concepts that organize this study. In these chapters I argue that for economic ethics to adequately recognize the place of desire and the temporal structure of desire in any community's account of human flourishing, it must work to "privilege a path" for every member of the community. The notion of "privileging a path" speaks to the logic of differentiation and differential gearing that every individual need in order to drive toward self-fulfillment and human flourishing at their own preference and pace within the context of a community that puts a premium on human dignity and equality.

The study concludes by articulating the philosophical theory that undergirds, informs, and impels the socioethical model we have developed for Africa's economic development in chapter 6 ("Naija-Dialectics: Theory and Methodology"). In this chapter I unconceal the core, fundamental theory of this book that not only informs the development paradigm I recommended in the preceding chapters, but also crafts a logic of reality, offers a hermeneutic of hope, and undergirds the methodology of this study. The methodology of this book performs a form of philosophy of economic development and reflects a certain logic and dynamic of reality that undergird social existence. My philosophical method is not just about reasoning and production of knowledge, but rather it is also a reflection of the structural core and rational movement of all reality as comprehended from the Kalabari worldview. The structure of reality is informed and shaped by hope. The underlying structure of all reality is hope, the possibility of continuance of human coexistence amid all that thwarts human flourishing. Thus, any socio-philosophical analysis that draws from this worldview is better served if it works from a knowledge platform where method meets content and cultivates a hermeneutic of hopeful human coexistence. Economic philosophy connects directly to foundational methodological logic and it is normed by hope-driven hermeneutics of reality (Being).

The Kalabari logic of reality could be cast in this way: thesis ➡ antithesis ➡ *transthesis* (*nuvothesis*). Four quick notes about this dialectic: First, unlike the commonplace understanding of Hegelian dialectics, the movement ends not in a synthesis, but in a new (*novo*) thesis, something new that explodes an inherited order of being. The *novothesis* is a thesis, an event, an ("terrifying") excess beyond the coordinates of the thesis and antithesis, and yet is inherent to the potentiality and im-potentiality of the order of being. Indeed, neither our past nor our present or future is closed.

Second, the novothesis posits that the system, order of being, is not structurally determined and closed and is not moving toward transcendence and totalization. Novothesis is the non-constructible set. A core belief of the Kalabari people is *Ngei konte*: there remains one more. There is always an unfinished business, one more thing to do. People in the culture are always reminded of this fact, and in Kalabari Ekine Society (an arts and dancing, and governing club) this belief is constantly broadcast via drum lore at the times of masquerade displays. According to the religion historian G. O. M. Tasie, amid drumming for the masked dancers, the chief drummer will punctuate "his messages with the conventional *Ngei konte* of the *Ekine*, meaning 'one more.' This is to indicate to the masquerade that there is always an unfinished business in the *Ekine* requiring the *Sekibo* member [dancer] to be on the guard all the time."[31]

Third, the site of new coexistence or possibility follows not from the trajectory of the thesis and antithesis, or the past and the present, but from an emergent site, a new way of being that is to come. The vision of this possible new site is always powered by hope and alternative logic. The movement from thesis-antithesis to novothesis is not accomplished by a parallax shift wherein we realize that the antithesis is already in the thesis and this recognition is the (basis of the) synthesis. The movement is by what I will call a *transfinite shift*. By this I mean the freeing of reality or ontology from a single structure or movement as we view it through the lens of the infinite.

The transfinite thesis implies, posits, holds that there is a least a thesis, a "site" whose possibilities, features, numbering, or *modus operandi* exceeds every configuration, order, or sequence of relations constructed or embedded in the thesis or antithesis. The transfinite thesis signifies the unreachable end of human flourishing going by the logic of thesis, antithesis, and synthesis or counting motion one by one. Even this unreachable end can be exceeded by generating ever larger vision of what already appears "infinite," ad infinitum. This means there is no notion of the biggest vision or most powerful thesis to attain. If we have one transfinite thesis we can always construct another that exceeds it. In itself, the transfinite thesis is an infinite sequence.

The infinite sequence does not imply that the motion or dynamic of the transfinite thesis goes beyond history or nature. There is no thing more than the common movement of and apposition to the finite in a life-world alone. The theory is that all order of existence, order of things, is transfinite, which implies that the usual motion of *thesis and antithesis to synthesis* is not the normal state of social existence, but rather an exceptional case forced upon an order of things, forced on the transfinite thesis, by limiting circumstances.

Finally, those of us from Africa to whom the world has said there is no hope owe it to ourselves, and the rest of the world, to pursue the un-foreclosed and un-foreclosable options of existence. We owe it to our children and grandchildren to imagine what is beyond the current horizon in our current phase of life and economic development. We have to think in terms of possibility—in possibilities only!

Chapter 1

Religion, Temporality, and Desire

Introduction

This chapter examines the place of desire and the temporal structure of desire in Kalabari accounts of human flourishing. It will look at the implications of these for the ethics of economic development in Nigeria. It begins with the temporal structure of the process of economic growth, a condition necessary for raising the levels of human flourishing.

Following philosophical theologian Robert Cummings Neville, I will investigate what holds together the three temporal modes of any economy: a thing I name the *human creative act*. The creative act is the ultimate reality of the economy. It is the context in which creative things, the creativity of the various sectors, and the temporal modes of the overall economy are relevant to one another. In section 2, I will ground this conception of the temporality of economy in Kalabari notions of God, divine creativity, and personhood (subjectivity). Desire, temporality, and human flourishing are rooted in one ontological principle: the *togetherness* of the three temporal modes of the human creative act that is itself undergirded by the *ontological creative act*. Section 3 examines the relationship between economic ethics and the ontological principle. In this section I argue that for economic ethics to adequately recognize the place of desire and the temporal structure of desire in any community's account of human flourishing, it must work to "privilege a path" for every member of the community. The notion of "privileging a path" speaks to the logic of differentiation and differential gearing that every individual needs in order to move toward self-fulfillment and human flourishing at their own preference and pace within the context of a community that puts a premium on human dignity and equality. The chapter concludes by highlighting the benefits of the alternate world of thought we have offered on economic development.

1. Temporality and Economic Development

Let us define economic development as the creation of special and novel possibilities in an economy. This definition suggests that an economy has developed a capacity to shift toward producing more goods and services and create possibilities of increasing the levels of human flourishing for all its citizens. This description implies a shifting of the *production possibility frontier.*

What economists call the production possibility frontier (PPF) of an economy is a graph (with a typically outward-bulging curvature) that shows the optimal allocation of resources in an economy given the effects of diminishing returns on production.[1] The graph shows how the total value of the output will change as different allocations of land, labor, and capital are made. It plots out the combinations of output at different allocation regimes of an economy's factors of production. All points on and under the curve are attainable levels of production, and those above it are not attainable owing to the limited supply of resources (capital, labor, technical know-how, management expertise, and so on).

Production levels that correspond to points on the PPF are theoretically considered efficient.[2] At those levels, an economy is considered to be producing without wasting resources. At such levels producers can increase the output of a product only at the expense of another product. Any attempt to increase the output of a product involves tradeoffs. But when the PPF of an economy shifts outward, it can not only increase the production of all items but also produce new ones. The PPF shifts outward when there are technical improvements in the economy, and it defines the boundary of a set of possibilities available for an economy to produce and manage its total output.

The PPF raises the issue of the temporality of the process of economic growth and development. It shows the formal possibilities of an economy, the possibility structure of an economy; therefore, it correlates with the conception of the future that I am using in this chapter, a conception that comes from Neville:

> The future is the temporal mode that constitutes formal possibilities. The possibility structure of any date in the future is relative to the temporal modes of the past and the present. The past consists of all things that have been actualized and the present is the temporal mode in which past things are responded to, reconfigured, added to, and integrated into the new present reality. When that present moment of creative harmonization is finished, the result is a past actual thing. The future provides the possibilities for a present moment of creative harmonization relative to the past things with which it has to work. The present moment of creative harmonization, it should be said, might be very destructive of past things and also lead to disastrous consequences; "harmonization" should not be assumed to be beneficent.[3]

Let us translate Neville's conceptions of past and present temporalities into the language of economics. The present tends to correlate with the focus of economic agents on short-term exchange. These agents tend to ignore the reproduction and improvement of the social order as a whole and in the long term. The short-term transactional cycle is concerned with short-term gains, quick profits, and individualistic transactions and not with the timeless order of the economy. The past is the set of built-in structural efficiencies, imbalances, ambiguities, and distribution of resources that the economic agents are responding to, reconfiguring, adding to, and integrating into the present order. The present is the becoming of what has been actualized in the past. The present is where the children bear the sins of their parents' past and add to the sins their own children will inherit. Conversely, it is where they all eat or add to the fruits of their parents. On the other hand, the future, the space beyond the curve of the PPF, is where they can transform the formal possibilities of the economy as given by the past and present.

These three temporal modes are always affecting one another. Once again Neville explains it in this way:

> The present receives conditional components from the past and the future. From the past it receives actual things as potentialities for integration in its spontaneous creativity. The present integration needs to add something to the actual past as given in order to give rise to a new thing. . . . The present receives

> as conditional components from the future the possible forms its spontaneous creative integration might take. These forms determine what consistent pattern might be actualized in the integrative process.[4]

He adds:

> The past receives as conditional components from the present the decisions determining just which possibilities are actualized. . . . The past receives as conditional components from the future the forms that the present has actualized for it. . . . The future receives from the past the determinate differentiations that constitute the specific multiplicity that it must unify formally as possibilities. If there were not the multiplicity of specifically different actual things requiring unification in present moments of spontaneous creativity, the future would have no structure. . . . The future receives as conditional components from the present the steady changes to its formal structure that come from present decisions being made. Each present moment results in an actual effect that alters the possibility structure of the future.[5]

Economic temporality means the interaction of the three modes of an economy's time. The time or modes of time of an economy flow together. Each mode embraces the other two modes that are within it. They are all rolling along, drawing from and feeding one another. Economic temporality is the *time's flow* in an economy. The past, present, and future of an economy are together. For the temporal modes to flow together they must be together. This togetherness is not temporal togetherness; there is a context of mutual relevance that enables each of them to be together with the others. This togetherness is the *human creative act*, or simply human creativity. This is what holds the three temporal modes of an economy together.[6] It is the ground of the possibility of their being and coming together. It is in the human creative act that all the dates of an economic activity have their threefold identity. The identity of an economy or any of its sectors cannot be contained within any segment (time's mode) of the temporally flowing economic life. Only in the context of mutual relevance of human creativity is an economy's identity concretely real or its flourishing properly assessed. The temporal modes of an economy are created together in the human act of creativity. The human creative act is not something separate from the economy—the world of determinate goods and services and their temporal flows—but rather the economy's social-ontologically unified depth. Goods and services are creative things that are bound by human creativity, from the beginning to the end. No creative thing takes up the whole of human creativity, but each creative act is creativity itself in its temporal finitude. Without human creativity there would be no creative products and changes in them. Therefore, a human creative act includes the extraordinary dynamism of the change in determinate goods and services and in the temporal modes of the economy. The creative act is the ultimate reality of the economy. It is the context in which creative things, the creativity of the various sectors, and the temporal modes of the overall economy are relevant to one another. This is a fundamental aspect of an economy that needs attention as we seek to understand desire and the temporal structure of human existence.

What does this basic creative process of change have to do with desire and the worldview of the Kalabari-Ijo? How do all these affect the way we think about economic ethics and economic development? The place to start responding to these questions is the philosophy of God.

2. God and Temporality

Though the pre-Christian Kalabari did not have a monotheistic religion, they had the concept of a god who is higher than the rest, a kind of *primus inter pares*, first among the equals. This god is conceived as a composite force, a combination of creative-destructive force and destiny, and a combination of person and directing concept. It is both *Teme-órú* and *So*.[7] *Teme-órú* (this word metamorphosed into *Tamuno*) is regarded as the female creative modality. *So* is the directive modality, the aspect of divinity that orders the created outcome, the neuter or male counterpart. Put differently, the *Teme-órú* part is concerned with creation, existence, and destruction (wrath). *So* is concerned with the destiny and behavior of people, groups, animals, and institutions. *So* (that is, uppercase *So*) fashions the primordial desire, the disposition to act in certain ways, the conatus of all persons, the inclination to his or her ownmost identity and place as a mode of God. Each one expresses the power (the telos) of *So* in its existential field. A person's flourishing consists in her capacity to preserve and actualize her own given *so* (lowercase *so*, destiny). The telos is a conception of the good, a promise of flourishing life that will bring a person into her own. It is thus the governing force that will bring her into view and reveal the "who" of her life.

The distinction between *Teme-órú* and *So* is not a speculative one. It is based on an acknowledgment of the freedom of divine decisions as well as that of humans in dealing with such (divine) decisions. It correlates with the religious anthropology of the people. *So* represents the fixed point (or rather the unfinalized constant) in humans' dealing with God, and *Teme-órú* is the fluid point. The individual is believed to have a two-part personality. The component parts of this personality act as separate "persons." One is conscious, the other unconscious. The unconscious part (the soul) before the birth of the person decides the destiny (*so* or *fiyeteboye*), the life-course of the whole person on earth. Before a person is born the would-be soul of the person goes before *Teme-órú* and speaks the entire course of the individuals it is going to inhabit. The other (the conscious, the physical being, the individual) only works out its fortunes on earth. If a person does not like the course of her life on earth, she goes to a diviner to change her *so* or *fiyeteboye*. The process of changing one's destiny is called *bibibari* (altering or nullifying the spoken word, recanting). The person visits a diviner to let *Teme-órú* (the fluid concept, the part capable of effecting change) know that the person would like to change how they want to live their life on earth. Once the person's destiny had been changed, the new *so* (which becomes a new point of fixity) determines the whole course of the person.

There are three principles or forms of relationship in what the Kalabari call *So*. First, there is an uppercase *So*, which is the creative force, the inexhaustible ground of (impossible) possibilities that overflows into human activities. When *So* is considered in this way, it becomes the shorthand for *Tamuno*. Second, *So* is considered as the principle of limitation—the part that gives meaning and structure to the infinite possibilities and results in modification and concretion so that there is no chaos. The third principle is *bibibari*, and it connects human beings and God in a sphere of sharing decisions that concern human flourishing.

Bibibari is a feedback mechanism that works to properly align the interaction of the first two principles in the context of a particular person or group's life. This is the continuous process of retooling the actualization of potentialities, the appropriation of possibilities, and their reshaping. *Bibibari* is the process through which past possibilities that determine a person, institution, or group are themselves retroactively changed. The Kalabari believe that a person is created to embody a certain destiny—there is a virtual self that follows her, and in this sense her concrete deeds do not add to her virtual past as they only unfold what she is, as she becomes what she is. The fact that *bibibari* is part of this process means that ultimately the Kalabari do not take a literal teleological reading of a person's destiny. Destiny as a necessity is an outcome of a contingent process. A person's deed is not a mere acting out of her atemporal encased set of possibilities, as any of her numerous acts can retroactively reconstitute her primordial past. She can change her eternal past, the transcendental coordinates of her existence. "We have thus a kind of reflexive 'folding back of the condition onto the given it was the condition for': while the pure past is the transcendental condition for [her] acts, [her] acts do not only create new actual reality, they also retroactively change this very condition."[8] This change in the condition for her acts now gives her life a new necessity (destiny), but it is only a necessity she contingently created. In this process of *bibibari*, there is unfolding, folding, and enfolding of possibilities that are reversing necessity into contingency, and in turn contingency into necessity. The point to note here is that the three principles of *Tamuno*, *So*, and *bibibari* are in a sense about the opening of possibilities for human flourishing within a community. At any point in time the Kalabari categorize the sum of possibilities available to them in three sets: (a) one that is open to all individuals; (b) another that is available to only a few, and thus the rest of society are excluded from it; and (c) the universe of possibilities that are yet to be fulfilled or not yet available to all persons and institutions. The "c" is actually the *horizon of unfulfilled possibilities*.[9] This categorization speaks to the possibility-character of being, desire as lying in the gap between the sum of "a" and "b" and the fullness of possibility indexed by "c," temporality of desire, and the nature of the sacred.

The Notion of the Sacred

While the conceptualization of the sacred in Mircea Eliade's *The Sacred and the Profane* (1957) is usually a good place for many scholars to start their discussions of the sacred, I would like to warn the reader that my use of word *sacred* is not necessarily beholden to religion as it is usually conceived by Eliade and his followers.[10] As I will soon demonstrate, the sacred is not equivalent to religion; religion constitutes only a certain constellation of the activities of the sacred. Though the sacred in Kalabari encompasses the ideas embedded in Eliade's conceptualization of the term (transcendent referent, hierophany, and *homo religiosus*), it is actually about the universal set of possibilities available to the community.[11] The sacred is a way of organizing their thinking about possibilities of human existence. Broadly, their notion of the sacred affirms that possibilities are part of human life, even if human life is in some sense greater than the sum of the possibilities. Their notion of the sacred is a theorization of how a society or culture actualizes its potentialities for human flourishing. Religion as a constellation of possibilities and impossibilities is a subset of the sacred. As sociologist Richard Fenn, my former teacher in a doctoral seminar on the sociology of religion at Princeton, puts it,

> Because the sacred always points beyond itself to possibilities that the social order can scarcely acknowledge or include, the sacred is always potentially subversive or antinomian. That is why it needs to be contained, and it is one function of religious institutions to provide such containment. Thus every social order is haunted by excluded possibility, and every form of language has meanings that point to suppressed desires, aspirations, and longings. Because sacred speech evokes the presence of invisible authorities and gives voice to suppressed or excluded possibilities, religious institutions authorize some utterances and place others in a barbarian limbo beyond the reach of known language. . . . However, when religion loses its monopoly on and control over the sacred, hitherto unheard of possibilities become common parlance.[12]

In the Kalabari worldview and philosophy, the notion of the sacred as a set of possibilities is encapsulated in one of the words for God, which is *So*. The word *So* refers to both destiny or directing-destiny and the sum of possibilities available to the people. In a sense, the two meanings of the word are not different. Destiny in the Kalabari understanding refers to the set of life possibilities allotted to a person before his or her own birth. *So* in the sense of destiny refers to the dialectical outworking of the telos of individuals, communities, and the world. It is an unfolding world process that is not confined to following a fixed groove. The shaping of destiny is done by or rather understood via the possibilities that *So* makes available to each person, group, or institution. (*So*, when applied to individuals, is called *so*; to households it is *wariteme-so*, and to communities it is *amateme-so*). The directing concept of *So* is not just about the working-out of a preassigned telos. The concept of *So* directs the people to note their limitations, that is, the set of possibilities opened to them or excluded from them; the liberating potential for the transformation of selves and the structures of society; and the total of the conceivable possibilities given their level of social, technological, and economic development. Let us say that *So* as applied to the sum of possibilities is spelled uppercase *So*. Uppercase *So* is the set of possibilities from some of which individuals, cultural institutions, and social structures are excluded. More precisely, it is the universe of possibilities some of which are available to persons and institutions while others remain either unfulfilled or simply the set of possibilities excluded to them at any given time.

When lowercase *so* and uppercase *So* are taken together, we get the sense that *So* is the ultimate source of possibilities and the principle of limitation or selection. This combination of infinity and limitation defines the structure of the sacred as lived experience in the Kalabari worldview, shedding important light on the idea of the three sets of possibilities that mark the sacred.[13]

I would like to note that the uppercase *So* and lowercase *so* are not opposites in Kalabari. Thus, what is not part of uppercase *So* is not confined to extinction. The uppercase *So* is the ground of lowercase *so*. The lowercase *so* is only a set of appropriated or available possibilities at any given time. For instance, a person may have the *so* to be a good dancer out of all the possibilities that are available to members of the community and even beyond. If the person dislikes being an artist, he or she can go to a diviner and ask that it be changed and thus select another career from that unlimited urn of possibilities that the uppercase *So* can give. It is a pool that can never be completely realized. A person can literally ask for any set of possibilities, but *So* has the right to defer or "project into the future whatever may be too much for any community or society [or the individual] fully to experience or acknowledge in the present."[14] Because an individual can only be given or allotted only a part of the set of all possibilities available to the community at any given historical moment, what he or she has "always points beyond itself to the full range of possibilities for either salvation or destruction."[15] As Fenn puts it,

> At some level, societies know that they are based on the foreclosure and postponed fulfillment of possibilities for both life and death. Every social system . . . creates an index of impossible

> or prohibited satisfactions. . . . The sacred always offers only a very limited embodiment of unfulfilled possibility.[16]

The individual may encode within her the possibilities allotted to her by the social system (or the gods), but she always stands to look upon the uppercase *So* as the embodiment of unfulfilled possibilities. Humans can imagine alternatives not currently available to them and can take steps to attain what is denied them. In fact, this is the whole impetus and impulse behind *bibibari*, the recanting of destiny.[17] (A similar notion of refashioning or recanting of destiny also exist among the Igbos of southern Nigeria, and it is captured in the complexity of the *Ikenga* symbol. The philosophy of *Ikenga* involves as a retrospective process of change in individual or group's destiny).[18]

What is remarkable about the operations of the three principles is that they offer profound hints about what Neville calls the *ontological creative act*. They show that human beings, human institutions, or creation as determinate things have both essential and conditional components. The essential qualities are those aspects of a determinate being that define its own reality. But nothing exists by itself without relating to other determinate things. So, the conditional components are the features that relate the being to other determinates, and it is by virtue of such a relationship that it is a determinate object in the first place. The essential components organize and integrate the conditional components to constitute the determinate being.[19]

We are getting ahead of ourselves. The next subsection is devoted to Neville's discourse on the essential and conditional components of determinate things. The subsection will enable us to demonstrate that *So*, *Tamuno*, and *bibibari* are principles of an integrated life on a path of human flourishing.

Essential and Conditional Components of Human Life

According to Neville, all determinate entities, persons, communities, or institutions are harmonies of what he calls *conditional* and *essential components*.[20] To be an entity, an individual or thing—that is, to be determinate—is to be related to other things or entities. Conditional components are those components that show how a thing is conditioned by other things and how it relates the thing to other entities. Essential components are what give a thing its existential identity, giving it its own being, its own place, and its own time. Conditional features tell us how a thing is positioned in space-time order and give context to the thing and prevent it from being an atomistic monad. Simply, the thing has a context—it affects others and others affect it. But without essential features a thing cannot be related to others in its context through their conditional features. A thing is more than the influences of others on it and its influences on others. "If there are no essential features things would not have their own being but would reduce to other things. Carried out seriously, the denial of essential features would entail that nothing would have its own being and nothing could condition or be conditioned by anything else."[21]

Neville goes on to ask this question: What makes for the togetherness of essential features of a determinate thing such that a given combination of them at any given moment constitutes a being? He also asks how essential features can be related to conditional features; how can they harmonize conditional features for a thing to have its own space and time? Every determinate thing, he maintains, is a harmony of essential and conditional components. What is the context for their relating, for their mutual relevance? He believes the context is ontological—they are a product of a single divine act. This ontological context he calls God, whose eternal creative act and dynamism allow things to be together. This context itself is not determinate. "If the context were itself determinate, such as a super-space-time, then some deeper context would be required to relate the determinate context of the determinate things it itself relates."[22]

From the foregoing it appears that *Tamuno* provides the conditional components of the human being (or any other determinate thing) and *So* provides the essential features to organize the components so as to have to be a determinate thing relative to others, to be a being. The basic operative creativity of the two principles of *Tamuno* and *So* is that if the essential components that make a determinate its own being are not suitable in a particular existential field or do not produce the right value-identity, there is a chance to alter it through *bibibari*, the third principle.

It appears at first sight that this split between essential and conditional components of human beings are built into the notion of God; therefore God appears as a composite being of *So* and *Tamuno*. When the Kalabari speak about God they also refer to her in two other ways. In theistic and personal terms, she is *Tamuno/Tamarau*, but she is also the ontological creative act, divine creativity (*Teme*, spirit of creation). Yet the Kalabari people always speak about God, the supreme being, as a singular being. Is there a conceptual confusion here? God (the ontological creative act viewed from the duck-rabbit perspective of *Tamuno* and *So*) is singular or a singularity, and the two functionings known as *So* and *Tamuno* are anthropomorphic symbols of speaking about the ontological creative act or God (*Temeso*) of the created world in the eternal-temporal act of existing. *So* and *Tamuno* are the names of the same being, same ultimate reality, same Creator-God.

Temeso (as in *Teme* plus *So*) creates all determinate things with their identities and differences. For things to be separate from one another, have identities, and exist together, they must be in an ontological context of mutual relevance. *Tamuno* and *So* provides the ontological context for the togetherness of all determinate beings. Yet *Temeso* is not a unified totality of all things. There is no totality in the sense that *Temeso*, as the ultimate conception of spirit, is not considered as a determinate and "it does not impose determinate unity on everything."[23] Herein is a theory of strong pluralism, necessary for understanding the conception of human flourishing in Kalabari. Since there is no unified totality of things, what we have are determinate things with their own identities and differences, pockets of order with radical differences, all made to exist as *harmonies* that involve *contrast*. Things, elements, persons, or beings are different from one another, but they are together.

The togetherness is provided by *Temeso* as the ultimate reality. As Neville puts it, "Ultimate reality is the reality that is ultimate or last in the seeking out of conditions, that which is presupposed by other things but has no presuppositions itself. Furthermore, ultimate reality is not merely accidentally last in the sequence of conditions but is ultimate because it has to be the last, because there cannot be some further condition behind it."[24] *Temeso* as the ultimate is a substance-subject in Kalabari philosophy. It appears that *So* is a transformation of a necessary-creating *substance* into subject-qualities such as internal self-reference, telos, or desire. With *Temeso* as substance-subject, the creative act is not totally contingent; it happens for a reason.

The word *Teme* means both "spirit" and "to create," a noun and a verb. To refer to God as *Teme*, as a spirit, is also to refer to the ontological context for the togetherness of all determinate beings as "spirit." In this habit of thought, the spirit underlies the movement and process of all determinate things, constituting the togetherness of all determinate things. Kalabari people reject the assumption that determinate things and the ontological creative act are two different topics; they refuse to separate determinates from spirit, the underlying ultimate condition within which a thing or the dynamic of a determinate takes place. The created world is the eternal and external terminus of the ontological creative act, which is God as spirit.

To think of determinate things in this core spiritual sense is to connect the *being* of determinate things to an understanding of the nonbeing of their past and future in their real togetherness. In Kalabari thinking, the spirit is the context in which a determinate is together in all its three temporal modes. Spirit is the togetherness of the temporal modes of any sense. The art of spiritual discernment enables certain persons, especially diviners, to "see" (to be interpretatively present with) the realities of past, present, and future nestled in a processual moment of a determinate. The diviners' perspective is not limited to the mere present of the determinate thing, but also involves the spiritual togetherness of all its moments in all the temporal modes.[25]

This naming of the togetherness of the three temporal modes as spirit is different from that of Neville, who names eternity as their context of mutual relevance. For him, eternity in certain respects is another word for the ontological context of mutual relevance or the ontological creative act.[26] Eternity also means the togetherness of the three temporal modes as per Neville. We chose the term *spirit* to name the ontological context of mutual relevance, as it fits better into the Kalabari conceptual framework than *eternity* does. This should not be construed to mean that in discussions below we will completely avoid using *eternity* as an alternate name of the togetherness of the three temporal modes.

We have so far examined the togetherness of both essential and conditional components of determinate things as well as the three temporal modes. Now the task is to explain how the temporal modes fit together in human work, grounded in self-identity, in a community. The connection of self-identity and work is an important dimension of the Kalabari account of human flourishing.

Work, Self-Identity, and Temporality

In this section I attempt to ground a standard of human flourishing—the pursuit of a person's own values in work grounded in one's useful conception of the identity of a person-in-communion. Ethical work consists in the efficient pursuit of one's values that defines what one wants to be in the context of a community. Such work is to leave a legacy for one's community. Work is meaningful when it generates and bequeaths a legacy to one's community so that the structures of communality and the community's well-being are made sturdier. The drive to leave a legacy shows one of the ways citizens attempt to contribute to the paramount goal of their communities, which is the promotion of the community's well-being. There is a link between the drive to leave a communal legacy in one's work and the matter of personal self-identity. In the Kalabari context, this is not the self-identity of the *separative ego* (as Catherine Keller terms it). It is a notion of identity that recognizes and embraces connectedness and accents virtues and self-esteem.[27]

To ground work in the identity of a person-in-communion or human flourishing as the pursuit of a person's own values, we need to develop a notion of work that takes within itself a view of time that incorporates time within eternity and the ontological context of creativity. The Kalabari idea of work and identity-conferring legacy cannot be properly understood without situating it in a concept of eternity that is a temporal wholeness of each of the three modes of time. As Neville has argued, "personal identity requires a peculiar transcendence of the present moment. A person's identity in the present moment, especially moral identity, is never merely the present moment but is also eternal togetherness of all the person's moments in all temporal modes."[28] I will speak of the conception of work I am developing here as "self-identity grounded" because it requires the individual to pursue the values that will give him or her the greatest freedom (to be all that he or she wants to be), and also because a person's values are grounded in his or her identity as person-in-communion in the eternal togetherness of the modes of time.

Given the perspective on essential and conditional components, a focus on self-identity is necessary so as not to deny individual personhood because of the communitarian emphasis in Kalabari society. As Neville has shown, to deny individuality or the individual pursuit of values that relate to identity is ultimately to deny community, the set of conditional features of individuality. We need to situate human flourishing in the harmony of essential features (individuality, person-communion) and conditioning features (community) to fully work out its ethical implications and relate it to the underlying dynamic reality of creativity, which we have termed *Teme*. Self-identity, when properly conceptualized, is, as I shall argue later, neither autonomous nor heteronomous, but theonomous.

This identity that a person acquires is not just temporal; it is eternal. It acquires a certain transcendence of the present in a twofold sense. First, it is in the sense of *essentialization* (strengthening the essential components of one's life). Acquiring an identity and sustaining it involves working out the possibilities and potentialities given to one by *So*, destiny. The results of the actualizations add not only to the sum of possibilities available to the community from which the person arose but also to the possibilities available to *So* to work with the community. This is an idea of essentialization that does not necessarily contribute to the divine ground of being but contributes to the possibilities of various forms of lowercase *so*. Further, a person's current moral identity in the present moment "is never merely that present moment but is also the eternal togetherness of all the person's moments in all temporal modes."[29]

It is difficult to get a good grasp of the eternal togetherness of the modes of time in identity without understanding the underlying ontological divine creativity (*Temeso*, ultimate reality) from which a person stands in and stands out into existence. Work as creativity leaving behind legacy is connected to the Kalabari understanding of ultimate reality. Through legacy, past work (actualities) enters the presence of the communal sociality so as to fashion and refashion it. Present ongoing work can only actualize itself as a finished product by taking account of the potential that past work offers and the potential and possibilities for future work. Past work is involved in present work, and future work is also involved as anticipated. But in what sense are past and future creativities (works) present in present work? Are they temporally present in the present? The answer will begin by showing the temporal togetherness and temporal wholeness of each moment. Neville argues that a person's moral identity (and in our case, that identity is forged through the drive for legacy) "requires not only the past that responsibly conditions the present, and the future that the present will condition responsibly, but [also] *the past and future dates in all temporal modes*."[30]

The Kalabari focus on legacy is neither about remembering a deceased person's work in a place beyond time such as heaven, nor a notion about a person's work abiding in historical time while the person's essence (whatever it is) abides in eternal time. Theirs is a notion of work that takes within itself a view of time that incorporates time within eternity. It is a view of work or, rather, the temporal products of work that incorporate diverse modes of time into the formation of identity. When life and the works it accomplishes are examined only *within time*, each present work is together with other works as actualities of previous creativity and possibilities for present work. From a different perspective, each temporal segment appears to be cut off from the others. But when life and work are viewed from the perspective of legacy, that is, *within eternity*, the narrative is different. All segments of work are viewed as one whole. A rich meaning and identity are conceivable from the eternal connections of temporality or temporal modes. "Eternally the individual is what the person could be, what the person comes to be, and what the person is and has been relative to what the person could have been. Within eternity, the person is never only at a present moment, never only faced with a future, never only a finished story but eternally all three."[31] It is within this comprehensive perspective that the meaning for human work is sought by way of legacy in Kalabari. Because all dates (future, present, and past) are present together—existentially and possibly—work is placed within a personal identity that is whole and the product of a whole community that links three generations (ancestors, living, and unborn) of residents with each generation. When the drive for legacy is interpreted in this way, and in its connection to moral identity, we see human work and its legacy as integral to the widest conception of communality. As Neville puts it,

> The eternity of human life is not merely the eternal togetherness of different dates of a person's life. Our eternity is also an eternal connection with absolutely everything else in the cosmos with respect to which we are determinate. Thus we are in necessary connection with one another, with nature, and with the social institutions and habits that mediate our conditional interactions. Our eternal individual identities are part of a larger eternal community of identities.[32]

We need a succinct practical illustration to make the foregoing conceptual arguments clearer. In light of the drive for legacy and its connection to eternity, let us examine a dance for which a man would be remembered long after his physical demise and map out its time components. Let us imagine a dance being performed on December 7, 2022.

1. On December 6, the dance is relatively open as source for the future dance in the community compared with its pre-performance. The man has promised the community the performance as part of its annual masquerade festival. Now this future date for the performance is part of the moral identity of the man. As future, the performance day

"lays a moral and legal obligation on the person between now and then. There is an obligation to come to that day ready and able to [perform], and this affects many things" in the man's life.[33]

2. At the performance on December 7 in the community square, the dance is actualized as a present act. It is a spectacular performance, lifting the spirit of all present at that moment. He has put the "old" future date successfully in the past.

3. Moments after the ovation, the dance has been performed (completed) and it is now identified with a particular dancer, the performer. The community now marks the man down as a possible candidate to pay off in the "new" future with some "memory" after his physical demise.

4. By his spectacular performance, the actual dance is an open future for which he may or may not be remembered, and for which its style may or may not be incorporated into other dances or community performances.

5. Years later, he is dead. And then comes the future possible date of remembrance. The "new" future has become actually present—the day (period) for the "payoff" has come. Call this the remembrance payoff day for the spectacular dance witnessed by the community on December 7, 2022. This day of payoff is actually a selection from all the days from the date of his passing. As long as the selection has not been made it is itself living in the not-yet.

6. This future payoff day can only become past (realized) when it is actually possible to know whether he has been remembered. Note that when he was performing the dance to the applause of his enthusiastic audience this community payoff day was still in the future; it was not yet determined whether society's debt to him will be paid when the day of his death is past. Nonetheless, the man embarked upon his venture with the possibility of future remembrance becoming a past fact.

To paraphrase Neville in another context, I will say that without the day of the dance as a relatively open future, the dancer cannot be noted as a possible candidate for communal remembrance in the days after his performance. Nor can he be regarded as a spectacular dancer without the day of his present actual performance. Without the future remembrance period as his actual time of living in the community's memory, his drive, preparation, and actual performance were meaningless, and without this future period of memory coming to pass there would never have been the hope of the community fulfilling its obligation (intention) to him. The point I am trying to make by resorting to Neville is that the past and future of any work cannot be reduced to its present consequences (utility) and anticipations in the present. The present is not its only reality. We cannot begin to investigate the serious moral and ethical dimensions of work and hope to properly understand them if we only examine the dimension in which work is temporally present in the present. It is also myopic to attempt to reduce past and present works to only the ways in which they are temporally or eschatologically present in the future. The meaning and purpose (end and end) of work is often conflated with a favored mode of time.

But the Kalabari philosophy of work being developed in this chapter sees work in all its three temporal modes together, as perichoretically united. The issue now is in what context or framework are the three temporal modes of past and future works present together with current work in the present. *Teme* is the non-temporal context in which current work exists together with all three temporal modes. *Teme* is the togetherness of the temporal modes of creativity of work. Creativity has three parts (differentiable but inseparable) that correspond to the three temporal modes. The first part of creativity I will call *practice*. It is where individuals interact and generate moments of actualization of potential and change potential. The second part is *tradition*, the putting into the past of the coming-into-being of present creativity. The last part is *form*, which is the sum of the developmentally relevant possibilities. Creativity of work needs to be understood in these three modes. No one mode by itself constitutes work. The creativity of work is about the actualization of certain possibilities, contributing the actualities to the past (the source of existence and progress of sociality and its accumulated responsibilities), and always changing future possibilities. The force of "always" is to remove any sense of fixed destination of work as in a new earth or heavenly city. Without current work nothing can be accomplished; nothing will come into being. Without gathering in what has been accomplished (that is, the creative impulses and pulsations that have come into actuality), the existence and progress of life cannot be sustained. If today's work cannot change the future, "it would be as if the happening [the actuality of creativity] made no difference to anything."[34] But in reality, today's work offers future possibilities to the individual and her community. The possibilities offered in the future that we are willing to accept depend on three considerations, among others. First, the kind of people we are going to be; second, our willingness to hold one another responsible for our actions; third, our willingness to be accountable to the norms of a given community's tradition.[35] What we accept and reject are parts of the basic changingness of the ontological creative act, *Teme*.

Teme is the dynamic principle, the condition for and inclusion of the pulsations for creativity. *Teme* accounts for the constant change of creativity from practices, past possibilities within history. Human creativity is part of the larger creative act we have talked about as the underlying reality of all existence. Divine creativity provides the infinite dynamism for human creativity or creaturely creativity. The divine creative act is not static. It embraces the changing nature and dynamic relationality of all creativities together in all modes of time. This does not mean that divine creativity viciously determines human creativity. My statement that divine creativity embraces all creativities together in all modes of time gestures to the following ideas: the power of being in one's own being; humans as bearers of divine creativity; users of actualities from the past that themselves have been influenced by spontaneous divine creativity, and as beings whose actualization of creativity is subject to the formal properties for things in the future. Even though human creativity has no ontological independence or distance from *Teme* in the sense that all creativity is rooted in divine dynamic creativity, what a person does and makes of her own identity and creativity is her own doing.[36]

In a nutshell, creativity *is* in beings and beings are *in* the ontological creativity of the underlying reality. *Teme* is the ontological context for actualizations, the accumulation of actualities, and the dynamic actualization that shifts the structure of future possibilities. *Teme* is the deeper ground that relates existents and creativity. In Neville's terms, *Teme* would be described as "an ontological context of mutual relevance."[37] We have clearly seen how *Teme* (*Temeso*) is related to temporality and work as a form of human flourishing. We are yet to show how desire fits into the discussion.

Desire, Religion, and Human Flourishing

What is desire in the light of Kalabari philosophical framework of God, determinate being, temporality, and human flourishing? Particularly, what place does desire have in flourishing human lives, and what significance does the temporal structure of desire—and of general human life—have for human flourishing? Finally, how do all these inform the ethics of economic development, which is one the essential components of human flourishing in the twenty-first century?

Here desire is not conceptualized as want for goods or fulfillment of needs, but as the passion for existence because of the perceived goodness of destiny or telos of individual lives. The Kalabari citizen is a being moved by her destiny (*fiyeteboye*). This is different from desire as seeking after goods because others in one's culture want them. Desire for the citizen is delighting in the actualization of one's potentials in the context of the wholesome integration of the essential and conditional components of one's life, "and thus occupying one's ownmost place and identity" in one's existential field.[38] Basically the person becomes the subject of the becoming of her own destiny.

Human flourishing is to accomplish desire as a state of the world, not as a virtue. Desire is existence as such. The Kalabari citizen's idea of actualizing her destiny or potential is founded not on needs or on the order of possession, but on the *justice* of the citizen's existence as a child of God and community with a particular destiny. It is necessary to make this fine distinction if one is to fully grasp the fervency with which traditional Kalabari people pursue what they think is their God-given destiny. With this orientation to life and the attendant view of *just* existence, one will say, following Giorgio Agamben, that there is "a striking contraction of ethics and ontology, [desire] is presented not as a virtue but as a 'state of the world,' as the ethical category that corresponds not to having-to-be but to existence as such."[39] This is not about the right of possession, but the right of existence itself, the right of actualization of destiny itself. And it is akin to how Walter Benjamin understands justice:

> Justice does not appear to refer to the good will of the subject, but, instead, constitutes a state of the world. Justice designates the ethical category of the existent, virtue the ethical category of the demanded. Virtue can be demanded; justice in the final analysis can only be as a state of the world or as a state of God.[40]

There is a mode of subjectivity that engenders this notion of desire as passion for *just* existence. Subjectivity is the event of apprehending that for which the person is apprehended by existence (or *So*, God). But whatever it is it cannot be fully apprehended, so the person presses on, pushing outward the frontiers of human flourishing, reaching forward for the prize of the apprehension. Subjectivity is an event, and the person is engaged in its unfolding. This is no homogenous empty subjectivity as in some strands of Western philosophy. Subjectivity in this construal is not an abstract void that can be filled by a Badiousian event. Nor is subjectivity an abstract void of personhood that awaits to receive content from the irruption of an event. In the Kalabari worldview, subjectivity is always already an irruption (*pakabo,* existence or birth of a human being, is an irruption), an ongoing event. It is an irruption of the person's telos into the fabric of social existence, and the miracle of natality that calls for something new amid ongoing social processes. Subjectivity cannot be separated from personhood, from what is happening *for*, *in*, or *with* the person.

Subjectivity is dialogic, polyphonic, and unfinalizable. There is a constant interaction between the self, the individual telos received from *So*, the telos of the house (*wari*) or group in which one was thrown into existence, and the dynamic balancing of essential and conditional features of one's life. The person in this Bakhtinian polyphonic tension is not required to abandon her own consciousness or conscious efforts to succeed in life but must work to broaden her mentality to accommodate the various voices speaking into her life. And she may not succeed in bringing them together into a coherent system; hence, the demand for *bibibari*, the redefinition of what one considers as one's essential components of life.

We have now come to the juncture where we can formally tie the notion of desire to the *Temeso* (*Tamuno* and *So*) insofar as she decides the destiny or telos of a person's life here on earth. Desire is about *So*. Desire is what *Temeso* adds to the determinate things as one of their essential components. Determinate things are infused with *lowercase so* to achieve a certain purpose, telos, in their respective existential fields. In Kalabari thought, determinates are organized to achieve given purposes. It is this purpose that acts as a determinate's animating force and serves as its ultimate good that is relatable to the telos of its corporate house (*wari*) or community.

In other words, the telos constitutes the desire for what is the final good, the ultimate good for the person. This is a good that is not external to the life of practice. In the Kalabari conception, the telos is an essential feature of a person's life, and it is not a demand that comes from a standpoint external to the person's life. Every good is directed to attain this final good. Insofar as such a conception of final good is rooted in and flows from the telos or destiny of one's life, it is unqualifiedly good. It not only stands as a measure of the person's flourishing, but also orders all other goods and desires. For Plato such a final good is grasping the Form of the Good. For Aristotle it is contemplation, and for Aquinas it is a vision of God.[41]

The telos and hence the desire that *So* puts into each Kalabari person is to enable her to do her own part in the actualization of the paramount goal of her community. The paramount goal (good) of every person is the promotion of the well-being of the community. The community in Kalabari is conceived as the proper place in which individuals can amalgamate their capacities with the resources of the social world to develop their personhood. A person's being could be more complete, more perfect in its kind by giving and receiving inputs, qualities, and characteristics from the communal milieu. The paramount moral goal of the person is to contribute her best to the well-being of the community, and the community's aim is to let her be all that she can be, developing all her capabilities so that her personhood is not diminished or threatened, but enhanced.

We have laid out the philosophical meaning of desire as it relates to human flourishing. There is more to learn about the words for "desire" in Kalabari. The native words that I have in mind when using the English word *desire* are *tari*, *gboloma*, and *belema*. *Gboloma* can also be translated as "eros" or "togetherness." *Belema* can also be rendered as "love" or "like." *Tari* (which also means beginning, original, the first or primordial, "long-for," "being-after-something," or "being-concerned-with") in its complex depths of meaning and nuance can carry most of the connotations of the others and go beyond them. *Tari* as desire is a potentiality, not a thing or substance but the contextual ground for things or substance. *Tari* is singular and indeterminate. When desire (*tari*) meets its object, it become *gboloma*, an actuality, producing a determinate thing.[42] *Tari* is an integral part of the divine creativity.

Tari is a flow; it is part of *So* that is ever flowing and thus can be molded and remolded into various forms, such as *waritemeso* (the telos, spirit of the corporate house), *amatemeso* (that of the town), or *se-temeso* (that of the nation). All this should be clear to the reader if she remembers that uppercase *So* is the universe of (creative) possibilities and lowercase *so* (as expressed or carried by a person or institution) is a part of that universe of (realized or not-yet realized) potentiality.

Tari is always used to convey a demand; desire that is not external to a determinate, a person. "I am hungry" is *buru-tari*. Sexual urge can also be rendered as *gboloma itari-ari*, meaning "I am hungry for togetherness." "I desire to love" is *belema itari-ari*, and so on. Always, it bespeaks a force (primordial power, the first principle of existence) coming from inside the person and reaching out into the world of existence to actualize itself.

Insofar as *tari* is the creative manifestation of *So*, like its motherlode, it conveys some sense of togetherness of the temporal modes of time. As we saw with the dancer, his ability to realize his telos as a good dancer involves the togetherness of the temporal modes of time. We also saw that the actualization of telos as work grounded in self-identity (or legacy) is part of a person's moral identity, which requires, as Neville taught us, "not only the past that responsibly conditions the present, and the future that the present will condition responsibly, but [also] the past and future dates in all temporal modes."[43]

The key insight from the foregoing is that a proper understanding of human flourishing involves a deep cultural or religious understanding of a people's conception of temporality and desire as rooted in how they explain human existence to themselves. Human flourishing is to accomplish desire as a state of the world, not as a virtue or vice. Desire is the unfinalizable working out of the ultimate joy of human existence and personal identity in the togetherness of the three temporal modes. Joy is an *affect* of being on the way to all that one can be given the quality, place, and time of one's telos of life. Joy is desire celebrated. Desire, telos, *fiyeteboye*, is the "law" of an individual's own development; this is a law that the individual and we (as a community) impose on ourselves as being necessary. Desire is a passion for existence, and without understanding the religious depths of existence we can neither satisfactorily penetrate the cultural symbols of temporality nor plumb the existential matrix of human flourishing.

Desire as the gap between what is realized and the total range of possibilities in *So*, or *So*'s promise to an individual or community, is structural. It is structural in two senses. First, the gap cannot be made to totally disappear. The object of desire—the pursuit of human flourishing—cannot become a permanent possession. An existent in the Kalabari view cannot completely realize her possibilities; the justice of existence can never become a fixed (complete) possession. There is always a new projection of possibilities after every actualization because possibilities always exceed actualities. Human existence (*sepakabo*) is being-concerned-with-this-gap. This being-concerned-with, being-after-something is what *tari* (desire) is about. In this space of *longing-for*, the temporal structure of desire consists in the retentive reaching back into the past and the anticipatory reaching out for the not-yet and possible from the present, the gap. The *long-for* also comes from *Temeso* (God) as a force that energizes human "possibilizing" capacity or human creativity. Indeed, a person desires because *So* desires her or first desired or claimed her. The community (whose being is *amatemeso*) also desires or claims her.[44]

Second, desire is structural with respect to the *rhythm* of existence as theorized by Giorgio Agamben. The temporal structure of desire or human existence also refers to the proper ("original") place of an individual or group existence, the inner rhythm that allows her (the group) to take the original measure of her (its) dwelling on earth.[45]

3. Economic Ethics and Human Flourishing

Having now identified desire as a key component of human flourishing and human existence, and clarified its link to temporality, we are in a position to explore briefly the role of desire and temporality in economic ethics. How might policy-makers incorporate a robust understanding of the interplay of desire and temporality in human flourishing in their economic reasoning or development projects? Simply, I want to draw out the consequences of the arguments in this chapter for the study of economic ethics. What might Kalabari-Ijo (Niger Delta) philosophy or philosophical theology contribute to this discourse?

There are three important concepts in the Kalabari philosophical system that go into the core understanding of their account of human flourishing. We have only analyzed two of them: temporality and desire. The other is power. Given all that we have learned about existence, divine and human forms of creativity, it is expected that power, as in the ontological power of being, the social power of a people to push for actualization of their God-given potentials, or the economic power of public policy-makers to expand the reach of the production possibility frontier (PPF), should come into focus.

Power is the capacity, capability, or drive to actualize the potentialities of a person or group. Every move of power from essence (or will-to-live, power of being) to existence privileges a path, creates a specific process of moods, modifications, and concretizing of existing data or entities to produce and guard its actualizations.[46] The notion of "privileging a path" speaks to the logic of differentiation and differential gearing that every individual needs in order to drive toward self-fulfillment and human flourishing at her own pace and preference within the context of a community that puts a premium on human dignity and equality. To "privilege a path" does not mean that there is a unique path that each person must follow to actualize her individual potentialities. It only means that a person should become what she is essentially and therefore potentially establish herself as a person and a person-in-communion.[47] Every person is a *miracle* of new beginning in the world and has the capacity to introduce something new, something totally unexpected into the world.[48] Thus, ignoring this purpose to do and actualizing what one is essentially and potentially capable of doing is deemed immoral.

The individual and her community forge the privilege of a way forward to realization of God's gifts in the individual. The privilege of actualization of potential is a moral act. Following Paul Tillich, I would say that every moral act is also an act whereby the community and the individual work together to establish the individual as a person capable of answering to the demands of life. And this takes place through the process of actualization of potentialities for the sake of the individual and the community. When an individual is given her due—her privilege—she also gains access to relevant communal-institutional forms in which everyday person-to-person encounters happen that make for human flourishing.

The concept of privilege recognizes the uniqueness of every individual and, accordingly, affirms Hannah Arendt's notion of natality, which nudges us to acknowledge that every human being carries the possibility to act in totally unexpected ways that might constitute a fresh start for our social existence. Every child is a miracle to the world and a potential source of miracle. When we as a community regard every child as a miracle, as something that has never happened in the world before, and thus remain open and willing to allow and support her in following the "law" of her own individual development, give her the right of exception to the actualization of her potentialities, and not consider her as a cog in a wheel, we are enacting privilege for her. Here privilege (*privus* + *lex/leg-*) gestures to the "private law," the force of the alternative, the underside of standards that deform and disrupt hegemonies and hierarchies that are proprietary to publicly, widely recognized, institutionally proper practices and appearances.

Economic ethics, as informed by our definitions of power and privilege, is the thought and practice of enhancing or returning power and privilege to every person so she can become all that her gifts and training can allow her to be in order to enjoy maximum human flourishing. Among other things, this involves expanding the PPF in directions and intensity that enable all citizens in communities, and nature, to flourish. Economic development in the concrete ethical sense of human flourishing will continue to elude Nigerians as long as their government ignores this inner truth of the ethics of development.

Concluding Remarks

We started this chapter with a definition of economic development as the creation of special and novel possibilities in an economy. In the course of our discussion we have demonstrated that an adequate philosophical understanding of economic development goes beyond mere technical manipulation of the gross national product to include a robust account of a people's conception of human flourishing, temporality, desire, and power. We concluded that the task of economic ethics that takes these four issues seriously will not settle for quantitative increases in national income but demonstrate a firm and prophetic commitment to the human flourishing of all citizens and nature across all temporal modes. We have also demonstrated that any theorization of human flourishing that ignores economic ethics is not adequate to its task in postcolonial, subaltern Nigeria. Finally, we have indicated to our readers that economic ethics that is not grounded in the tradition or philosophical construct of a people cannot really address the demands of the human flourishing of such a people.

As I stated in the introduction, this chapter presents the whole book's arguments in a nutshell, setting out the logic and experience of the Kalabari people in the movements and counter-movements of destiny, desire, temporality, and economic development. Chapter 2 deepens our knowledge of the interactions between destiny and desire as they are conceptualized in this indigenous African community. I search for this deeper understanding so I can craft a philosophical framework for interpreting economic development, a process, impossible to complete, of the actualization of human potentialities or the creation of special and novel possibilities in an economy for the human flourishing for all citizens in a nation.

Chapter 2

Destiny and Desire

An Ontology of Human Flourishing

Introduction

"Destiny" in everyday English does not have the resonance that *fiyeteboye* has in Kalabari. In English we visualize it as a constricting, inescapable power, a vise around our decisions or actions. But in Kalabari *fiyeteboye* gives us an image of encircling power in which the person ensconced in it can break free of its pulls and reshape the webs that network the circle. Man/woman and *fiyeteboye* give us an image of a spider and its webs. The web is the immediate circumference of the spider's world, but the spider is not trapped in it. This circumference is much larger than those who are not familiar with the Kalabari culture data can imagine. Philosopher and theologian Paul Tillich agrees with the Kalabari conception of destiny when he writes:

> Our destiny is that out of which our decisions arise; it is the indefinitely broad basis of our centered selfhood; it is the concreteness of our being which makes all our decisions *our* decisions. When I make a decision, it is the concrete totality of everything that constitutes my being which decides, not an epistemological subject. This refers to body structure, psychic strivings, spiritual character. It includes the communities to which I belong, the past unremembered and remembered, the

> environment which has shaped me, the world which has made an impact on me. It refers to all my former decisions. Destiny is not a strange power which determines what shall happen to me. It is myself as given, formed by nature, history, and myself. My destiny is the basis of my freedom; my freedom participates in shaping my destiny.[1]

What Tillich means by saying that destiny is a not a strange power is that it is not heteronomous. Kalabari does not see it an imposition that is beyond question. It is not an unalterable entity, totalized and bound. Many readers may argue that by saying destiny is not heteronomous in Kalabari I have divorced it from its divine provenance or rejected the notion that is from *Tamuno*. As I will argue later, the Kalabari understanding of destiny is more complicated and complex than what the simplistic resort to God can resolve. First of all, as we shall demonstrate below, although *fiyeteboye* is said to be negotiated outside any specific historical or worldly realm and expressed in deeply spiritual terms, it is not actually independent of historical reality. Second, Kalabari do not believe that they are under the strange power or "law" of destiny that is greater than them as a collectivity. The Kalabari idea of destiny as not heteronomous is best understood when we view it through the lens of Stathis Gourgouris's definition of heteronomy:

> I understand heteronomy . . . simply according to the word itself: being under the law of another. This does not pertain merely to religion. . . . Heteronomy pertains as well to any worldly conditions in which the law is, in the last instance, beyond question. Any sense that the law is ultimately unapproachable, inalterable, and, institutionally speaking, greater than the society that has consented to this law it has ultimately created is a heteronomous condition. In fact, heteronomy exists from the very moment a society refuses to acknowledge that it and no one else has created the law of its God, its state, or its universe.[2]

The Kalabari who can "kill" their gods when they become too dangerous or assume heteronomous powers over their worshippers do not interpret the "law" or course of destiny as inalterable, as greater than them.[3] In fact, the Kalabari idea of destiny encourages a certain sense of autonomy of persons. We understand this clearly when we place *fiyeteboye* side by side with *bibibari. Bibibari* is about self-alteration, the dynamics of thinking of the self as otherwise irrespective of what destiny might have decreed. Destiny is all about an ideal, not a fate. The movement from destiny to *bibibari* is caused by alienation from this ideal. Alienation is primarily caused by time and the incompleteness of any existent, as we will see later in this chapter and the next. *Bibibari* is a correction course that aims to eliminate alienation by constructing another ideal type that is always keyed to an understanding of human flourishing. Human flourishing is the reduction or elimination of alienation. Human flourishing is an immunization against alienation in the community through a short-run series of completeness, self-alteration, thinking of oneself as otherwise in the long run of incompleteness of actualization of human potentialities. This is the dynamics of autonomy "as enacting oneself as other to oneself."[4] As Gourgouris argues, "understanding autonomy as self-alteration dissolves the notion of the . . . 'outside' in the very process or practice of transformation, of the radical capacity to imagine and enact oneself and one's world in a way . . . unimaginable" to a person under the totalizing grip of a heteronomous fate.[5]

Apart from the tension of heteronomy and autonomy in the *fiyeteboye-bibibari* syntagma, there is also the tensive relationship between competition and cooperation—all these giving us fodder for the analysis of agonistic communitarianism as a fundament of Kalabari to national economic management in chapter 4. *Fiyeteboye* signifies both division of labor and competition, specialization and selection, the distribution of places and competition, aesthetics and chance, destiny and freedom. These properties should not be considered contradictory.[6] They are moments or dimensions in the process of actualization of human potentialities. *Fiyeteboye* points to the idea of the specialization of activities or functions by members of the community. But it also evinces the belief that certain people are considered to be fittest and strongest, most endowed by the "gods" for the competitive life driven by the commerce and entrepreneurism of nineteenth-century society. *Fiyeteboye* points to the tension between mere arbitrariness and mechanical necessity in human social life, in the actualization of human potentialities, in the structure of finite being, to use Tillichian language. *Fiyeteboye* and *bibibari* is a play on destiny and freedom. Once again let me quote Tillich at length to drive home this point. He writes to alleviate any concern about destiny as contradictory to freedom:

> Only he who has freedom has a destiny. Things have no destiny because they have no freedom. God has no destiny because he *is* freedom. The word 'destiny' points to something which is going to happen to someone; it has an eschatological connotation. This makes it qualified to stand in polarity with freedom. It points not to the opposite of freedom but rather to its conditions and limits. *Fatum* ('that which is foreseen') or *Schicksal* ('that which is sent'), and their English correlate 'fate,' designate a simple contradiction to freedom rather than a polar correlation, and therefore they hardly can be used in connection with the ontological polarity under discussion. But even the deterministic use of these words usually leaves a place for freedom; one has the possibility of accepting his fate or of revolting against it. Strictly speaking, this means that only he who has this alternative has a fate. And to have this alternative means to be free.
>
> Since freedom and destiny constitute an ontological polarity, everything that participates in being must participate in this polarity. But man, who has a complete self and a world, is the only being who is free in the sense of deliberation, decision, and responsibility. Therefore, freedom and destiny can be applied to subhuman nature only by way of analogy; this parallels the situation with respect to the basic ontological structure and the other ontological polarities.[7]

Let me now state how the rest of the chapter will unfold. I will continue exploring the tensions of polarities in the *fiyeteboye-bibibari* syntagma. This time I will explore them under the rubrics of religiosity and secularity. It is not legitimate to use the word *secularity* when in the traditional Kalabari society there was no readily available distinction between religious and secular spheres. Yet I will proceed to use these categories in this chapter because the distinction between religion and secular helps to deepen our interpretation of the social philosophy of the syntagma. It also enables us to transfer ideas from Kalabari worldview to modern pluralistic society in which it is necessary to translate ideas from any religion into a common language so other citizens can appropriate them without being required to betray their own deeply held religious views.

I have divided the rest of our discussion into two sections: (1) Religious Dimension of Destiny and (2) Secular Dimension of Destiny. This division does not mean there is a watertight separation of the religious and secular ideas in the discussions that follow. The sections are meant as broad categories for heuristic purposes, so ideas interpenetrate one another in fluid movements. I need also to warn the reader that ideas of time, the connection between time and destiny, and the imbrication of destiny and time in economic development are discussed under the broad category of the secular dimension of destiny. This is done for two reasons: first, to ensure that every chapter is helping to build our understanding of split time and what it holds for conceptualizing economic development; second, to prepare the reader for the more technical discussions of split time that come in chapter 3. In any case, ideas of time, and the incompleteness of self, time, and reality, are embedded in the two sections. In them there is a sort of constant background hum going on about these terminologies.

So far in this book we learned that destiny (*fiyeteboye*) refers to a telos, a central purpose for human beings, but it is a goal that is never fully known for sure and it is not singular. There is room for failure and correction and a new beginning through *bibibari*. What if the process of *fiyeteboye* and *bibibari* is not really about the individual and her fortunes, but about the reality of time? What if it is all about the dynamics of a given society or fantasy that complements reality or the pure negativity of time? What if we interpret the dual process of *fiyeteboye* and *bibibari* as the fantasy of total, absolute control of one's purpose or life-course projected back into the distant past, a mythical period preceding the birth of the subject into the social setting with restricted possibilities? Here I am hinting that external dynamics or necessities are transformed into internalized psychic dynamics. This is to say that when we are discussing destiny and desire in Kalabari we should not locate them outside time or history in order to draw conclusions.

1. Religious Dimension of Destiny

The search for destiny is very well an expression of religiosity as well as the very essence of religion. The question of "Why do I exist?" cuts through or beyond the point where the self is seen as the center of existence and speaks to the belief that everything has necessity and utility. The self is now questioned to discern what it exists for; its existence is put into question and thus it is an awakening to a religious quest that is at once personal and social.[8] This self-questioning is remarkably different from that of Descartes. It is not a drive toward a self-centered assertion of the ego, the internal ego as the central position of all that exists. It is a quest to decipher the living connection of the ego to the natural, social, and spiritual worlds. The essence of this internal ego is not in thought (consciousness) or in physical extension, but in circulation of life. Life is the ground of consciousness (self-consciousness) and matter, *res cogitans* and *res extensa* of every consciousness confronting its objective world.

This orientation of African traditional religion (ATR) is transferred to African Pentecostalism. But there is a difference. The prosperity gospel introduces a fundamental tension in Pentecostalism. ATR's quest for destiny forces an orientation toward the world in which the self is not the center of existence; an inclination to penetrate into the heart of self-questioning "at the level of life at which everything loses its necessity and its utility."[9] The prosperity gospel, with its focus on the necessity and usefulness of things, on material things as the contents of individual living, and on how they relate to the welfare of the self, fights against the basic thrust of the fundamental religious quest. The axis on which the self turns is no longer the *telos* of the self, but the self as the *telos*. In Kalabari the notion of destiny (*fiyeteboye*) is about revealing the telos of the self as a bearer of possibilities from *So* (*Tamuno*), the creative ultimate.

Fiyeteboye has the sense of a *definition* that discloses the "essence" of a person, that is, allows her to appear (*pakabo*). It discloses the attributes, partial elements, and predicates of *So* (universal set of possibilities) to appear as a unity of being (person). By disclosing certain features or presuppositions, it excludes others, features or elements, that do not belong to this unity. *Fiyeteboye* defines, delimits the distinguishing character, characteristics, or presuppositions of a particular unity, gathering, and assembling of elements of *So*. It defines the unitary character of the elements of being assembled in a person.[10] It determines or conditions the predicates of being. It is the whole of predicates that the Kalabari understand as the essence of the person. *Fiyeteboye*, "which is declaratory of essence, *defines*, that is, circumscribes and distinguishes, the elements which 'signify' the uniqueness and unity of the essence. It separates and differentiates these elements from other elements which 'signify' other essences."[11]

All these preceding discussions may give the impression that a person's being and meaning is coming from outside the person or society, but it is not. One can easily give three reasons why destiny is, arguably, not fundamentally coming from outside history. First, never mind that if you asked the average Kalabari person why she believes that destiny comes to her from the outside, from the transcendental realm, she will likely reply that the belief came from the ancestors. But it is not so. The belief in destiny and the interpretation of anyone's destiny or its failure is always in response to the challenges the person is facing today. We have here a culture that is always in the frame of core-periphery. The core is what their ancestors did in response to the challenge their ancestors faced, to which they produced positive outcomes, which is why it is being retained. Only that which has proved valuable to the environment is retained and carried forward. If such an item came in 1920 and they are in 2020 dealing with the same environment, they will of course transfer what was valuable in that environment in 1920 to the 2020 situation, to see if it continues to be valid. However, the ingenuity of the Kalabari order is that alongside the transfer is the periphery of the individuals identifying and making a decision: how much of this 1920 element (wisdom) is pertinent to my solution. This is the way Kalabari have survived every variety of environments with flexibility. They will bring only those things that have proven valuable. They bring all of that to the present situation. When they check out their heritage solutions vis-à-vis their present situation, they start discarding those that are not pertinent and start looking for what in their own understanding is applicable to the current situation. At any given moment they are telling you what the ancestors did or believed, and all that is to provide legitimacy for the current decision. It does not in any way interfere with them applying their own understanding for addressing the moment.

Second, in fact, *bibibari* reveals that destiny is socially constructed. In the *bibibari* rituals, the person seeking to change her destiny talks to a priest (not directly to God, though the priest pretends to be a mouthpiece of God). The priest or his power represents society. The priest is also a reflection of his society. A good diviner (religious specialist) is acclaimed for his capacity to see and understand the whole social order as it is and to interpret it according to its history, ethos, and paramount goal. A good diviner is often a person who claims or is believed to be capable of grasping the unmediated spiritual orders of things through creative imagination. Religious imagination is not only about re-presenting (reproducing) in the mind the interlocking whole of cosmos, nomos, and ethos. It is also a creative locus in which people instantiate (in the particular sense of carrying a universal import) the order that can produce something new and unprecedented. And in extending this order (even if it is all mental) to encompass the new case or the case in question, it extends and completes the whole—often in a significantly new way. The diviner, in helping a person to alter her destiny to initiate something new amid the continuity of the social processes, must comprehend this social order and enable his client to place her initiatives, her figuration of something new in it even as she attempts to reconfigure the whole of her life.

Third, the notion and practice of destiny are, in a sense, an effort to deny, mitigate, and avoid the contingency of our existence by seeking the recognition or affirmation of one's existence by the other (God, society, diviner, or *amatemeso*). Recognition "saves" existence from contingency and forgetfulness; it frees a person, her accomplishments, and continuance in being from the abyss of contingency. Jean-Paul Sartre says that in the absence of God, who sees the value of work, any attempt to justify existence through the recognition of the other is futile.[12] Kalabari solve this problem or bypass Sartre's advice with their orientation to the legacy of work. Having no conception of a god who institutes divine trial to affirm or condemn human deeds, the only trial they have is that of legacy, the legacy of work (as a path to social immortality[13]). The matter of legacy concerns how one's name or actions will be seen, evaluated, and remembered by other human beings after one's death. This is their only trial. Work or deed is not experienced as only one's own but as reflected in the experience and evaluation of the community, the "plural us."

The community's evaluation of legacy sets a clear boundary for the pursuit of legacy for the purpose of recognition of a person's existence. What are the barriers or boundaries? The true barrier to birthing legacy is legacy itself. The true project of infinitely expanding one's legacy to society encounters the barrier of society's needs for human flourishing for all. The development of acts that perdure and conduce to legacy must harmonize with the valorization of human flourishing and existing human beings. This limit is not external but results from a person's striving to transcend existing work, human selfishness, or apathy. The image of the future is not the unrestricted accumulation of individual achievements that jettisons the connections to or limits of human flourishing and communality. This is so because the very idea of legacy speaks to the generation of achievement that is in concert with communal norms and human flourishing. The ideal of legacy does not remove all restraints on the generation of legacy. This limit is not contingent but is internal to the structure of legacy; it is not an external obstacle but a necessary, constitutive obstacle through the ideal's own ethical or logical requirements. The one who is deemed to have left a legacy, accomplishments worth remembering, did not eliminate this limit but embraced it as the very condition of possibility of his or her work. This person recognized human flourishing and the paramount goal of the community as the necessary limit that not only functions as boundary to the generation of her accomplishments but also constitutes the generation as its possibility.

This effort to seek recognition from others is in tension with the act of choosing the self in the prenatal realm represented by *fiyeteboye*. The interpretation of destiny as a purpose or function that justifies a person's existence (somewhat) runs contrary to the philosophical impulse of *choix originel*, the freedom to choose oneself. Constructing oneself before *Tamuno* by crafting one's destiny is an original form of freedom, freedom as self-choice, as Sartre argues in his *Being and Nothingness*.[14] *Bibibari*, following a period in which the individual felt that she had been abandoned or forsaken by good fortune, is a reminder to choose the self again—this is to say, to determine her essence by her existence. At another level, there is really no tension in the Kalabari system between the original self-choice and the quest for recognition from God, the priest, or society. From the beginning the Kalabari self chose itself "from the hand of God."[15]

Let us tarry a while with Sartre to explore briefly another area in which his ideas help us to shed light on the Kalabari conceptualization of destiny. He argues that choosing oneself is to be grounded in nothingness. At one place in *Being and Nothingness* he states that "human reality is free to the exact extent that it has to be its own nothingness."[16] Elsewhere he writes, "by going further and further back we have reached the original relation which the for-itself chooses with its facticity and with the world. But this original relation is nothing more than the for-itself's being-in-the-world inasmuch as this being-in-the-world is a choice—that is, we have reached the original type of nihilation by which the for-itself has to be its own nothingness."[17] In terms of the original self-choice, nothingness in Kalabari may be likened to forgetfulness. At birth, the self-choice, the destiny, is forgotten by the person, and the person, while alive, bears the anxiety that she might be forgotten after her death.

So instead of the Sartrean sequence of Nothingness ➡ Being ➡ Nothingness, in Kalabari we have Being ➡ Nothingness ➡ Being. The person "existed" before birth and exists after death. The Kalabari person is a beingness that tends to beingness. Yet nothingness separates the person from herself, split by a nothingness that marks the contingency of existing as a particular self. The space between the two phases of beingness is traversed by nothingness, the forgetting of the prenatal wishes, a "plan" that is now at a distance from the self-in-the-world. The plan (wishes) that is supposed to be the prime mover of personhood is forgotten at birth but is "creatable" as a second act of self-choice in *bibibari*. In this second act the person's deeds perpetually will being into being. This is the import of the Kalabari moral imperative *tombo tombo so*, meaning let a person be a person. This summons makes sense because the nothingness that is sandwiched by the phases of being does not allow being or a person to coincide with itself or herself in full equivalence. This nothingness itself is supported in its functioning by the negativity, nothingness of time. The self, the identity of the self, is always caught in the in-between space of time, ensconced between the "not-yet" and "already-no-longer." Indeed, to "fall" into the world in the midst of time is the precondition to falling into the nothingness that is the forgetting of prenatal wishes. The nothingness that sutures or splits the two phases of being is only a variation of this original nothingness.

Between one phase of being and the other, the Kalabari person is haunted by forgetfulness, which hints at a lack of completeness of self, of the subject. There is a desire not only to *re-cognize* the purpose justifying one's existence but also to eliminate the gap between the "ideal I" (that is, the "I" presupposed by destiny) and the "existential I." Or since the "ideal I" is basically forgotten, the desire is to translate the deeds of the "existential I" into the essence of the "ideal I." But this essence is always ambiguous, always incomplete because of temporal finitude, because of the split-ness of time itself.

Forgetfulness is the precondition and consequences of the pursuit of destiny. Forgetfulness reveals the possibility of freedom and anxiety, the latter because of the infinite possibility of actions that opens up—the vertigo of freedom that reveals itself—in the face of the forgotten stream of potentialities. Despair is the recognition of the person's mis-relation to her destiny, a manifestation of the qualitative leap from being into the guilt of nothingness as a result of forgetting the assigned path for moving from mere being (existence) to being-more-abundantly. *Bibibari* is an attempt to sociologically heal this anxiety. It is a society's way of giving a person's finiteness something to grasp to support the self in the dizziness of freedom and despair. In relating herself to herself, that is, in relating herself to her destiny, the person relates herself to her community and to God (*Temeso*, *Tamuno*). In eliminating or reducing her mis-relation to herself through *bibibari,* she relates herself to a newfound personal will to be herself and to the "foundations" of her own being. *Bibibari* is an attempt to heal the wound of forgetfulness, to heal the loss of memory.

Unlike the dominant Western conception of being (whose opposite is nothingness), the Kalabari conception of being has as its opposite *forgetfulness.*[18] And forgetfulness is this: that being in manifesting itself, in the task of actualizing its potentialities, betrays or deviates from its preconstructed path. Being in manifesting itself as a being, as a human being, bears a hole of incompleteness at its core. Forgetfulness in this sense is an undoing of being. It represents spaces wherein being breaks down, the point/spaces within Being where being itself, that is, the order of being, breaks down. Forgetfulness is the freedom to not take one's place in the order of things. Being carries within it that which it must avoid; incompleteness, indeterminateness, the freedom to not-be.

Once again, forgetfulness is the undoing of being within Being. This occurs when the flow, the dynamic thread of being comes undone, loses its form, or becomes confused, undifferentiated, such that it does not tell a story or show a pattern or structure. If being (like the human being) is an expansion of Being, then forgetfulness is the contraction of Being, the return to singularity, hiddenness, non-manifestation. (In Kalabari, existence is *sepakabo* or *emi,* meaning to stand out/manifestness, or thereness/hereness, aliveness/livingness. Inexistence is *fi,* which connotes hidden essence, loss, non-manifest essence, loss of identity or key function, brokenness, death.) Forgetfulness is the loss of structure or pattern. If we compare Being to a star, then forgetfulness is a black hole. A black hole has no structure.

This forgetfulness is human. It appears in being only as the gaze and concern of human beings. It appears as nothingness in being: it is not an opposite but a contrast in the phenomenal realm. It is within the human gaze and care that it penetrates into Being. It is with a deep recognition of the contingency of existence that it most deeply appears as fissures in Being that swallow memory. Indeed, human beings and Being have an internal relation. Humans and Being are like figure/background ambiguity; if one is removed, the other disappears.

This forgetfulness is evidenced by desire in human reality. The Kalabari person desires to accomplish her potentiality. *Tamuno, So* (God) endowed her with the desires to act, to establish, affirm her essence (that is her identity) by her deeds. She desires not to be forgotten after her death. She is haunted in her being, "essence," and existence by forgetfulness, by what she desires to remember, to gain, or to eliminate. To confront forgetfulness is to come face to face with desire.

Forgetfulness: feeling like a long way from my home (destiny), a motherless child, uprooted from her home, from her very own anchoring in Being. Forgetfulness is a feeling of homelessness. The African American sense of homelessness and feeling like a motherless child in America capture some of this sense of spiritual straying in concrete terms in America. When I hear "Sometimes I feel like a motherless child a long way from home," the word "home" for me means both physical and spiritual home. Slavery takes you away from both your spiritual and your physical home. It certainly makes you a motherless child. Unlike slavery in America, *bibibari* in Kalabari provides a way to return home and provides hope.

Destiny: A Search for a Lost Religious Object?

In line with received wisdom, we have so far interrogated (represented) destiny as a goal, an object (of consciousness). The real psychic aim of the subject is to create a satisfying relationship with this "object." *Bibibari* is therefore a process to create this goal, this object that has been lost or distorted; it works to restore a subject's relationship with this lost object. Destiny, before or after *bibibari*, serves to orient the subject's desire.

Let us stop for a moment and rethink destiny. Was the object ever lost? Was there, in the beginning, a goal to be lost? The object or goal that constitutively forms the subject and is installed at the center of her meaning-making system was never there to be lost. Destiny is only a lack that is constitutive of the subject and acquires a substantial status that it never really possessed. It is a lack that is retroactively created as the price of a "soul's" entering into existence, into a community or world of signification, an ontological lack that assumes an empirical and objective character. Actually, destiny does not precede *bibibari*. Destiny assumes its substantive character "only in the act of losing" or in the retroactive recognition of a lack. Destiny lost is the speculative equivalent of *bibibari*.[19] This is to say, the so-called loss/distortion of destiny does not represent disruption of a pregiven plan, but "the emergence of the possibility for satisfaction" with one's life.[20] It is not a loss or disruption, but the limit of one's subjectivity, the "self-limiting structure of subjectivity,"[21] a barrier to existence that the subject cannot overcome. (In a sense, destiny speaks to the constitutive finitude of the subject.) This barrier or obstacle that confronts or haunts the subject also constitutes the subject. To regard the failure to attain destiny "as a loss of something is to fail to recognize" forgetfulness as constitutive of subjectivity.[22] This forgetfulness animates subjectivity. The subject creates what she thinks she has forgotten, and this drives her to act. Destiny is an attachment to (ontological) forgetfulness at the existential level and the subject's satisfaction is tied to it. Put differently, destiny is a sickness unto death as a result of a subject's confrontation with forgetfulness.[23] *Bibibari* only configures the contours of the frame of forgetfulness and fills it with new contents. *Bibibari* is never about regaining or redeeming what is lost; it is a superimposition—the old disappears so that the new takes its place. And forgetfulness is not about a lost object that the subject must pursue forever. It speaks to split subjectivity, that is, to the idea that a person never fully coincides with herself.

Destiny in a sense is the nonidentity of the self with itself. Destiny targets the subject's life at the point at which the promise of potentialities exceeds the self's accomplishments (level of flourishing), such that the promise of the self exceeds the self, and the self is not identical with itself. Destiny is always that which is in the self that is more than the self. It is the subject's nonidentity with itself. A Kalabari person posits destiny to "escape the constraints of [her] symbolic identity and to enjoy [her] nonidentity."[24] In the pursuit of destiny or *bibibari* the person abandons the annoying self for the ideal of something better.

Sculpture and Destiny

Let us turn to another aspect of Kalabari traditional religion to further explore further the philosophical density of destiny: sculpture. The theory of sculpture offers insights to how they understand destiny in their everyday practices. They use sculptures to control and direct spirit, the immaterial, the invisible toward human flourishing through the instrumentality of the material and the visible. The material is used to fix the immaterial. As Robin Horton explains it, "sculpture is a necessary instrument for controlling the spirits and . . . any spirit without a sculpture to represent it is dangerous because it cannot be adequately controlled."[25]

A sculpture is an instrument for "bringing the spirits into spatial confinement," and they are effective in so summoning them when needed by human beings because sculptures represent the "names" of the spirits. So just as human beings respond when their names are called, spirits are wont to do the same thing when they are summoned before their signifiers.[26] "First of all, there is a Kalabari saying 'the spirits stay and come in their names.' And sculpture is often compared with the name of a spirit, or even said to be the name. Hence it enjoys the same intimate link with the spirit it represents as would any other kind of name: whatever is due to the one *ipso facto* affects the other. As to the nature of this link between sign and referent, Kalabari do not speculate. It is something almost implicit in the meaning of 'name.' "[27]

Before I turn to explore the common ground between sculpture and destiny, I need to make two quick points about how Kalabari relate to the powers of their gods or spirits. They believe that the power of a god depends on the quantity and quality of the worship and attention bestowed on it by its followers. They say *tomi ane oru meye duwa mare*, meaning it is human beings that make a god to be great. They maintain that gods have no intrinsic powers of their own; withdrawal of worship deprives a god of its power and authority to act on human beings or control human affairs.[28] The argument goes on to say that they build up the power of God to benefit them as its worshippers, and if such a god were to forget itself, to become too demanding, they will tell it from which wood it was carved (*agu nsi owi baka kuma en ke o kara sin en dugo o piriba*[29]). This means that a community can unanimously annul the power of a god by refusing it worship.[30] Robin Horton interprets the aphorism this way:

> Literally, if a spirit's demands become too burdensome, the whole congregation can join together to destroy its cult objects, and by this unanimous act of rejection render it powerless to trouble them further. . . . Broadly, then, the more people lavish offerings, invocations, and festivals upon any spirit, the more powerful it becomes both to reward and punish them. And conversely, the less they attend to it the less powerful it becomes—up to the point at which unanimous rejection results in the complete loss of power. Generally, of course, a single man cannot reject a spirit at will; for while he is only one among a congregation of many, it will have the power to punish him.[31]

Horton even relates the story of how a spirit who misbehaved was summoned before an assembly of its worshippers, found guilty, and fined.[32]

In Kalabari, destiny as a repository of possibilities, like the gods, comes and goes in its name.

We have already learned that a sculpture—a material object, a wordless figuration—is used to "fix" spiritual beings, to make them available to human solicitations. It is used to fix (principally) non-material beings. Destiny—spoken words that are living, that embody spiritual powers—is used to fix material possibilities. Destiny is a word-sculpture in heaven or in a spiritual, invisible realm. A sculpture conjures a spirit. Destiny as an event-structure conjures or promises a future, a dynamic set of possibilities. Possibilities (favors and disfavors) come and go in their names (a name that harbors an event or promises in the future, to use John Caputo's words), in their wordless figuration.[33]

Sculpture and destiny are forms of call, inviting the bearer of the name summoned not only to actualize the content or possibilities harbored in it, but also to enact or otherwise signal possibilities. Sculpture and destiny in this sense are ultimately calls for transformation for justice for the person as a community member. Sculpture or destiny as a variation of figuring beings issues a call to extant beings or shelters a call in the name of heaven as a power immanent in the human existential condition. Destiny and sculpture establish, signify a relation between heaven and earth, transcendence and immanence, or gods (spirits) and humans. They work to hide (or eliminate) the discontinuity between these spheres or realms, to signify continuity between past and present, material space and immaterial space. In spite of this co-functioning, there is still a differential margin between the realms (space). Without this margin there cannot be any signifying relations between them. Destiny does not always perfectly coincide with life on earth. And the sculpture cannot capture the spirit without an excess, a remainder. There is always a gap.

Destiny and sculpture are ways of transforming words into flesh (body) and flesh (body) into word (spirit). In the enactment of destiny, words (spoken in heaven) are transformed into flesh, into a human body. In sculpture a material body is transformed into spirit (word). The wood becomes *the* spirit, a carrier of the immaterial god. The relation of destiny or sculpture to its medium is contingent, unstable, deconstructible; they could be separated when the human is not happy with the connection. If a god becomes too furious or demanding, the Kalabari say they can tell from which wood it was carved; in the same way, if a destiny causes too many problems for its bearer, it could be replaced in a process call *bibibari*.

At this point we may do very well to view the age-old Kalabari understanding of destiny and sculpture through the postmodern term "hashtag": In this special sense—and in this special sense alone—destiny and sculpture are like hashtags in our twenty-first-century social media (Twitter) world. These ritual "objects" (that is, destiny and sculpture) were created to enable possibilities to coalesce around a key person or spirit. This is similar to what hashtags do around trending or viral topics. While hashtags do this with memes that have powerful semiotic charges, destiny and sculpture as "texts," as "objects," as foci of emphasis and concentration of potentialities, promote and provoke interaction and dialogues across realms of existence. Destiny and sculpture as hashtags are forms of apparatus that collect and organize human voices, words (prenatal and postnatal) to instantiate, enable, or drive natality (initiate something new, opening up a path of blocked or etiolated possibilities, the capacity to begin). Interpreting destiny or the pronouncements from the "voice" of sculpture, like a hashtag's message, is not about revealing or recovering the supposed objective or original meaning but about deciphering the dynamic preferences, the reenactment of the words of human beings—whether spoken in the distant past or at present in existential contexts. Destiny or sculpture is an assemblage of faith that the Kalabari float in the ocean of uncertainty of lived experience to seek understanding, to create islands of promise, and to condition that lived experience. In this task, a faith assemblage such as destiny or spirit-in-sculpture does not work as a unidirectional vertical model that provides answers to questions. It is dialectical and mutually correlational. The questions and insights and answers posed by human experience are a factor in conditioning the nature of pre-natal wishes and spirits. Destiny, spirit, and human experience constitute a critical realistic bundle that operate empirically, imaginatively, and theoretically to respond to existential situations.

And destiny as a response to an existential situation conveys the idea of the presence of the divine in cultural forms or finite persons. The Kalabari notion of destiny, as I have interpreted it thus far, is a sacrament of a sacrament. It is a sign of a sign. It is not only the sign of the spiritual presence in a finite reality (a word generated in the spiritual realm embodied in a living human being); it also points the "human-as-sacrament" (the human being who is herself a sign) to its abyssal depths of the incompletable actualization of human potentialities. Destiny is a sacrament of God's infinite, universal possibilities and actions in the world. In this sense, the person, the bearer of destiny as a finite, particular subset of possibilities, is the sacrament of the pneumatic Creator. *Bibibari* may well be all about freeing the immediate connection of a person to a particular subset of divine possibilities, re-engineering the relation between a set and a subset of possibilities. Like sculptures of gods, pre-natal words as destiny, as a visible realization of possibilities on earth, are efficacious conveyers of the power of the universal set of possibilities. At a deep level, they demonstrate the desire for co-inherent union with or interpenetrative docking with the capital-S Sacred.

Before we leave this section on destiny as a religious quest, I need to clarify a point here. Some may argue that the whole idea of destiny or *fiyeteboye* wherein a person is given a divine or supernatural purpose to live for on earth points to a religious sense of life lived as an ontological lack in any failure to fulfill it. I would like to respond to this in two ways. First, the said destiny is always forgotten when a person reaches earth. At best, a diviner is called upon to (socially) construct it. As it is so derived, it is not the same thing as the explicit religious goals of, for example, Christianity or Islam. Second, destiny in the Kalabari conception is never presented as exempt from time and finitude. It is not conceptualized to transcend these. The highest good of destiny is the flourishing of human life in all its finite form and limitations on earth. Destiny as a notion in the Kalabari context does not orient community members toward an absolute fullness of life outside of history. The highest good of both destiny as a religious idea and of the community as an existential collective is the flourishing of human lives as connected and embedded in nature, environment, committed to past human beings who are in communion with the living, dedicated to future human beings who will carry forward the legacies of the past and present members of the community and to forces that either enhance or thwart this paramount goal.

2. Secular Dimension of Destiny

Destiny is judged by its effects rather than by its intention as spoken by the pre-natal person. The mere fact that it is forgotten at birth and can only be properly inferred by the concrete deeds of the person means there is a split between the intention of destiny and its effects. Destiny is a reality produced by deeds behind a veil of ignorance. Yet, individuals acting in this way produce the *waritemeso* (destiny of the house group) or *amatemeso*[34] (destiny of the town or village), suggesting that destiny is a kind of Hegelian universal produced by concrete individuals who are not self-consciously aware of their deeds working to produce the universal. Each member of a house (*wari*) or town (*ama*) seeks their own betterment—and in the competitive Kalabari society this is often at the expense of another person. There is here a theory, even if inchoate, about the discrepancy between intention and consequences that produce some form of universality. This idea reminds me of Adam Smith's invisible hand—at least, its basic logic and its pragmatic commitment to the finite life of human beings.

The belief about destiny should be construed not only as theological (religious) propositions but also as a passionate practical commitment to finite life, to living with loved ones and the community. Destiny speaks to our finitude, precariousness, and vulnerability as human beings. Uncertainty, fragility, and changes in life courses are intrinsic to what makes us human and are not extrinsic to our nature as finite beings. The theory of destiny speaks to the "value of a life that *can* be irrevocably lost."[35] The theory says that every person who is born to experience the temporal process of living-on is susceptible to loss. Thus, the theory or belief in destiny is most intelligible only in terms of these commitments to finite life. If you propose destiny (as secure in some realm outside history), it means you believe not only in the value of a well-lived life as part of a community of lives but also in the possibility of a threat to that life. Nobody will be concerned about the precariousness of life lived in finitude if she believes that life is not vulnerable or that changes cannot be experienced as tragic negative loss. If she believes that finite life is like eternal life (life beyond history, timeless life) where nothing can be permanently lost or can go wrong, she is not going to be worried about finite, temporal life. It is temporality, finitude that leads her to value life and to value it for its own sake.

The belief in destiny takes each person as an end in themselves; each person has a purpose, an end in herself. The finite life of a community member matters for its own sake. Each life comes to earth as an end in itself as it is not a means to some salvation, history's march, or some purposes not intrinsic to the person. The person's life is not expressed as a lack of eternal life. We care about this particular life because of the positive and negative qualities ascribed to it in its foursquare reality. An integral part of why we care for these qualities is that they can be irrevocably lost in themselves or in the community of which their bearer is an intrinsic part.

The belief in destiny at its deepest levels goes well with the ethos of communitarianism. This is an ethos that commits Africans to treat their fellow community members as ends in themselves. We care for them because they are subject to irreparable loss.

The belief in destiny is an acknowledgment of a person's or people's dependence on the vagaries of life and the possibilities that exceed their control. This is only one part of the belief. The other is confronting the vagaries, the courage to take on life, living on, and a commitment to life that that is vulnerable, finite, and dependent on others. Yet there is no idealization of courage, or of any attitude toward life that either embraces sufferings or denies them or advocates equanimity or the passions to undergird agonizing loss. There is no appeal to eternity, the eschatological providential settlement of wrongs to obfuscate the suffering that is part of life. In Kalabari traditional religion there is no religious devotion to eternity and no dependence on a god that provides a path of salvation and blessedness in his or her timeless presence. There is no transcendental afterlife of endless repose. Kalabari traditional religion is a religion that has no love toward or passion for the eternal. Everything is worked out within the bounds of finite life with all its messiness and impurities.

Bibibari is not a practice aimed at escaping vulnerability of life. It is rather an announcement of recommitment to finite life through a different engagement with the world and its prospects. *Bibibari* is a reorientation of a particular life toward the future that is not certain and is still bounded by a retained past that has value, and a distended present is between them (past and future). As philosopher Martin Hägglund puts it,

> The commitment to living on does not express an aspiration to live forever but *to live longer* and *to live better*, not to overcome death but to extend the duration and improve the quality of a form of life. The commitment to living on bears the sense of finitude within itself. However long the movement of living on may last—and however much the quality of living on may be improved—it can always end. Even when we fight for an ideal that extends far beyond our lives—a political vision for the future, a sustainable legacy for generations to come—we are devoted to a form of life that may cease to be or never come to be. This sense of finitude is intrinsic to why it matters that anyone or anything lives on. If we seek to engender, prolong, or enhance the existence of something—to make it live on in a better way—we are animated by the sense that *it may be loss* if we fail to act. Without this risk of loss, our efforts and our

fidelity to the project would not be required.[36]

Destiny and *bibibari* and the existential commitment to life speak to one issue: that is, to what a person ought to be. They constitute a quest for a particular normative stance toward human sociality and flourishing amid uncertainty, promises of coexistence, and intersubjective dependence and risk of loss

None of this means that Kalabari believe in the nonexistence of God or eternal life. It only means that life is not lived in the grip of eternal life under the vision of a perfect life in heaven, and certainly worldly existence is not commandeered by God as a mere site for the faithful to display their religious faith. The Kalabari entertain no theory of loving the eternal or the supernatural God through life or people. Persons are ends in themselves. There is no religious doctrine that calls human beings to transcend finitude, no dogma about the attitude of detachment to material existence for the sake of peace of mind. Religion is an affirmation of the fragility and messiness of life. Simply, it all means that life is worth living for its own sake. It is because life is worth living and matters a great deal that destiny and *bibibari* are matters of grave importance. "It is because [they] believe that life is worth living that [their] life can appear *as* unbearable in the first place. If [they] did not believe that life is worth living, [they] would not experience [their] lives either as fulfilling or as unbearable, since [they] would be indifferent to the quality of [their] lives and unmoved by anything that happens."[37]

Destiny and Bibibari: A Conception of Time

From the foregoing, we have learned that the notions of destiny (*fiyeteboye*) and *bibibari* speak to a conception of time that is contrary to eternity. Destiny and *bibibari* combine events that have passed away and a projection into or anticipation of the future—with the present as an in-between. At any moment these two notions require a person to retain something of the past and anticipate the future amid the present that cannot be in repose. Thus, embedded in the two notions is the idea that time is a succession of moments or units—in other words, that no concern, project, or program of a person can be sustained without care and tending. Any or all could be lost. The risk of loss is intrinsic to what it means to be a temporal being. Destiny and *bibibari*, though having their provenance and sustenance in religion, do not allow a notion of time when all units will be gathered in an instant, when existence or life will be timeless, and when any particular interaction between human beings or between human beings and God will be endless. If time were to be gathered into a unit where the present does not cease to exist and is thus unable to move to be the past or to permit the coming of the future, then the events that engender, define, or constitute destiny or *bibibari* cannot come into existence. This is all so because destiny and *bibibari* are temporal. Neither of them is an expression of desire for eternity. They each and together express an affirmation of the temporal and an exposure to the risk and vulnerability of humans as finite beings. Thus, the conception of time embedded in the twin notions of *fiyeteboye* and *bibibari* rejects eternity or does not privilege or foreground eternity.

The process of destiny (a desire for mortal life, a pledge aimed at a finite moral being), which is said to begin in the realm of the supernatural, a timeless place, actually follows a temporal logic. It is haunted by temporal finitude from its inception, from the very moment the words, the pledge came out of the mouth of the would-be human being. The word or promise of destiny is a commitment toward the future. But it is also a bond to remember the spoken word, the promise, the covenant made before *Tamuno*. The person promises to keep in memory what she has promised. "There is thus an interval of time that divides the promise [the destiny] within itself, which answers to the interval that divides every now from its inception."[38]

Now, someone might argue that there is really no promise to keep in memory what was promised, as the child, on making the journey to earth through the mother's birth canal, always forgets the promise. This forgetfulness actually affirms the temporality of the promise, the temporal finitude that is intrinsic to everything in mortal life, the double bind that every life or desire confronts in finite existence. Any desire of a mortal involves both a love for the object and the simultaneous realization that it will be irrevocably lost.[39] The double bind of destiny shows that it is "mortal in its essence."[40] The point I am making here, following philosopher Martin Hägglund, is that destiny as promise is "a *promise of time*. If the promise (whatever its content) is a promise of time, it follows that even the most ideal fulfillment of the promise must be haunted by the possibility of nonfulfillment, since the temporal must remain open to its own alteration."[41]

There is another fairly loose thread from our earlier discussions that we also want to tie up now. Earlier we learned that the notions of destiny (*fiyeteboye*) and *bibibari* speak to the idea of incompleteness of reality, time, and subjectivity. Destiny could be described as the diagonal between time and potentiality. It is the path of incompleteness of actualization of the potentiality of any human being. It is the path of incompleteness, inherently incompletable because, among other considerations, time, which is inherently unstable, traverses the process of the actualization of potentiality. The line of destiny is the line of time. It is always split by time; potentiality is always split by time.

Potential is both potentiality and impotentiality (adynamia). Potentiality (to be or do) is capable of not passing into actuality. Potentiality can actualize itself, it can succumb to the urge of fulfillment; but in doing so it does not exhaust itself. It is always in play. As Aristotle put it, "What is potential can both be and not be. For the same is potential as much with respect to being as to not being."[42] A potential can pass into actualization whose conditions of actuality demand that the creative actualization cannot exhaust the potentiality or destroy the impotentiality. It means that a potentiality doubles as both potentiality and potentiality not to be, that at every moment of realization, pure actuality is indistinguishable from pure potentiality. We might call these two sides or dimensions of potentiality "fulfillment" and "impotentiality."

Impotentiality remains due to the split between present and future as time units; the future is always open. Generally, things move from potentiality to actuality, but potentiality does not exist only in act. When potentiality passes into actuality, does it exhaust itself? Giorgio Agamben, following Aristotle, says "no."[43] Potentiality does not exhaust itself in actualization. A part of it will always remain, that is, the impotentiality (to "be able not to-do," potentiality to not-be, potentiality that "conserves itself and saves itself in actuality"). There is also another dimension of time that comes into play here. An act or actuality can retroactively create its own possibility.[44] This does not mean that the person magically changes her past; it only implies that a decision today can retroactively (re)constitute the past itself. Destiny in Kalabari is seen in terms of possibilities and potentialities. Some of these preexist their manifestations and others happen without a place in any preexisting set, only retroactively creating their conditions of possibility.

Bibibari is the process through which past possibilities that determine a person, institution, or group are themselves retroactively changed. The past in this process becomes something like Deleuze's pure virtual past. The Kalabari believe that a person is created to embody a certain destiny:

there is a virtual self that follows her and in this sense her concrete deeds do not add to her virtual past, as they only unfold what she is, as she only becomes what she is. The fact that *bibibari* is part of this process means that ultimately the Kalabari do not take a literal teleological reading of a person's destiny. Destiny as a necessity is an outcome of a contingent process. A person's deed is not a mere acting-out of her atemporal encased set of possibilities, as any of her numerous acts can retroactively reconstitute her past. She can change her eternal past, the transcendental coordinates of her existence. "We have thus a kind of reflexive 'folding back of the condition onto the given it was the condition for': while the pure past is the transcendental condition for [her] acts, [her] acts do not only create new actual reality, they also retroactively change this very condition."[45] This change in the condition for her acts now gives her life a new necessity (destiny), but it is only a necessity she contingently created. In this process of *bibibari*, there is unfolding, folding, and enfolding of possibilities that are reversing necessity into contingency and, in turn, contingency into necessity.

The notion of *fiyeteboye-bibibari* in Kalabari as we are conceptualizing it here as a pair captures the restlessness that is characteristic of the infinite fabric of life. This relates to the material and efficient causes in the collective and individual transformation of existence. It also offers a lure to all transformation in the reality of the world insofar as it relates to potentiality and impotentiality. It has the power of lure that draws forward the infinite fabric of life to full actualization, to its destiny of asymptotic full realization.

We have now set the stage to properly elucidate our earlier statement: Destiny is a diagonal between time and potentiality. *Fiyeteboye* in Kalabari thought and lived experience points to a tension between the infinite past and the infinite future. The future is infinite since there is no end to history or at least to rectilinear history. The infinite future is represented by the notion of social immortality (work as legacy), and the infinite past is the incalculable past that includes the time of the ancestors. In between these infinites is the infinity of the natality (a new beginning, the birth of something new because of *bibibari*), which is a *diagonalization* of the space between the infinites. The notion of natality (*bibibari*) puts the accent of life on new beginning, on the actualization of potentiality. Every end has only one option to be a new beginning. Because of the emphasis on new beginning, more is expected from every moment and every life. The practice and discourse of the syntagma *fiyeteboye-bibibari* is located between potentiality and impotentiality, between infinite past and infinite future. It is a schema of discourse that is on a diagonal trajectory between these two historical (philosophical) referents and between potentiality and time. It opens up or searches for a new alternative ("otherwise possibility") when the present intersection of possibilities-at-hand and time is not coming up with *co-promising* options for the individual-in-community. The syntagma is a kind of a *diagonalization* at a 45-degree line between potentiality and time. *Fiyeteboye-bibibari* as a guide to personal decision does not motivate a person to inscribe present failures within the coming flow of time. Nor does it encourage people to seek final satisfaction or a sense of completion or to see their life as goals that must be achieved. The proper position is a triangulation of endless actualization of potentiality and a *subject* bound by time, which is nothing more than a commitment to sustain life as a purpose but not a goal.

> Being a [Kalabari] person is not a goal that can be achieved but a purpose that must be sustained. . . . Leading my life is not a process that ends in a final fulfillment, but an activity that I have to sustain for the sake of something that matters to me. Even if a defining purpose of my life breaks down, the breakdown matters to me because I am striving to have a purpose. The activity of leading my life—my striving to have a purpose—cannot even in principle be completed. If my life were complete, it would not be *my* life, since it would be over. In leading my life, I am not striving for an impossible *completion* of who I am but for the possible and fragile *coherence* of who I am trying to be: to hold together and be responsive to the commitments that define who I take myself to be. Leading a satisfying life is not to achieve a state of consummation but to be engaged in what I do and put myself at stake in activities that matter to me.[46]

Africans Dwelling in a Time Gap: The Impress of Economic Underdevelopment

We have just related that the fundamental experience of temporality from the perspective of the inherent incompleteness of actualization of potentiality is bifurcated. The same is true for another experience of time in Africa. In this case the experience arises from a gap—a tiny unbridgeable space—between two "arrows" of time. Our analysis in this portion of our chapter will focus on Africans. The African subject is never thrown into the full enjoyment of the present moment nor fully inclined to an escape from earthly time. These two extremes are kept from crashing into each other and are kept in their places by the expectation of *novum*, which is undergirded by what I have elsewhere called the *Pentecostal Principle.*[47] Borrowing the words of Stéphane Mosès in his description of Jewish messianism, I will characterize the Pentecostal experience of time in this way: In African religious consciousness there is "a very strange experience of time: it is lived, in its very nature, in the mode of *expectation*; neither the pagan joy of the present moment, nor a spiritual escape beyond time, but an always renewed aspiration for the emergence, in the very heart of time, of the brand new."[48]

The brand new, the *novum* never emerges from a pure state. It must always contend with the preexisting history, structure, or order. There is always the tension of being and becoming, the expected and the unexpected. Two models of spiritual orientation, two models of explanation-prediction-and-control of history, life, or social totalities, appear to compete in the time gap, in the experience of time. One model holds that every existent has a destiny and whatever is happening to that being is in harmony with its destiny as divinely determined. The divine destiny, which is primordially good, is only marred by sin, by disobedience to God. The work or adventure of a believer in African religion is to follow the fixed divine plan, making repairs when it is broken. The other model maintains that the divine plan for an entity or a person is evolving, becoming, changing as it is concretely realized. In his study of Jewish messianism, Mosès describes these two models in this way:

> The first model is *archaeological*: the world is the expression of a divine plan, and from the beginning of things, this is inherent in the secret structure of Being. The harmony of this plan was destroyed by a primordial catastrophe (which can be reproduced in some form, throughout history). The human adventure, then, will consist of repairing what was broken, that is, always recovering anew the original landscape of truth. For this truth exists, it was set from the beginning, and it remains unmoving even when it seems to evade us. The other model is *eschatological*: truth is in becoming; it is constituted day after day, as the invention of the new goes along. Even in this escha-

> tological model, there is certainly an original structure of truth; but it is only a purely abstract form, without an identifiable semantic content. Symbolized by the Tetragrammaton, this may be said to resemble a mathematical formula; to be filled with a meaning accessible to man, it must be embodied in our empirical world, that is, unfolding in time, a source of infinite renewal, in which it reassumes ever-changing forms. It is at the ideal end of this process, when it will have known all its possible incarnations, that truth will appear in all its universality but also in all its concrete abundance.[49]

We should bear in mind that these models are operating at the same time, in a time gap between pagan enjoyment of the present and spiritual escapism that aspires to jump beyond time. The two models are indicative of the relation and tension between being and becoming that is shot through with a break of time. This is the break in the time continuum (to be exact, the break in the perception of homogenous flows of instants of time) that engenders the new, which must struggle through the birth canal of the given to actualize itself. The new is seen as an interruption of evolution, an explosion of the continuum of history. " 'While the idea of continuity crushes and levels everything in its path,' wrote Benjamin, 'the idea of discontinuity is the foundation of authentic tradition.' It is not from the endless flow of instants that the new can reappear, but from stopping time, a break, beyond which life begins again in a form that constantly eludes all prediction."[50]

The reader who is not conversant with African history might conclude that my excavation of the deep time structure in the African religious consciousness is only the fruit of philosophical training. Alas, my analyses are rooted in history, in historical experiences of failure of economic development colliding with an exploding devotion to expectation of the miraculous in everyday life in Africa. This peculiar encounter of economic dynamics and religious consciousness has on the one hand "stretched" time and on the other intensely condensed time. National life, social life, and personal life can now only strive in the warped space left by these two altered times. The separate stories of Franz Kafka and Jorge Luis Borges appear to capture the simultaneous experiences of endless extension of time and extreme condensation of time.[51]

In a remarkable reversal of the biblical story of the building of the tower of Babel, Kafka's story "The City Coat of Arms" tells of the non-construction of the tower. The story in Genesis tells us that the people were in a hurry to build the tower to reach heaven and to serve as a symbol of their unity. In Kafka's narrative, they were plagued with hesitation and endless postponement. "At first all the arrangements for the building of the Tower of Babel were characterized by fairly good order . . . as if there were centuries before one to do the work. In fact, the general opinion at that time was that one simply could not build too slowly."[52] This failure to build, this erasure of purpose is akin to the projects of economic development in Africa. Economic development evokes notions and memories of non-development and underdevelopment. African states could not develop their economies too slowly. African states and their leaders, unlike the residents of the biblical Babel, could not be accused of impatience. God could not be alarmed by how fast they were building anything; rather, the powers of heaven would accuse them of the sin of non-construction and the embodiment of hesitation. Kafka's description of the history of the non-construction of the tower is remarkably prescient of the "non-construction" of viable economy in African countries where their leaders maintain that economic development is the most primary, urgent, and essential task before all citizens of their nations. Kafka writes,

> People argued in this way: The essential thing in the whole business is the idea of building a tower that will reach to heaven. In comparison with that idea everything else is secondary. The idea, once seized in its magnitude, can never vanish again; so long as there are men on earth there will also be the irresistible desire to complete the building. That being so, however, one need have no anxiety about the future; on the contrary, human knowledge is increasing, the art of building has made progress and will make further progress, a piece of work which takes us a year may perhaps be done in half the time in another hundred years, and better done, too, more enduringly. So why exert oneself to the extreme limit of one's present power? . . . Such thoughts paralyzed people's power, and so they troubled less about the tower than the construction of a city for the workmen. Every nationality wanted the finest quarter to itself, and this gave rise to disputes, which developed into blood conflicts. These conflicts never came to an end; to the leaders they were a new proof that, in the absence of necessary unity, the building of the tower must be

> done very slowly, or indeed preferably postponed until universal peace was declared. . . . In this fashion the age of the first generation went past, but none of the succeeding ones showed any difference; except that technical skills increased and with it occasion for conflict. To this must be added that the second or third generation had already recognized the senselessness of building a heaven-reaching tower; but by that time everybody was too deeply involved to leave the city.[53]

What is most important about this narrative for our interest in orientation to time and time gaps is that the people thought that time was unlimited; they were living in the "space" of endless extension of time. This orientation is basically linked to the awareness that nothing of importance is ever going to happen, nothing is going to change. We observe this kind of resignation to economic underdevelopment by the masses in Africa; there is massive disenchantment with government and its capacity to deliver economic development or public services. The link with the future is broken, hopes are frustrated, and time is an empty form that can be indefinitely extended. There is a complementary aspect to this disenchantment. "When the social compact no longer rests on anything but the disenchanted awareness that nothing essential will ever change, that is, on the frustration of all hopes, the [former energy and expectation for economic development in the early years of independence] that henceforth [have] no object will be invested completely—as if in compensation—in eschatological [miraculous] daydreams," in expectation of relief from the poverty and daily trauma of postcoloniality.[54]

While the failure of economic development has delivered Africans to the experience of living in an endless extension of time, the rise of virile (virulent?) Pentecostalism has delivered millions of them to its opposite form, the experience of extreme condensation, concentration of time. Social life appears to be functioning in a tiny space between these two extremes of orientation to time.

To tell the story of Pentecostals' imbrication in the extreme condensation of time that is also inimical to the socioeconomic development of African nations, let me turn to the tale of another writer, Jorge Luis Borges. In his novella "The Secret Miracle," Borges tells the story of Jaromir Hladik, a Jewish writer in Prague sentenced to death by the occupying Nazi forces in 1939. He was to be executed on March 29, 1939, and in the ten days leading to it Hladik's most important preoccupation was to finish a three-act tragedy he was working on before his arrest. "He had already completed the first act and a scene or two of the third. The metrical nature of the work allowed him to go over it continually, rectifying the hexameters, without recourse to the manuscript. He thought of the two acts still to do, and of his coming death."[55] He prayed to God in the night before his scheduled execution to grant him just one more year to finish the drama, which he hoped would bring glory to God, who owns all centuries and all time, and to himself. Then came the morning of the day of execution and at 9:00 Hladik stood before the firing squad, expecting an answer to his prayer.

> The firing squad fell in and was brought to attention. Hladik, standing against the barracks wall, waited for the volley. Someone expressed fear the wall would be splashed with blood. The condemned man was ordered to step forward a few paces. Hladik recalled, absurdly, the preliminary maneuvers of a photographer. A heavy drop of rain grazed one of Hladik's temples and slowly rolled down his cheek. The sergeant barked the final command.
>
> The physical universe stood still.
>
> The rifles converged upon on Hladik, but the men assigned to pull the triggers were immobile. The sergeant's arm eternalized an inconclusive gesture. Upon a courtyard flagstone a bee cast a stationary shadow. The wind had halted, as in a painted picture. Hladik began a shriek, a syllable, a twist of the hand. He realized he was paralyzed. Not a sound reached him from the stricken world.
>
> He thought: I'm in hell, I'm dead.
>
> He thought: I've gone mad.
>
> He thought: Time has come to a halt.
>
> Then he reflected that in that case, his thought, too, would have come to a halt. He was anxious to test this possibility: he repeated (without moving his lips) the mysterious Fourth Eclogue of Virgil. He imagined that the already remote soldiers shared his anxiety; he longed to communicate with them. He was astonished that he felt no fatigue, no vertigo from his protracted immobility. After an indeterminate length of time he fell asleep. On awaking he found the world still motionless and dumb. The drop of water still clung to his cheek; the shadow of the bee still did not shift in the courtyard; the smoke from

> the cigarette he had thrown down did not blow away. Another "day" passed before Hladik understood.
>
> He had asked God for an entire year in which to finish his work: His omnipotence had granted him the time. For his sake, God projected a secret miracle: German lead would kill him, at the determined hour, but in his mind a year would elapse between the command to fire and its execution. From perplexity he passed to stupor, from stupor to resignation, from resignation to sudden gratitude.
>
> He disposed of no document but his own memory; the mastering of each hexameter as he added it, had imposed upon him a kind of fortunate discipline not imagined by those amateurs who forget their vague, ephemeral, paragraphs. He did not work for posterity, nor even for God, of whose literary preferences he possessed scant knowledge. Meticulous, unmoving, secretive, he wove his lofty invisible labyrinth in time. He worked the third act over twice. He eliminated some rather too-obvious symbols . . . There were no circumstances to constrain him. He omitted, condensed, amplified; occasionally, he chose the primitive version. He grew to love the courtyard, the barracks . . . He found it: the drop of water slid down his cheek. He began a wild cry, moved his face aside. A quadruple blast brought him down.
>
> Jaromir Hladik died on March 29, at 9:02 in the morning.[56]

Hladik thought he had a miracle. God stopped time for him, giving him a whole year to finish his drama. He thought he had finished his tragedy, but for posterity he left behind an incomplete literary work. In the interval of seconds between when the sergeant gave the order to shoot and the time he fell dead, time, it appears, had condensed into one infinite segment, and he was working, writing at incredible superhuman speed. But all this was in his mind; objective time did not change for him. His experience of time as condensed was only subjective, a mental one. As Stéphane Mosès puts it his "mind was cut off for a moment from external reality and the instruments that measure it and withdraws completely into itself: a suspension of physical time whose counterpart is an extraordinary intensification of mental time. To speak here of a contraction of physical time or an extension of mental time amounts to the same thing. For the few seconds that separate the order to fire and the arrival of the discharge,

Hladik's consciousness is exacerbated to the point of accomplishing in a few brief moments the work of an entire year. But in this mind, it is the lived content of an entire year that is condensed in the lightning speed of a moment. 'For his sake, God projected a secret miracle.' "[57]

What is important for us here is not whether or not miracles occur, but the effect of the religious consciousness of the extreme condensation of time on social-political consciousness. Reframing the two types of time orientation in a different register, I venture to say that Pentecostals appear caught in the rotary drive of Schelling's two forces of contraction and expansion, the movement between necessity and natality, between the "infinity of a point" and the "infinity of line," thus a privative relationship to the public square, trapped in contracted reality. The positive will (expansion) cannot overcome the antagonism of the negative (contraction), and in this fundamental deadlock, the two wills frustratingly move in rotary form so that the positive will not be able to break out. African Pentecostalism cannot withdraw completely into itself or open itself up, to admit Otherness. But there is a potential for creativity, for breaking the rotating drive and initiating something new as the Schellingian God who had the two forces within him was able to do.[58]

More importantly, we need to focus on the effect on Pentecostal social psychology of (a) the resignation, the disenchanted awareness that substantive economic development will not come with its resultant endless extension of time, and (b) the concentration of time, the illusion of the contraction of physical time due to the widespread inordinate interest in the miraculous. African citizens now live between the endless time of the corrupt political leaders and the condensed time of thaumaturgical preachers. This in-between is what I have named as time gap. The task of an authentic or radical African economico-political philosophy is how to think of this time gap as a "space" to interrupt history, as the juncture where emancipatory politics burst forth into the African political scene. Otherwise, the time gap in which Africans dwell will become the valley of the shadow of death of social transformation, economic development, and human flourishing in the continent—with no exit and *novum*.

In the next chapter, we will treat the notion of split time. We have touched on it here and there in this chapter. In the next one, we will lay out the philosophy of split time and clearly demonstrate how it enables us to understand not only the intricate connections between temporality and desire, but also the philosophy of economic development. I make the argument that time, temporality crafts a lack, a gap within the human being, a shocking space around which desire circulates and pushes forward the horizon of human flourishing.

Time is disjoined within itself. Its presence is always what it is not (past) and what it is yet to become (the future). This is time's basic split or essential negativity. It never grasps itself as a harmonious whole, as an entirety, or even as self-identical. This is all so because it has gaps within it. This negative character structures human existence; striving for survival is about inhabiting these gaps, making provision for the gaps, putting themselves between the past and the future. Human beings are always struggling not only to relate to the world as it *is* but also *as it can be*, given a particular vision of unexplored possibilities. In this venture of mediating the worlds of "is" and "as," they insert themselves between the past and future of the time spectrum. From here they push toward a new horizon of possibilities for economic development or human flourishing.

Chapter 3

Temporality and Desire

Introduction

Human temporality is often interpreted as an irreconcilable tension between eternity and time, between the drive for absolute fullness and repeated failure at obtaining satisfaction.[1] Psychoanalysts tell us that this tension is a major force of the human psyche. The driving force within the psyche creates a split, the split subject. There is a subtle shift on how the split is theorized in Kalabari notions of *fiyeteboye* (destiny) and *bibibari* (recanting of destiny). The primary tension is not between timelessness (eternity) and temporality but, rather, within time itself. Time is split within itself due to the inevitability of the succession of time units. The present now—always distended—is haunted by the traces of the past and the expectations of the future. Time is not present to itself; it is not self-identical. The ultimate driving force of the psyche owes itself not to the split between time and eternity, but to split time. And the drive has as its goal not absolute fullness or attainment of a lost object ("the Thing") or the overcoming of finitude, but *survival*, the ability to live on. The goal is about care for life as a matter of negotiating existential conditions: that whatever they care for is subject to irreparable loss and that whatever there is does not and cannot transcend temporal finitude. The goal of living on is not to overcome temporal finitude for eternal repose or to achieve timeless perfection, but how to grapple with the condition of time that is constitutive of every human desire. The notions of *fiyeteboye* and *bibibari* are not about covering an ontological lack but about generating social constructs to explain and manage the elemental struggle to survive amid the ravages of time's intrinsic negativity. As we will demonstrate later, the notions fundamentally speak to what a person, community, or people should do with their time, what they should do with their lives, and how they do all these. This concern in a very basic sense connects with their economy. As philosopher Martin Hägglund writes, "The economic organization of our society is not a mere instrumental *means* for the pursuit of individual ends. Rather, our shared economy is itself expressive of how we understand the relation between means and ends. Economic matters are not abstract but concern the most general and concrete questions of what we do with our time."[2]

The lessons from the Kalabari understanding of temporality, desire, and human flourishing are used to frame an innovative hermeneutical perspective to interrogate the meaning of economic development in Africa later on in this chapter and in the next two. The object of my exercise is to offer a rethinking of the link between time, desire, and economic development.

Split Time and Human Desires

The theme of this chapter is temporal finitude. And how does this relate to desire and to the belief that whatever exists in the temporal presence suffers from *lack* of fullness? What is the nature of desire in the temporal mode? Is desire a matter of constitutive difference; that is to say, we desire things that we do not have, or what we are not? Does constitutive desire testify to an ontological lack or to the condition of time? Does the answer to all these vexing questions lie in the split nature of time, a process (phenomenon) marked by relentless succession of time, every unit of it ceaselessly disappearing and negating itself?

Plato in the *Symposium* tells us that all that exists lacks the fullness of being, and the proper telos of desire is to come to repose, to come to eternity that is timeless and changeless. Psychoanalyst Jacques Lacan argues that our existence or being is, properly speaking, a lack of being as we desire to reach fullness. Our desire seems to be a desire for a lost object ("Thing"), but we never had the object in the first place. We are only cut through as temporal beings, as lack of being. According to Lacan, "it is not the lack of this or that, but the lack of being whereby being exists."[3] This ontological lack of fullness is the *cause* of desire, which can never come to satisfaction. Precisely, desire exists in us because there is no proper destination for it insofar as there is a lack of fullness. Desire is a response to lack of being itself.

Time may not only be split; it is what split everything. The unit of time that cannot be self-present, that cannot be indivisible but must immediately cease and negate itself, is what unsettles and destabilizes all of what is in itself. To continue in time, to survive and keep living on, is, for any living being, to exist in a distended present, bound on one side by a past that is no longer and on the other a future that is not-yet. That which survives cannot be present in itself. The thing or person cannot always be the same. It (she) is always becoming by ceasing to be and carrying forward traces of the past into a future in which it will ultimately die. Time makes everything to not be in itself and hence exposes its lack of fullness and thus its desire to be what it is not. Because of time nothing coincides with itself. Time inherently divides life. Every being and its desire for fulfillment is traversed by a split within. Every moment of the state of being and fulfillment is constantly disappearing, ceasing as it is becoming and experienced as a loss.

The split time that provokes desire is temporal and not metaphysical or ontological. This is Martin Hägglund's core argument. It will handsomely advance our discussion at this juncture to quote him at length:

> The condition of time thus allows one to account for the constitutive difference of desire without interpreting it as an ontological lack. It is indeed true that desire cannot coincide with its object, but not because the object of desire is a timeless being. On the contrary, both the subject *and* the object of desire are from the very beginning temporal. They can thus never be themselves, but not because they have lost or aspire to reach a being-in-itself. Rather, they can only be themselves by not coinciding with themselves. This constitutive difference is what makes it possible to desire anything in the first place. Without a temporal delay there would be no desire, since there would be no time to reach out toward or aspire to anything whatsoever. Even if I only desire myself, auto-affection presupposes that I do not coincide with myself—otherwise I could never affect or be affected by myself. The point is thus not that the fulfillment of desire is impossible to attain. Rather, what is at stake is to rethink fulfillment as essentially temporal. Even the most ideal fulfillment is necessarily inhabited by

> non-fulfillment—not because fulfillment is lacking but because the state of fulfillment is temporal and thus altered from within. Even at the moment one *is* fulfilled, the moment is ceasing to be and opens the experience to loss.[4]

Owing to this, no desire or state of being can reach the state of "consummation of desire."[5] To put it as I have done is to imply that the telos of desire or state of being is to reach eternity, timelessness, or immortality. When a person says she wants to continue to be rich, healthy, or strong, she is not wishing to transcend finitude or condition of time but only to survive, to continue living on. Survival or living on can only take place in the conditions of time. For in eternity nothing flowers, nothing fades, nothing passes away, nothing is born, as nothing lives on in time.[6] What motivates a being to strive for survival, to desire to live on, to aspire to enjoy or change any extant state of being, to care for its sustenance and those of others, is the very impermanence of time—temporal finitude, the susceptibility to change and loss. To live, to be a living being, is to have "a structural relation to loss even in the persistence of the 'same' being across time. Every moment of living on necessarily involves a relation to what does *not* live on, and this negativity already constitutes a minimal relation to death. If one survived wholly intact—unscathed by the alteration of time—one would not be surviving; one would 'always be the same in every respect.' By the same token one would not be susceptible to any form of change, since nothing would happen to one."[7]

All this motivates us to care for life. Because we know that life is short, that it could suffer irrevocable loss and is not present to itself, we care for its sustenance. If, on the contrary, we know that nothing can happen to it, that it can go on forever, always the same yesterday, today, and forever, we will not be motivated to invest in its survival. No wonder the religions that disdain earthly life and emphasize the state of eternity, of detachment from any form of care for temporal things or life, do not want to invest in things that can be lost.[8] To invest in finite life is to live on desiring, and fearing that what you desire in life can be lost. It is to live with courage amid being wracked by the tension between love or attachment to finite life and the fear that what one loves or cares for can be lost.

How do societies generally respond to this vexing problem of the permanence of the impermanence of time, to the temporal finitude of living on? They seek either survival in time or timelessness or immortality.

"To survive is to live on in a temporal process of alteration, where one is always becoming other than oneself. In contrast, to be immortal is to repose in a state of being that is eternally the same."[9]

The Kalabari of the Niger Delta, as I interpret their data, have opted for the strategy of survival. Their notion of destiny, though couched in religious language, is not about the denial of attachment to temporal life. The notion or belief about individual or group destiny is an effect of a mindset that emphasizes survival, and religion, with its typical emphasis on eternity, is not the originary cause of it; indeed, religion, as we know it in the West, is far from it. This is so because Kalabari traditional religion does not have theories of eternal life that imply sites of repose outside of the material realm. Not even the gods exist in timeless places. Although some of their gods may not organically die, they are susceptible to change. Mortal human beings can even make the immortal gods powerless by either "killing" and "eating" them or telling them from which wood they were carved.[10] For the Kalabari the notion of destiny is neither to temporarily or ultimately deliver them to eternal life nor to deliver them from the problems of time but, rather, to support the time of mortal life, to undergird the desire for survival, for finite life to continue, for individuals and communities to keep living on.[11]

The goal of destiny is not to extinguish desire itself. As we learned in chapter 2, the very notion of destiny promotes desires within finite life. Desire is not a dead drive; it is a desire to live, to live a flourishing life. In a certain sense, the notion of destiny speaks to a constitutive desire for survival. Let me quickly add that this desire or drive for survival does not come with a fixed teleological principle or purpose. Yes, there is a desire to live and to flourish, but the exact form this should take is not open to alteration; hence we have the accompanying notion of *bibibari*, which serves precisely to alter any purpose that is not working well in the finite life. Since destiny is about surviving in the temporal realm and not about repose, the notion of change or alteration is built into it. Destiny is threatened from within itself by *bibibari*. *Bibibari* indicates that destiny is not the movement of an eternal substance in the material realm. Whatever "substance" destiny is, it does not exist absolutely in itself; it requires material support in order for it to exist. It is not indifferent to material reality. In fact, its actualization is threatened by many things. Also, the bearer of a destiny is not indifferent to his or her survival. The bearer of a destiny is by definition already temporally bound to it (without this she cannot experience it as a finite being) and already invested in it. As it is common with finite life, destiny is marked by "the bond of temporal life and the investment in living on."[12]

Bibibari acknowledges that temporal life or psychic life is subject to chance and cannot be absolutely preceded by any principle or purpose outside of material life itself. The embeddedness of *bibibari* in the notion of destiny means that ultimately destiny cannot be decided. This way of explaining destiny and *bibibari* is not an extrinsic theory that I bring to bear on them, but an insight that derives from the notions (beliefs) themselves. They offer themselves for in-depth exploration of the deep and complex connections among time, desire, and human flourishing. My hope is that they will lead us to important insights into the prospects for economic development in Africa. In a period when Africans and many scholars studying Africa think that Africans are attached to immortal life and eternity, it is critical to explore the indigenous religious and philosophical "library" for insights into Africans' attachment to mortal life and its implication for economic development.

The notion of destiny is both an acknowledgment of and apprehension of the slippery ways of time. Because time splits everything and renders all things impermanent, the apprehension exists that what we have will be taken away, disappear, cease to be. The business of living on, of keeping and caring for what we have, faces constant precariousness, and destiny (thought couched in metaphysical language) is only an expression of *secular faith* that what we have will not last.[13] What we have will last not because the gods are going to guarantee it (if not, what is the point of *bibibari*?), but because we are going to construct and care for it. Because of the movement of time we are afraid that whatever state we are in will cease and be followed by another. We cannot repose in any state, condition, actualization, or gift. Take health or beauty, for instance. The one who is beautiful or healthy today knows that her desire to be beautiful or healthy forever will not be fulfilled. In fact, she fears that her beauty or health might even cease to exist in the next moment. "This anticipation of loss and concomitant desire to persist are unthinkable unless the experience of health [beauty] is always already *divided within itself*."[14] Every state or desire is threatened from within itself. Destiny is a construct to understand this threat, confront it, and manage it without resorting to the illusion of transcending it, overcoming finitude, and seeking repose in eternity. Destiny is a materialistic, earthy construct and not a heavenly dogma that asks us only to look forward to overcoming finitude in the afterlife, in a timeless realm.

The notion of destiny (phantasmatic in nature, a retrospective illusion) points us to a societal effort to transform its members' experience of passive exposure to the passage of time, the tension of finitude, into a deliberate, active choice. The members of a society pretend to stand outside of time to make a choice for activities in time. Rather than being seen as powerless in their experience of temporal finitude, they stage this "metaphysical game" by taking command of life in a timeless place. This care and concern for life arose out of investment in survival or a positive affirmation of life. The pretense of an active choice testifies to an attachment to finite life, an attachment that is prior to the birth of the individual, the coming of this present generation,[15] and that does not desire to obtain absolute completeness. This is an attachment that actually exposes their lack of fullness, the inability of their desire to be fulfilled.

Incompleteness of Desire

Desire here is not a yearning for completion, a return to some superessentiality. Rather, it is a longing for what breaks into the economy of existence, holding it open for human flourishing. Destiny, which we have argued is connected to desire, is ultimately not about the relationship of God to the world but about the relationship of individuals to the world. There is a subtle movement of thought in the Kalabari notion that renounces any claim to speak of the human condition, of the vicissitudes of life from the divine perspective and the quest for total satisfaction (completion). The movement of thought is discernible from the apophatic underlining of the belief in destiny. The pre-spoken word, *fiyeteboye*, is never quite known, is always forgotten in remembrance, and hence, putting its emphasis on unknowability or retrospective illusion, is affirmed in the negative about what it is not. This is an acknowledgment of its ineffable mode of being. Yet it has existence and essence as a finite category. It *is* and it is *not*. *Fiyeteboye*, which at first blush appears to settle certainties, actually unsettles them. *Bibibari*—*fiyeteboye*'s partner—says we must act despite failures, have the courage to go on with finite life in the midst of difference and vulnerability, delay and deferral, potentiality and uncertainty. *Fiyeteboye* is the spacing of existence, the crack immanent in an order that allows for the necessary actualization of potentialities conducive to human flourishing. It is the gap between what the subject thinks is her core identity or essence and the struggle to translate such a construct into reality, practice, or word. It is a space between her perception of her being and her actual conditions for flourishing or survival. The quest of or for destiny is to find this incompletable space, this differentiating space within the tempo, rhythm, and temporality of living on so personal existence can be considered meaningful. The apophatic impulse of destiny and desire is not a ruse to cover some ontological gap, to aspire to be one with God. It articulates a certain hesitancy to name a definite content for the idea of destiny. Indeed, rather than aiming for closure and exclusiveness beliefs, *fiyeteboye* and *bibibari* may be aspiring for radical openness. The notion of destiny, when properly interpreted as we have done throughout this book, is "deprived of any positive onto-teleological content status: [Destiny is not the inexorable power watching over the quotidian life of the Kalabari person], but a name for radical openness, for the hope of change, for the always-to-come [possibility]."[16] There is an invitation to *event* housed within the two beliefs, notions, theological constructions, or names: *fiyeteboye* and *bibibari*. As John Caputo would say: "The name is the historically inherited form of life, what is handed down to us by the tradition. Then there is what is astir within this name, its inner energy or life, what I am calling the *event* within it."[17] The genius of the Kalabari notion of *fiyeteboye* or *bibibari* is that there is no chasm between the name and the event as in the Christian opposition between dead letter and the spirit in the word, because the distinction between name and event is not meant to assert an ontological gap that prevents desire (materiality) from reaching fullness or eternity. Appropriately, the distinction is to fold "transcendence" (if any) into immanence. *Fiyeteboye* and *bibibari* are entangled in the dense relationality of social existence, the give and take, the joy and loss of living. They are entangled in the world. They constitute an *ethic of possibility*.

The quest for *fiyeteboye* is the desire for the socially constructed object—a person's life ideal. Both *fiyeteboye* and *bibibari* are constituted by the symbolic order marked by the constitutive temporality of human existence. They are created as narratives of social identity. The narratives are arbitrarily dividing up the field of possibilities in one way rather than another. To repeat *fiyeteboye* is the desire for a social object. Many people repeatedly fail at their attempt to obtain satisfaction from this object. *Bibibari*, which at first seems an attempt to change the object, is in reality an alternative way of obtaining satisfaction from this repeated failure. Insofar as the so-called new object set in place by *bibibari* is a life ideal, the individual is still seeking an arbitrarily created life-purpose.

Bibibari is the movement of the same object—a symbolic representation of failure, of desire, of the split subject and her determination to repeat the process and derive satisfaction from her circular motions. The fantasy of *bibibari* is a "means for [the] ideology of [*fiyeteboye*] to take its failure into account in advance."[18]

In the language of Lacanian psychoanalysis, the transformation of *fiyeteboye* to *bibibari* is also akin to the shift from desire to drive. *Fiyeteboye* and *bibibari* are also akin to another psychoanalytic pair of concepts: object and sublime object. While the subject claims a set of possibilities constructed out of the universe of possibilities as a destiny—*fiyeteboye*, supposedly prearranged before her earthly life—all other parts of the universe of possibilities are excluded as not part of her identity. But once destiny, *fiyeteboye*, fails and she switches or scrambles for *bibibari*, the excluded (a subset of the excluded) is now named as the truth of identity, herself as a whole. The new set of possibilities fills out gaps in her identity, the sublime fantasy harmonizing the whole order of her being. The originary identity as the sublime object of fantasy turns into an abject figure once it is declared a failure, once it shows itself inadequate to the place it occupies. This is the fate that awaits the post-*bibibari* identity.

Bibibari at another level reminds the Kalabari that the world is basically incomplete—there is no perfect order of cause and effect. There is a crack, a split in the basic economy of cause and effect that makes human freedom possible. If the world functions without this crack, no free acts will be possible. All acts will be decided ahead of time and everything will inexorably lead to predetermined, ironclad deterministic conclusions. This is the condition of death and the dissolution of the subject of destiny. *Fiyeteboye* (destiny) is the illusion of a perfect chain of cause and effect, a chain that precedes the subject and remains inviolable and rules from heaven with no space for human agency. *Bibibari* is a reminder not only of the failure of *fiyeteboye*, but also of the failure of a perfectly harmonious, complete world, indicating the radical incompleteness of the world. *Bibibari* reminds us that there is always a violent intrusion into the homeostasis, the phantasmagorical construction of ordinary life. Thus *fiyeteboye* "does not deny the place of history and change but occurs precisely at the point of transformation, of the unsettling of the existing order of things. 'It is the hard and arduous work of repeated uncoupling.' "[19]

Bibibari is a philosophical challenge to the theory of the ontological completeness of the world. The world never fully coincides with itself. It is perforated by time and gaps and divided excesses that defy and escape its grasps, or rather the grasping or control by the subject. It is haunted by reviled, abject objects. The joint incompleteness of the material world and the subject is the concealed truth of Kalabari ontology. Philosophically, where does this leave the study of Kalabari (African) traditional religion? Philosophy or theology must seriously consider that the study of destiny, *fiyeteboye* (completeness, fullness, fantasy of wholeness), is inseparable from *bibibari* (incompleteness, disruption). This perspective is often missed in scholarly work because these concepts are investigated outside the purview of temporal finitude, attachment to finite life, the desire for finite life to go on, and the pursuit of human flourishing that is marked by a succession of time units. Both our nature as human beings and our desires are time-bound. The necessity of the succession of time units conditions the character of our desires and temporal experiences.

The key point of our discourse (the split nature of time) so far in this chapter is that transience is in any thing, object, or value that human beings desire. We experience this transience as a limitation, but this limitation is not an ontological lack, it is not a measure of the distance between what we desire and the ideal of its eternal nature or that of an eternal being. Or is it because as finite beings we suffer a lack of being? No, *nein*. Everything that we desire is affected by the succession of time. It is never present to itself as such. Delays, deferrals, destruction, and anticipation of loss due to the passage of time always create a gap between desire and its fulfillment. Thus desire persists in us not because we suffer an ontological lack and consequently have a passion for immortality or fullness of being. As Hägglund teaches us, "The reason desire persists even in the most ideal fulfillment is *not* because it fails to arrive at the desired destination but because the arrival at the destination—the experience of fulfillment—is temporal in itself. Even at the moment one *is* fulfilled the moment is passing away. This immediate passing away opens the difference that sustains desire."[20]

The temporal process of destiny is never seen as a search for the part of the self that is lost forever. The object of desire that is encapsulated in (as) destiny neither is opposed to proper immortality (in the sense that it does not seek it) nor stands as a representative of immortal life. It is not an object subtracted from a person because he or she is a sexed living being, separated from immortal life or absolute self-sufficiency, absolute fullness or emptiness. Destiny in Kalabari is never portrayed as a return to some original plenum. It is seen as internal to the temporal process of living on. It derives from the necessity of the succession of time units, from the bond to the mortal life.[21] For the "truth" of desire is the temporal finitude of survival, "a response to the investment in the undecidable fate of survival."[22]

Some may argue that my interpretation of destiny to exclude the desire for immortality contradicts what I wrote about the Kalabari in my 2008 *Depth and Destiny of Work*.[23] There I argued that the Kalabari strive for social immortality, that they consciously work to leave legacies behind so their names will not be forgotten. The reader might ask, is this desire not an attempt to overcome temporal conditions? But this is not a constitutive desire to transcend time, to hunger for a timeless state of repose, eternity, or immortality. The desire for social immortality is perforated by succession of time. It is animated by temporal finitude. The desire is a passion not for immortality, but for survival. A Kalabari person seeks to ensure that her works are not lost but that they persist in the memory of living beings, because she is invested in temporal life and knows that they are susceptible to loss. The person who is gunning for repose and fullness in a timeless being beyond history who can guarantee survival of her soul and its lifetime works will not care about social immortality. "When we fight for an ideal that extends far beyond our own lives—a political vision for the future, a sustainable legacy for generations to come—we are devoted to a form of life that may cease to be or never come to be. This sense of finitude is intrinsic to why it matters that anyone or anything lives on. If we seek to engender, prolong, or enhance the existence of something—to make it live on in a better way—we are animated by the sense that *it may be lost* if we fail to act. Without this risk of loss, our efforts and our fidelity to the project would not be required."[24]

Split Time in Everyday Language Use

The Kalabari understanding of split time, the spacing of time that prevents being or life from self-identity, can also be teased from examples taken from their everyday language. Their everyday description or language for pregnancy is telling in this respect. When a woman is pregnant, they say *akalu aborote*, meaning the moon went past her, it bypasses her, or she missed the moon. She is no longer a closed entity because the moon passed her; that which represents time, the past and future that exceed her control, has violated her circle, cracked it. It prevents her from being in herself and thus open to a relation to a child, an immanent other, so to speak. The circle of menstruation can no longer continue in its repose and released from relations. Time skips her and she stays in this skipped time (situation), skipped circle, broken circle for nine months.

Pregnancy is also described as *a saki kira-a*. This means that her time is incomplete; time is out of joint. Her time is disjointed; there is a disjuncture in her time. They also say *a bu kira-a:* her body is incomplete. The arrow of time, the infinity of time breaks into the cycle of her womb. Pregnancy is the inherent incompleteness of time breaking into the harmony of the womb to destabilize, disturb, and displace it toward a new creation. Here the disjuncture of time is seen as an incompleteness of the body, rather than as a woman's time. Her body that embodies time is now disjointed as time itself. Her body is conceptualized or viewed as "cracked," in a state of incompleteness, of non-harmony with itself; she is not self-identical. The logic of bringing forth is incompleteness. Here incompleteness is not in the pursuit of or the step before fullness, nor does it seek the recovery of a lost object. It is about the hope and fear of that which, even when gained, could be lost because of temporal finitude. Incompleteness is not a means to an end, it is not an end in itself; it is only a pure means. It is a medium (without finality) by and through which fullness arrives and disappears, and disappears and arrives, and registers its inherent instability, precarity, and vibrancy.

When pregnant, a woman is not identical to herself (more obviously than ever before), and thus this condition allows for alterity, the other to emerge. The idea of incompleteness of time or identity is an ode to life. The absence of movement of time, the disjuncture of time, or the full presence of the self to the self is complete death. In a state of being where no change is happening, where there is an unmoving now, where the present is not haunted by the traces of the past and the anticipation of the not-yet, nothing ever happens. It is the state of absolute death. It is "*one* absolute presence that is unrivalled by succession."[25] Temporal finitude, the spacing of time that prevents everything from being fully present to itself, opens everything to discord, breach of integrity, and eventually to death is the condition of possibility and impossibility of mortal life.

The words or descriptions for pregnancy not only speak to the incompleteness of time, but also to the undecidability of survival; the coming of time is undecidable. Pregnancy is seen as an exposure to the unpredictable future. Kalabari say *Furo te erebo ari nyin-mariye oyibo erebo nimibo ofori* (No one knows whether a pregnant woman will put to bed a boy or a girl) to talk about undecidability, the complete knowability of the future, the absence of definitive assurance for the future. They use this proverb to say that the coming of time to everything puts it into a state of unpredictability. The undecidability does not prevent them from making decisions because of "the bond of temporal life and the investment in living on."[26] Kalabari say *ngianya toru ngianya kun*, boldly make a decision in the midst of uncertainty, make a decision when the consequences cannot be known; thus, recognizing that decisions are "precipitated by the undecidable coming of time."[27] Hägglund puts it well when he writes, "There is no opposition between undecidability and the making of decisions. On the contrary, it is *because* the future cannot be decided in advance that one has to make decisions. If the future could be predicted, there would be nothing to decide on and no reason to act in the first place."[28]

The economy is structured around the fundamental impossibility of the *futureness* it tries to cope with. There is the fundamental impossibility of knowing (mastering) the future. It is the obstacle to the future that sustains the future. The future is the *a-present*; the negation of the present, and this negation is strictly immanent to economic transactions. The present never attains its goal or finds satisfaction within itself. In this case, the present and the future are not two segments but the present and its impossibility (its failure) posited as separate; the present and its impossibility of existing as master of the future is externalized as the other. The future is the abyss in which present human economic activity that never reaches its goals performs its repetitive gesture and finds satisfaction in the very repetitive failure. Owing to the invocation and provocation of the future, the present never coincides with itself. Futureness is "nothing but a split between two forms of otherness"—the unsatisfactory present as other and the uncertain, uncontrollable future as the other.[29] The split is not only this structure, but it is also in excess of structure.[30]

This issue of undecidability and making decisions or provisions for the future is at the heart of all economic problems and the forms of life a community wants to lead. How should economic decision-making relate to the undecidable future, the incalculable coming of time? The split time, the undecidability of the future, is the very condition of possibility for economic development. What does it mean to think of Africa's (Nigeria's) economic development in terms of temporality as an irreducible condition of human interaction? The next section will begin providing responses to these questions to set us up for the more detailed treatment in chapters 4 and 5.

Economy and Split Time

In *The Split Economy: Saint Paul Goes to Wall Street*, I examine how the primitive economy emerged as a process of making provision for the future. The process is remarkably defined by the split of finance from the economy or the appearance of asset and liability, credit and debit in the primordial economy. What I did not do in that book is to acknowledge that the split economy was preceded, undergirded, supervened, and driven by split time. Our finitude is the source of our entanglement with the future. Making provision for the future always takes place in time, always subject to the unstable remembrance of the past, and always wracked by the uncertainty of the future. Provision for the future neither guarantees the future nor promises that those that are making the provision will be around to enjoy it. The daily grind of providing for the future only indicates that our survival is at stake in the future. The future matters to us, and our survival (especially as individuals or a limited set of individuals) could be lost. This risk is not ontological, eternal, or external; it is internal to our nature as finite beings, persons bound by time, dependent on one another for survival, and liable to death.

Providing for the future is not only for survival, to satisfy the demands of the realm of necessity. Economic actors as human beings are subjected to what they do, to the process of production, consumption, and investment. The process could be driven by physical needs, profit-seeking, power-seeking, *creative destruction*, or communal commitments. It all depends on what purposes matter to them, on what is at stake. Indeed, as both Aristotle and Karl Marx thought, human beings as a species have no fixed essence, nature, or calling. What they do depends on what they value as finite beings. Thus, human beings do not pursue the process of production, consumption, and investment as the ultimate end, but as a means to a life of freedom, a spiritual life. In other words, economic activities do not only help us to self-relate and self-maintain, but they also relate to our life-activity as a free activity; that is, they call us to question the very process of production, consumption, and investment, to ask questions or transform the purpose of the process. As Martin Hägglund puts it,

> Rather than treat our own survival and the survival of our species as the given *end* (as the ultimate purpose of our

> life-activity), we can treat survival as a *means* toward the end of leading a free, spiritual life. For the same reason, the question of what should count as a satisfying, successful form of life is never finally settled for us. Like other animals we have to satisfy our needs and reproduce our life form, but *how* and *why* we should satisfy our needs and reproduce our life form is always at least implicitly at issue. We are not simply consigned to reproduce a given form of life but capable of calling into question and changing our ways of living. This is why our life-activity fundamentally is a free activity.[31]

The dynamics of the split economy compel us to ask what motivates the making of provision today and consumption tomorrow, to divide surplus into consumption and investment in the first place. Why do all these matter to us? What is at stake? Our life is finite, time-bound. We are not just in time; time itself is split and this split provokes and defines the character of desire and temporal experience. Our economic activities—as a form of dependence on others and as an urgency to do, prioritize, and value things because we can lose them in the future—"depends on economization of time," as Marx argues in *Grundrisse*.[32]

It is not only that economic production is grounded in split time; the process of production, consumption, and investment splits time, that is lifetime itself. As living beings, humans need to engage in the activity of self-maintenance, of sustaining life. Without this activity they would die. With dexterity in the production, consumption, and investment process they learn to produce more than what it costs to keep themselves alive. The experience gained starting from primordial times up to the present has meant that it now takes less and less time to produce the resources humans need to maintain life as societies. The process of production itself generates surplus time, a surplus of lifetime. Their lifetime is not consumed by efforts to stay alive; rather, the surplus time that is generated allows them to pursue other purposes in life. We see here that finite lifetime is split; it is divided between *necessary* time and *free* time. The production process is liberating time, divided time. Human beings do not spend the whole of their lifetime in the pursuit of self-preservation. Some of their lifetime is spent in self-enjoyment, relating to their free time as free, and they "*do* have the capacity to ask themselves how they should spend their time."[33] We see that while the production-consumption-and-investment process itself started as a response to time, as a response to finitude, a response to split time, it is imbricated in generating structures of time that make life meaningful to us as beings bound by time.

Without understanding the various types of temporal processes in the economy, we cannot fully account for the generation of value. From primordial times until now, time has been at the center of the economic process.

In this book I am trying to grasp the relationship between human flourishing and time. What does it mean to interpret finitude as the condition of possibility of an economy? As temporal beings our economic activities are implicitly affected by time. The Kalabari conception of destiny and desire make explicit the imbrication of finitude in economic activities. They necessarily understand their practical activity of leading an economic life as time-bound from the first-person standpoint.

The question "What does it mean to interpret finitude as the condition of possibility of an economy?" also means "How does a people's understanding of time and its induced incompleteness of desire inform their conception of human flourishing?" Human flourishing cannot be reduced to the means of capital accumulation, since both desire and how we organize societal resources to satisfy it depend on split time. Finite time—split time, our shared finitude—and activities devoted to living on in finite time are to be treated as ends in themselves. Even our bodies are to be taken into serious consideration in any account of human flourishing, desire, and split time.

Split Time and the Human Body

The human body in Kalabari is the seat of time. It is neither the seat of sex, as in psychoanalysis, nor the seat of death, as in the biopolitical definition of bare life. Time is immanentized in the human body. How is this so? The body does not encounter a single, complete time; it encounters partial times, fragments and successions of time. Thus, complete time is always a retrospective illusion. Time inhibits its very movement toward completion: as a part of its very activity or movement it obstructs the achievement of its completion. It moves as divided into three units. The human body, the human subject forced to live in the time gaps, is the bond of time. The time gap traverses the human subject; she lives with it, lives within it, and it lives within her. The split in time opens up a split in her. Time is always slightly opening up fractures within her and between her and others/things. Indeed, it is not time alone that is "split from itself; the split subject is fractured through" time's repetitions of splits.[34] The hole in her is a *void* that permits her not to stubbornly stick to her personal history or repeat in the present the predictions, trends, and dictates that are reaching her from the past. Like time she transgresses herself. Time always transgresses itself. Time does not coincide with itself. The "is" of time is split.[35] Any unit of time always has something more than itself, "always slightly different from or more than" itself.[36] Time always contains an excess that cannot be fully articulated within any one of its three units. Each unit bears a necessity to go beyond itself. The time-bound subject-in-economy in the present has to make provision for the future and its excesses, and in this unsubduable task she is (should be) driven by the difference between the human flourishing that is demanded (or could be achieved) and that which has been attained. It is also driven by the quest to secure (or care for) what has been achieved but is susceptible to loss.

Let me restage this brief commentary on time and the human body (the subject) by stating that the subject is not just the seat of time and that time is not simply immanentized in the human body. We will be mistaken if we construe my commentary to mean that the body is simply an internalization (interiorization) of time. The transgressive excesses of time, its capacity to force or nudge the subject to make provision for the future, and the subject's propensity to be dissatisfied with her provisions are interpreted, fabricated, or appropriated only on the basis of the norms, laws, hopes, experiences, and ideals of her community.[37] Besides, although there is no outside of time for the subject, with the interiorization of time there is now an outside within time. To construct a human abode within a time gap, within the minimal gap that divides time from itself (as we shall learn later), is to conceive of the "passage of time" as distinct from the "time of passage." The time of passage is not the opposite of the passage of time, the inverse of the inescapable movement of time. The time of passage negates the passage of time not from outside, but limits the negating, annihilating effect of the passage of time from within. Human beings, in building institutions, rituals, practices, promises, and other constructions, leach negativity from the negative, the contingency of history.

Institutions (a short term for everything mentioned in the last sentence) are the forces that step into the small tears in the fabric of time and pull human beings through to some vaster tapestry so that when they arrive, the same human beings find themselves retroactively constituting the very same institutions. Institutions are always half-said or half-done, not fully said or fully complete, because they require our actual experience through time to complete them. There are no fully constructed institutions—they all need our actual acts or experiences through the passage of time to complete them. When time passes, our institutions step into the tears of time and become our times of passage between the cracks that exist as the units of time move. In a sense our institutions do not only live in the cracks, they also become "times." Institutions—as responses to the passage, damage, and surprises of time—symbolize as well as instantiate the freedom to begin a new kind of time and to effect the passage to new conditions of being or existence. Their devotion to managing the constant passage of time is itself an act of constituting themselves.

The overall image of human beings and time in the Kalabari society is not that of a people disdaining the sense of finitude because of some promise of timeless repose, but that of subjects who have found a place in time, not a timeless place; who have come to terms with their passionate practical commitment to finite life. While time-bound, they struggle to find spaces, cracks in time—empty places in time—in which to plant themselves and their institutions in order to complete or suture the units of time as a work of completing their world or standing in a new relation to the world. The subject-time relation we have here is not a structure of opposition in which Kalabari and finitude battle against each order, but a "topological structure in which the subject appears twice, first, as subtracted from and second, as added to [time]."[38] By subtraction I do not mean that Kalabari subjects are removed from time; rather, subtraction here means incompletion. The subjects cannot, on the basis of their relation to time, define themselves completely. Time, the subjects, and the social signifiers they use to define the time-subject relation, or their identity, never constitute a complete system, a totality. To be a subject in time is to be *non-all*, to be traversed by split time that unglues the subject's unique identity not by denying her existence, but by making the care for her finite life a disruption of her self-sufficiency, her wholeness. All this is not to talk about the common Hegelian-Lacanian psychoanalytic observation that the subject is always caught in her image, here in her image of time. She, as one that has a perspective, is always caught in the field of vision of time, contributing to what she sees.

Let me conclude this section by returning to where we started. We stated that time has no body but only a frame. When human beings and their institutions step into time, when they intervene in its flowing, floating kind of frame, they give it a body. This synthesis of frame (form) and body (content) is only a poor attempt to lock reality in place. But (time-drenched) reality in its precariousness and instability is always slipping through their fingers. Their work of responding to time, to living on, is never done. In general, how a society responds to this task will shape its orientation to time and hence its orientation of economic development.

Time Orientations and Economic Development[39]

There are, broadly speaking, three perspectives on temporal orientation. First, that which is discernable from Hannah Arendt's work pertains to establishing a gap in the continuum of time so as to "subdue temporality . . . to consolidate and stabilize a moral existence, rendering it less fleeting, ontologically less insecure."[40] The point of temporal orientation is to make the world of appearance more durable through human action.

Second, Mircea Eliade taught us that time orientation is toward the beginning or origin of time, which is a fixed point, ordering all human times. In his analysis, the beginning is the most important point in the time continuum—or the point that gives orientation to all times. This beginning is decided once and for all. The value of any time segment is related one way or another to this break, which is the center of time and is regarded as sacred. Eliade made a distinction between sacred and profane time with sacred time erupting into the continuum of profane time to renew, recreate, and empower it through worship and rites. Arendt does not make such a distinction between sacred and profane time. For her, it is the immanent and transfiguring human action that erupts into the time continuum, into the automatism of existing social and natural processes that creates a durable time (gaps in time) so as to sustain the being of politics.[41] The gaps enable men and women to show the "who" of their individuality in the world of appearance.

Finally, the view of temporal orientation usually common in economic science is about revealed preference for a time segment in decision-making. Temporal preference is usually considered to be the segment of time (past, present, or future) that agents choose or find most important when responding to exogenous stimuli in their environments or when making decisions. This perspective on temporal orientation ignores crucial dimensions and preconditions of the choice of any segment. The choice is not merely a result of focusing on a continuum that is alongside human beings.

The decision-maker is not of the life that shrinks from time as it flows by but, rather, is of the life that cuts it and inserts itself into its gap and endures the forces pulling and pushing from both ends. In grappling with exogenous stimuli, in being oriented toward time itself, the community plunges into time. The choice is decisive for every society. Through the choice the society penetrates time; if it does not choose, time runs out on it, and it withers. It is the choice that creates time (nonobjective time) for it. The choice is always a cut in time through which agents "abstract one time from the possibility of another" so as to encounter "eternity" in time, to construct connection between eternity and existence.[42] Choice is always the cutter and connector between time and eternity.

Deciding about a time segment is one thing, but existing in the time one decides about is another entirely. Societies not only make decisions about time—choosing what segments to focus on when making investment decisions—but also construct the time in which they live. Only the time they construct or build up is time for them. This is an essential predicate relating to time as an experience of Being-in-appearance. In this idea we hear the echoes of Søren Kierkegaard, for with Kierkegaard the ethical life is to summon those radical choices that make us encounter eternity in time. The possibility of the radical choices is sutured to an exception that happened in time; the Eternal itself appeared in a moment of time. (This is the so-called Christian paradox.) This break-in leaves a gap that must be experienced as subjective inwardness, and it is this experience that commences or recommences the gap for each person. It is only by his or her choice that the subject exists in commitment to the exception.

Alain Badiou, a dominant twenty-first-century French philosopher, also holds that to live is to live in a certain type of gap, in an exception; to live is to incorporate oneself faithfully into a discontinuity (or, more precisely, incorporate oneself into the evental traces of a discontinuity) inscribed on a world (or *situation*). As he puts it:

> Ultimately life is the wager, made on a body that has entered into appearing, that one will faithfully entrust this body with a new temporality, keeping at a distance the conservative drive (ill-named 'life' instinct) as well as the mortifying drive (the death instinct). Life is what gets the better of the drives.[43]

Contrary to economists' conception of temporal orientation as a focus on a particular segment of an infinite succession of segments and Eliade's sacred beginning, I consider temporal orientation to be fidelity to gaps in the infinities of time. There are only infinite past and infinite future, except that there are gaps, on which I wish to focus scholarly attention. What kind of thought and praxis can authorize and sustain the continuation of gaps? What does it mean to be free? Is it when we can punch holes in the continuum of time, in the automatic processes of social existence? Freedom is to know this gap and to understand just how to participate in it in order to initiate a new beginning amid the continuity of worlds or physical life. As Arendt argues, freedom presupposes an actor who articulates his subjectivity upon this gap or even initiates the caesura. Arendt and Badiou both explore how subjects live and thrive in exceptions in order to redo human existence. This gap, this break, appears in the immanent world or *situation* for both of them. But for Arendt it also appears between the past and future—in time—but can only be indwelled by what she calls the "thinking ego," not by complete corporeality that can incorporate itself into the gap.

In her *The Life of the Mind* Hannah Arendt conceptualizes the gap between past and future as the dwelling place for the thinking ego that withdraws from appearance. For Arendt the gap is a form of withdrawal, and in this she is right. But what kind of withdrawal is it for the acting man or woman (the full complement of the mind—thinking, willing, and judging—and the body), not just for a part of the mind? Unlike her, I conceptualize this gap for the whole acting person, whose freedom consists in initiating something new, as a withdrawal from omnipresence (from the chiasmic intersections of appearances that forever must mark the past) and from omnipotence (the absolute freedom of the Will's projects to determine the future and absolve itself from all consequences of action in the future). It is in this *tzimsum*-like withdrawal of the human that a person's creativity brings forth, that is, that a person is born to begin.

These two withdrawals from the relentless flow of time are also the ground for the principle of limitation and ordering in the creative advance into novelty made possible by the exercise of freedom. Because a human can dwell in this momentary gap away from the infinite, chaotic, creative possibilities that are in the nature of pure Being at the extreme edges of time, the human's momentary achievements can be preserved and enjoyed.[44]

I believe that the body, the full person, can be incorporated into the gap by exceptional decision. The gap is "transcendent immanence." It is a kind of border-experience, not only that human beings mark and inhabit it, but that it is also inscribed on them as a form of space, so to speak.

The gap presents a border onto experience, a spot where fullness confronts poverty. The gap is a limit that is accessible but cannot be possessed or abolished. "[This] is the significance of the construct 'transcendent immanence.' To place a border ready-to-hand, to posit a limit immediately at your face, and in your hands which you cannot transcend, but have to carry with you, wherever you walk. . . . An old vademecum of possibilities and of the very limitation of experience handed over to you."[45]

The gap is the border or common limits where human beings are exposed to time and where time is exposed to them. Arendt says that the gap gestures to human existence between two absences, birth and death. If time or the gap presents to us our birth and death it is really revealing in facticity our existence outside ourselves. The gap is an exteriority, "the spacing of the experience of [absence], of the outside, the outside-of-self," in Jean-Luc Nancy's language.[46]

Humanity is always exposed in the *now* of the gap. To be in the gap is to be posed in exteriority. I have said earlier that humans not only exist in this gap, but also bear it on themselves. The gap gestures to "an outside *in the very intimacy* of an inside."[47] By, in, or through this gap humans have access to what is proper to their own existence, "only through an 'expropriation' whose exemplary reality is that" of their being and sociality always exposed to time (time gap), always turned toward time as an other and faced by time, never facing themselves.[48]

The gap never disappears. The gap is resistance itself—as Arendt appropriately notes with Kafka's parable of the "HE." Without the gap there would be no time, or rather, nothing but time "appearing to itself, not even *in common* with itself, just immanent [Time] immersed in a dense pearance (*parence*). [The gap] resists this infinite immanence." The gap "keeps open a space, a spacing within immanence."[49]

It is important to clarify immediately what is meant by space here, since time by definition cannot be intrinsically spatial. The space is not a place but the sharing of the edges of Being of beings, their spacing. It is a locus or nexus of mutual interactions, a condition of possibility for the existence of interactions. Conceptually speaking, where is this space or locus to be located? There are three possibilities: a space outside of humans; a space within humans in some sense; or a space identical to humans. The first is not acceptable because it means that human sociality is grounded in an external source. Nor can the space be identical to human beings, since it is itself the result of interactions between human beings and time, an other. Thus, I suggest that it is within (as being-with, "an outside in the very intimacy of an inside") humans, more precisely *within* human sociality where time and humans are not just juxtaposed but are actually exposed to one another. The space is the basis of interactions, inseparable from human beings, to be sure, but nevertheless distinguishable from them.

Is the gap, properly speaking, a cut, a laceration of time (time flow)? Properly speaking, there is no cut in which the insides of both past and future infinities of time "would get lost in the outside (which would presuppose an initial 'inside,' an interiority). The laceration that . . . is exemplary, the woman's 'breach,' is ultimately not a laceration. It remains, obstinately, and in its most intimate folds, the surface exposed to the outside. . . . [Similarly], the open mouth is not a laceration either. It exposes to the 'outside' an 'inside' that, without this exposition, would not exist."[50]

The gap as a *now* is a breach. In a certain sense the now (the gap as the place of sharing of the infinities of time) is the origin of time. The "origin is the tracing of the borders upon which and along which" past and present infinities of time are exposed.[51] The *now* is the limit where human beings experience time's alterity and are exposed to time. What holds it together is the identity, the identity of being exposed—exposed to the outside. Bodies (as spaces) and time are exposed alike and therefore share the common identity of exposition. The *now* is the ontological order in which humans and time are alike.

The *now* is a singular-plural (being-with), bare, intense presence. This presence (this "it is") is detached from the *coming* time by the encounter with human beings that *finishes it off*. It is detached from nothingness as it discloses itself to human beings. This detachment, which is finite, takes place infinitely as time comes (appears) and goes (disappears).[52]

Let us garner more valuable insights about time by joining Ole Fogh Kirkeby's notion of "transcendent immanence" with Arendt's thought on time gap. Arendt calls the time gap "the standing now," *nunc stans*.[53] This now is also the place of the new, the new beginning. The etymological origin of the word "new" relates to now; " 'nun' in German, 'nyn' in the Greek, namely, 'now': that which is here forever."[54] The Latin *stans* (standing) comes from the Greek word *stasis*, "(that which stands still), i.e., the centre, the middle. But 'stasis' also means 'the getting-up,' 'the insurrection,' 'the rebellion,' 'the struggle.' "[55] This means that the center is not immobile, in movement it balances itself as a middle; the center cannot be irrevocably enforced into time once and for all so that humans can take a vacation and step aside for a while. Human beings cannot jump out of the struggle without past and future infinities crashing in on them.

The human insertion into the gap—the human as image of time—enables us to *see* time, find the invisible within the visible. In humanity time is invisibly manifest. The Kalabari word for menstruation is "saki-eri," literally "see time." The periodic flow of blood from the woman is a form of seeing time: the invisible movement of time is manifest at a site of the female body.[56]

Time as *now* discloses itself to humanity and by means of humanity. (This is also true for humanity.) It is the human body—in humanity, in human life—that the movement of time echoes, where its depth can be sounded, where its waves become visible. Humanity gives perspicuity to time by setting new beginnings before our eyes, by receiving kairos, and by *unconcealing* time's methodology (*meta-hodos*, "after-the-way-gone," the way it walked, what it actually did).[57]

The insertion of humankind as time and as center of time gives content to temporality by initiating the new. And it is by actions (in Arendt's terminology, initiating the new) that human beings as temporal beings act as a center to stabilize and strengthen itself in the struggle between the two infinities of time. A balance that acts as a middle, as a center, must move to maintain its position when the limits on the scale are mobile. The time gap is maintained and is maintainable only by decisions. The kind of decisions that keep the gap alive are not merely hinged on projecting prospects of the past onto the future, but on initiating new set of possibilities. For Søren Kierkegaard, in choosing to choose, the decision-maker acts in an "unconditioned way," negating the thralldom of determined past and future, and thus the crucial moment of decision is "situated outside of time," in the time gap as per the language of this study.

One of the tasks of this study is to investigate the ethics of consisting in that in-betweenness inscribed in the continuity of time. This task involves, at minimum, understanding how a human being can inscribe and articulate his freedom upon a break (gap) in time in order to define his subjectivity as actualization of potentialities. How does a human being, a victim of automatic natural and social processes, emerge as a *subject* who initiates a new series?

The subject is in history—not outside of history—and is in a specific world. It is from this localization in the automatic processes of world and history that the new world-making person must emerge. A subject emerges as she becomes faithful to an *event* by interpreting, intervening, and extending it. The event itself is born in the first place by the *actions* of men and women as they initiate the new amid the automatic processes of life and the hanging-together of life (sociality). The subject is subject insofar as he is committed to founding something new, a new criterion of action. This interaction of self, event, history is located in a specific space of the *self-world correlation.*

The human being as a being-in-appearance lives in a world marked by restlessness. The boundaries of this world are continually redrawn, for the self as subject is marked by *fidelity* to the discerning of possibilities visible from particular locality in the self-world correlation. Subjectivation is basically a process of pushing the boundaries of the world further outward, creating and actualizing possibilities, which remakes social coexistence for the sake of human flourishing. The subject bursts forth from the self and in the breaking-forth it does not break forth into the world of the old self but actually simultaneously steps into a new world dragged out of an old world.

This complex admixture of founding and fidelity to event and repatterning of a society's responses to the passage and pressures of time is the *origin* of the self and history.[58] Origin does not connote causes. I am, indeed like Arendt before me, using *origin* neither to suggest that the term is identical with essential nature, ontological point of departure, or historical causality, nor to give the impression that the factors I am going to list have the character of a chain of causes that must inevitably lead to a particular self. The origin is used in the sense that from the vantage point of the present we can recognize founding(s) in the past that have permitted augmentation and amendment of the self. This is about tracing the elements that have crystallized in it and not about an evolutionary narrative of causally related events that birthed and now sustain the subject. Origin is about formation, not genesis—how sociocultural sources crystallized.

How has the subject been formed by time as its other and as a source of ethical imperative? How is the difference between subject and this other negotiated and what are the demands entailed by this difference? This other is not a strange object thrown in front of me but, rather, stands actively alongside me, shaping my relationships with my world and even my understanding of my world and myself. Posing the question about the origin of the subject or self in this way requires that we seek the answer from an ethics that incorporates time into its formulation in new ways.

Ethicists do not usually think of time and the problematic of the ethical in this way. Time has been incorporated into ethics at best as that which provides a future horizon for the fulfillment of meaning, for the development of virtuous (noble) character, or for nothingness (that is, for the realization of the possibility of impossible existence). If it is not about any of these, it is then about the time horizon for moral deliberation or hope. Is hope or the binding ethical imperative within human history or outside it?[59] But it has never really been about conceptualizing the ethos of a society, first of all, as response to the passage of time itself. With a focus on ethos as a result of response to passage of time or to the choices that create and perpetuate a rupture in time, there is no longer any doubt as to the source of ethical imperative. The binding ethical imperative never arises from outside history but, rather, always from the human vulnerability to time (passage of time) as an other. The ethical imperative is to be free from this vulnerability, to transcend time within time and not to some eternal repose. At the social level (intersubjectivity), the task is for the relational structures of everyday existence to withstand and overcome the blows of decay that come with the passage of time as well as to renew themselves. At the individual level it is the exercise of the human capability of beginning something new. This freedom to posit the new is tied to the freedom to disclose oneself, the distinctiveness of one's individuality that demands new beginnings even as time chronically marches on.

This difference between the social and individual in response to time is founded on the dual nature of human existence: finite and infinite. The individual is caught between being and nonbeing and her existence must reach its limits one day. But she wants to survive, live on, flourish in this confinement. Proposing new things to one's environment, initiating the new, is part of the ecstatic temporality of human nature. Human beings are also ecstatic in the sociospatial dimension. If the individual person is finite and therefore his "existence appears to be for death," his social institutions are infinite, and their "existence is for life."[60] From the standpoint of the whole society, existence is in perpetuity; the common world lives forever. The Japanese philosopher Watsuji Tetsurō is eloquent on this point:

> Men die; their world changes; but through this unending death and change, man lives and his world continues. It continues incessantly through ending incessantly. In the individual's eyes, it is a case of an "existence for death," but from the standpoint of society it is an "existence for life."[61]

In conclusion, temporal orientation is neither considered to be a culture's focus on sacred beginning (although this is important) nor recognized as the preference for a particular segment of time (important still for investment decisions). It is, rather, seen as the disruptive ethics of founding and sustaining gaps in a time continuum. We have not yet carefully described the process of creating the gaps, and this remains the task ahead. Speaking of gaps, one is reminded that in the history of ethical discourse, gap is a common metaphor, often deployed as an arsenal of conformity. Let us destabilize the discursive calm and arrange gaps on the side of social transformation.

Ethics of Time Gap

Ethics is about gaps. The gap of the wholly-Other and the gap of the human-Other are the two most famous gaps. In the instance of the first gap, the Wholly-Other, theologians tell us that grace or certain approved deeds bridge or supplement the gap between humans and God. But Karl Barth argues that no matter how hard we try, the gap cannot be closed. Humanists tell us that in order to close the second gap, the gap of the human-other, we need only recognize (witness) the otherness of every person, vigilantly responding to it without denying or totalizing the difference. But Gayatri Chakravorty Spivak—in what appears to be an echo of Barth—says the gap between the self and the other cannot be bridged. "By definition," she says,

> [m]an lives in this in-between, and what he calls the present is a life-long fight against the dead weight of the past, driving him forward with hope, and the fear of a future . . . driving him backward toward "the quiet of the past" with nostalgia for and remembrance of the only reality he can be sure.[62]

We can now assert that in addition to the Barthian gap (qua theologians') and the Lévinasian gap (qua humanists'), there is another gap. This third gap we may need to consider as the founding gap and also as constitutive of being-in-ethical-relations. You know it already. It is the gap of time. Every society creates institutions, enacts rituals, and performs praxis to transcend the passage of time, but temporal leaps always fall short of the boundary of time. Humans live in the gap between two absences or limits (birth and death) defined by time. This gap is not something that is merely an object of response but is something that they create and nurture. This gap cuts into time to resist the finitude of time.[63] Human institutions acquire their own time, a new temporality. It seems that time has been abstracted from the possibilities of the factical-historical situation of social existence. The gap is, indeed, originary ("*ursprunglich*," taking "leap" from "*sprung* in in *Ursprung*, origin").[64] Following Krzysztof Ziarek, I assert that

> the word "originary" designates the temporality of how the familiar structures of everyday being—and the various practices and orders of conceptualizing them in ordinary language, scientific rationality, or philosophical reflection—have in each moment unfolded out of the factical-historical situation of human existence.[65]

Here Ziarek is in the good company of Hans-Georg Gadamer, who informs us that "the fundamental character of historicity does not depend on the fact that the human being has a history; rather all history depends on the originary temporality and historicity of the human being."[66]

It is important to remind ourselves that the purpose of this study's conceptualization of time gap, the creation of temporality, is geared toward understanding human subjectivity in an encounter with the fundamental other (time). Human agents create gaps and incorporate themselves into them in order to articulate their subjectivity. By making disruptive and subtractive time gaps the locus of ethical thinking, I hope that the philosophy of economic development does not focus only on technical capabilities to the neglect of how the links between ethos and social transformation are forged and articulated in order to open up futural possibilities for emancipatory economic development. The preceding statement summons me to clarify how my basic understanding of economic development or human flourishing remains open to political contestation and emancipatory praxis. In responding to this call, I want to show that economic development is not a project of driving Africans to the ideal fullness of the market, to pursue the market as "the Thing," but to focus their attention on their *living on* as beings perforated by temporal finitude and incompleteness and oriented toward human flourishing.

Economy Development, Human Flourishing, and Desire

Economic development is a desire for human flourishing that is marked by a threat of poverty that is feared. Economic development is not threatened by poverty as an external agent. There is also an internal division within economic development that makes it susceptible to turning against itself at any given moment. It is open to the unpredictability, corruptibility, and instability inherent in time. Economic development depends on decisions or strategic interventions. These are haunted by the undecidability of time, the condition of everything finite and mortal. It is because of this undecidability that economic development is a matter of articulatory practices, the bringing together of appropriate elements of private and public sectors that do not have necessary connections in order to form an innovative platform for human flourishing that could not exist without the articulation. How can this bringing-together of a plurality of actions be constructed and mediated as an aggregation? The neoliberal market model says actions with particular aims converge automatically as a result of the price mechanism. But there is also a way to approach the negotiation and mediation of actions that does not rely on spontaneous unity of actors and does not cancel out politics. There is always a need for a political articulation of the appropriate elements. There is always the question of how the struggles for economic development or the quest for human flourishing can be politically constructed and mediated.

This second approach does not aspire to cancel out capitalism or market hegemonic articulation of the heterogenous actions; rather, it aims to infuse its hegemonic articulation with an appropriate comprehension of the unpredictable coming of time and in this way to propose an alternative set of articulatory practices. This articulation would not be driven by a desire for the absolute fullness of market domination of the historical terrain.[67] Economic development is not a desire to cure any economy from the disease or dissatisfaction of the *lack* of market-being. And human flourishing is not a desire to bring infinite fullness to individuals or society. The idea that the desire for economic development, especially in poor African countries, is a desire to reach the fullness of market-being and that the "mortal economic being" of such countries is a lack of market-being is wrong. Economic development is not a "Thing" that Africa lost (directly or retrospectively) and that must be recovered or reached. The market is not the original plenum. In fact, neither economic development nor human flourishing should be thought of in terms of lack of being or lack of fullness. This kind of thinking only leads to the experience (or the rise) of satisfaction from such partial objects as growth of gross domestic product, stock price indices, or new housing starts. As Lacanian psychoanalysis has taught us, every desire for "the Thing" (*das Ding)* is soon corrupted into a drive—and "the elevation of ordinary object to the dignity of the Thing."[68] And what is touted as investment is only a revolving investment in partial objects for the mythical fullness of the market that always evades the fullness of the stomach of the masses. Revolving investment posits profit or economic growth as the "incarnation of the desired fullness" of economic development or human flourishing.[69]

While the neoliberal approach is predicated on the illusion that revolving investment is universal (in the sense of satisfying the needs of the whole economy/society) and embodies the fullness of market-being, the alternative theory I am advocating here says economic development or human flourishing remains open to contestation and it is not universal. My interest is to demonstrate that instead of economic development becoming a project of driving Africans to the ideal fullness of the market, we should focus on their *living on* as beings perforated by temporal finitude. I am not advocating that Africans should reject the market or saying that they do not deserve robust human flourishing. Rather, I am arguing that the desire for economic development cannot be a desire for absolute fullness of the market.[70]

Economic development and human flourishing are matters of survival, that is, making provision for the future, asking for a better future, being vigilant over the forces threatening to thwart well-being, and openness to the unpredictability of time rather than to the closed telos of the market. Chapter 5 will dwell on how best to connect economic development with human flourishing. Before we address this issue, we need to understand how the Kalabari address the thorny question of coordinating individual desires to produce and sustain the collective economic order for the production and distribution of wealth. They evolved a system that I have named *agonistic communitarianism*. Chapter 4 provides an analysis of agonistic communitarianism as a fundament of the Kalabari approach to national economic management.

Chapter 4

Economy and Destiny

A Theory of Agonistic Communitarianism

Introduction

We have seen that the dehiscent succession of time forces a wedge of division in desire, destiny, recanting, and subjectivity. The economic organization of society, the immanent co-implication of cooperation and competition, mirrors this temporal division. The traditional Kalabari economy in its libidinal dimensions carries the mark of the splitting of time and the subject. The split in time or the subject is reflected in the division of communalism and individualism that runs in the economy. The dehiscence between time itself, between whatever *there is*, is subsumed under the heading of economy itself. As we shall demonstrate further on, the structure of Kalabari economic subjectivity is split by communalism and "individualism." The desire of the economic subject is to return to the lost primordial (socially constructed) object of communalism, but it is inaccessible. Profit, the pursuit of economic gain, is the drive around this object. Profit as a drive is fixated upon *das Ding* of communalism, and it is successful if it can help to obtain or regain the lost object. But in reality, desire has been transformed into drive, as the inaccessible *Ding* (the Real of their community) is transformed into an object, the socioeconomic flourishing of the *wari* (the canoe-house corporation). The pursuit of profit through the concatenation of the house system serves as only a "trick," a futile motion of the drive to repeatedly circle around the irrecoverable Real. Indeed, the aim of profit-making only reflects the loss of the *thing*.

The economy is structured like destiny. The economy is the latent possibilities of destiny, that is, the interpersonal (transindividual) destiny of a community. The statement that the traditional Kalabari economy is structured like destiny is (almost) equivalent to saying that the economy is structured like time. Time is a treasure of latent possibilities, motions that erase and create, and rhythms that doubly bind the hope of care and the fear of loss of what is being cared for. Time with its infinite, indefinite successions, with its play on creative destructions, with its power to deny whatever there is, with its capacity to undermine the self-identity or uncracked presence of any existant, undergirds and supervenes the economy. An economy is a set of indefinite plays of values, differences, and splits. The economy, like time, is never fully present to itself. The analogy should not be construed to mean that time or destiny is a structure, an external order that imposes itself on individual subjects, decisions, or interactions. Destiny is not secretly determining conscious economic actions (agents). We are only saying that just like living on has to be attended to, so does profit-making.

Profit could be lost or something can go wrong with it. So like all finite "objects" it has to be attended to with care and passion. Profit requires that I sustain it. The profit that I make, like my finite life, is dependent on others and can be irrevocably lost at any time. If I believe that my profit is eternal, that its stream will exist forever, I may never be motivated or animated to care for it and it could never be considered to be at stake. The pursuit or preservation of profit could not be separated from the sense that it could be lost. The project of taking care of my profits gives my economic activities a purpose. It gives me, a mortal person—the one whose life is lived in relation to death and is dependent on others and who needs to take care of it—a purpose. The incessant preservation of profits tells me I am doing something with my finite lifetime. From here it is a small step to elevate this care and passion for profit to the dignity of the paramount goal of society, the preservation of communalism. Or, since profit is made in the name of the *wari*—the canoe-house corporation with its chief (manager) and the house members—the ideal of preserving and augmenting profits binds me to the normative ideal of communalism. The ideal of communalism is inseparable from the fidelity to the practice of profit. Communalism as life together bounded by time is an end in itself. In fact, the ideal of communalism is believed to live on through the practice of profit or practice of faith in profit.

The fidelity to fragile profit in the name of the so-called community well-being necessarily coexists with individualism (positive agency), a dimension of shared lives. Individualism in Kalabari is a commitment to lead a free life, which does not mean liberation from all constraints. Rather, it means each individual is free to "ask themselves what we ought to do with our time."[1] Is this not the fundamental question the notion of destiny asks? "Only in the light of the apprehension that we will die—that our lifetime is indefinite but finite—can we ask ourselves what we ought to do with our lives and put ourselves at stake in our activities."[2]

Communalism and individualism are dimensions of shared, finite lives that are ends in themselves in the Kalabari society. The community of finite beings—the purpose of what they do and how they do them—is not considered as a means of reaching some greater end, such as eternity, eschatology, or the end of history. Neither Kalabari religious faith nor the notion of *fiyeteboye* (destiny) or *bibibari* (recanting) denies that the lives and projects of finite beings are ends in themselves. Nor does Kalabari religion deny individuals the space to lead their own lives cognizant of the interdependence on community members' need for participation in worthy collective (communal) projects. Individualism (positive agency that is always contestable) is an intrinsic part of the Kalabari commitment to the form of finite life they pursue and the practices they have instituted to uphold and justify it. This individualism does not depend on a contrast to communalism, since individualism is intrinsic to their collective life, which is always turned to finite life and invested in a commitment to living on rather than reposing in a timeless presence and everlasting existence. The care and commitment to life that theologians like the Cameroonian Laurenti Magesa[3] celebrate as indicative of African traditional religions is sustained in faith in finite life lived as temporal experience—and not lived in anticipation of the "consummation of eternity."[4] As Yale University philosopher and literary critic Martin Hägglund argues, "There cannot be any meaningful activities in eternity, since nothing can live on in a timeless presence and nothing can matter in an everlasting existence. . . . For anything to be at stake in maintaining a life, it must be running the risk of death."[5]

The relationship or tension between individualism (as we have construed it) and communalism in the traditional Kalabari economy is indicative of the relation between parts and whole in any economy. The question that this relation addresses is, how do you coordinate individual desires to produce and sustain the collective economic order for the production and distribution of wealth? The combination of communalism and individualism in nineteenth-century Kalabari—which I have called agonistic communitarianism—is an attempt to forge a co-promising system that combines the satisfaction of needs and the accumulation of profits (economic wealth), and the quantity and quality of time for cultural development (or what Hägglund calls "socially available free time"[6]).

The traditional economy was animated by three *oughts*: the ought of necessity, the ought of profit (which contributes to the common good of the *wari*), and the ought of enjoyment of culture, sustaining practical existential identities and refining values.[7] These oughts are embedded in both *-isms*, communalism and individualism, and they live in agonistic tension with each other. So not only there is an agonistic struggle between communitarianism and individualism, but also such tension exists within each of them. These tensions are driven by the co-implicating questions of what to do with our finite time and what to do with our lives, what we prioritize or what we value. These questions are fundamental to any economy and to how a people choose to live together and relish cultural enjoyment. And they are at the heart of Kalabari agonistic communitarianism. Communalism was not organized in nineteenth-century Kalabari to banish individualism or to be released from the risk of straying from the collective goal of the community. Rather, the point is to enable the community to own the risk of individualism by owning the fundamental questions of the economy. Just as destiny was not a craving for eternity or repose in a timeless place, communalism was not a desire to overcome the uncertainties, risks, and vulnerabilities of a temporal economy.

Now that we have set the theoretical stage for our analysis of Kalabari agonistic communitarianism, let me state how the rest of the chapter will unfold. In the first half of the chapter I will investigate Kalabari history, culture, and social philosophy to contextually situate the theory of agonistic communitarianism. In the second half, I will discuss agonistic competition in an ethic of excellence (*arete*), which I am interpreting as actualization of potentialities, to set the stage for chapter 5, in which I examine the connection between excellence and economic development.[8] In my 2009 book *The Principle of Excellence: A Framework for Social Ethics*, I argued that the goal of politics is the creation of possibilities for all to participate in the polity and to realize their potentialities and, in so doing, to enable the community to realize its potentialities. Science is an engagement with nature so as to fully understand, realize, extend, and create possibilities buried in the potentialities of all beings and processes in the universe. Education (*e-ducere*) is to draw out and lead forth the potentialities of a person. The organization of market competition is also oriented in this way—it is *agonistic*. The Latin source of our English word "competition" is *con* plus *petere*, which means to seek together. In competition the participants help each other to stretch their skills as they meet the challenge posed by the other. What each participant is seeking is the actualization of their own potential and to help the other person attain his or her best.[9] In the same vein, an excellent friendship is the type of partnership and fellowship in which each person aspires to bring to realization the latent potentialities of the other. An individual's life will be adjudged excellent if it is a life that is engaged in the pursuit of ever greater development and the creative realization of his or her potential. This involves, among other endeavors, overcoming challenges to create, manage, and sustain possibilities for responsible personal development.

In this light, the task of economic ethics—and, for that matter, social ethics as a whole—is to direct thinking on how to develop the best society for the releasing of potentialities of all persons and institutions for the common good and for human flourishing. Alternatively put, the object of the ethicist is to create a society that not only is attuned to the possibilities for full development of potentialities, but also enjoys excellence (such as the self going beyond itself to participate ever more fully in its world). Taking one's stance in excellence is one veritable way of calling into account all of society's institutions, laws, religions, relationships, and so forth. Do they facilitate the release of potentialities and the creation of new (alternative) possibilities for a more perfect human flourishing, or do they require the suppression of them? Those that fail this test merit being set aside. The ethicist is also to evaluate all emerging possibilities amid the range of all present possibilities, so as to project the direction of human flourishing of a particular community in relation to his or her sense of what its citizens want to become or want their society to be.[10]

1. The Theory of Agonistic Communitarianism

As I contemplated the subject of agonistic communitarianism, I knew that I was going to say something that might annoy many specialists in African social ethics. I want to begin this chapter with a provocative statement; to some it may, indeed, be deemed shocking. Now wait for it:

It is time to stop this bromide about all authentic African social ethic being about communitarianism. Those who advocate this ethic define it as one that accents the community as the ultimate concern, pronounce it as the criterion of truth, and laud it as the source of value; and they hold that its structures constitute the meaningful order for individual lives in it, secure the integrity of interpersonal interactions, and provide the foundation for communion. With this definition they deny that individualism ever had a place in precolonial Africa, and, as such, they insist that any scholarship today about social ethics in contemporary Africa must have communitarianism as its point of departure and destiny for it to be considered authentically, indigenously African. But I strongly disagree with this view. There are individualistic, competitive aspects of African moral philosophy, both in the past and in the present, and many scholars who write on the subject have conveniently ignored this fact.

African social ethic is (was) not purely and thoroughly communitarian. There were societies in precolonial times that had spheres that were competitive and individualistic; at least, they were branches that were grafted onto the root and trunk of the communitarian tree.[11] Yes, there were societies in which individualism and communitarianism coexisted and the competitive spirit was regarded as valuable. For instance, the Kalabari-Ijo of the Niger Delta, Nigeria, was one such community. As far back as the 1960s anthropologist Robin Horton had pointed this out. The precolonial Kalabari society was very competitive and fluid. Horton has this to say in comparing Kalabari culture with that of the Tallensi of Ghana: "Kalabari society, whether in its village or in its city-state variant, encourages aggressive individualism and personal achievement. If the emphasis in Taleland is on 'fitting in,' in Kalabari it is on 'getting up.' "[12]

Contrary to what some scholars are telling us, Africa was not an uncontaminated haven of communitarianism. Indeed, as Peter Ekeh has taught us, in many parts of Africa the state and society drifted apart starting in the era of slave trade, which only intensified in the colonial period and was exacerbated by post-independence politics. The forces of the state, which have refused to recognize a person's worth or citizenship, have steadily attacked the individual. As some precolonial African states engaged in the slave trade, they became hostile to their citizens and did not recognize the worth of the individual; and their politics were driven by the calculus of profit and power. The terms of exchange between the individual and the society or state in these states were not always on communitarian terms.[13] Some scholars miss this insight because they are diverted by the "shining object" of communitarianism at one level of sociality to the neglect of other levels. In the precolonial and colonial periods, the moral focus of individuals was on the *primordial public*, such as kin and ethnic groups, and in this context communalism prevailed. This is well and good until you realize that the so-called triumph of communalism at the lower levels may well be the fallout of citizens' alienation from their states. Thus, the very triumph of communitarianism that some scholars celebrate at the local (village or ethnic) level may well be an indication of the failure or decay of "pure" communitarianism at the higher reaches of social totalities. This much is implicit in Ekeh's seminal essays.

The problem that confronts scholars who emphasize communitarianism to the exclusion of other forms of social ethic in Africa is fourfold. First, implicit in this emphasis is the notion of "I am because we are" that they have stretched to the point of distortion. At the extreme uses of this notion of the intersubjective formation of humanity, individuals in traditional African communities are not considered as having value or worth in and of themselves. Individuals are made by the community, belong to the community, and have value because they are embraced by the community. While I do not deny that a human being becomes a person only in a community of other human beings, I refuse to accept that individualism necessarily thwarts the process of human personhood. For instance, in precolonial Kalabari society individualism occurred as individual fulfillment in the context of community, as an expression of the substance of justice and actualization of human potentiality in ways consistent with human dignity and with the unity of community members. The individualism in this context is not the *expressive individualism* wherein the needs of the self trump those of the community. What I have in mind is what I will call *covenantal individualism*, wherein the needs of the communal relationship and social justice take priority over the needs of the individual without necessarily stifling individual creativity and actualization of potentiality. The take-home point here is that communitarianism in Kalabari did not operate at the exclusion of (every sort of) individualism.

Second, too often scholars of African communitarianism ignore the historical records and refuse to acknowledge the coexistence of competitive individualism and communitarianism, especially in some communities that were engaged in long-distance trade. This kind of communities recognized the uniqueness and difference of each individual and the value of her individual self-interest or good within the ethos of communitarianism. The Kalabari was one such group.

Third, the advocates of African communitarianism have mistaken the notion of individualism as operated in African societies such as the Kalabari for the narcissistic individualism at work in contemporary Western society. In Kalabari, individualism was the play of dialogical subjective autonomies where each player agrees to rationally and consistently will that which coheres with the common good (broadly defined) of the community.[14] Individualism was the means or freedom by which Kalabari citizens were allowed to invent, discover, deliberate, and seek to attain their various goods within the non-totalitarian meaning-making framework of their community.[15] This form of individualism (always embedded in social practices that are largely defined by shared norms and a sense of mutual belonging) was a good internal to the values of the Kalabari and was grounded in the individuals' striving to be good human beings, virtuous agents, and persons in right relationship with others.

Finally, scholars talk about communitarianism as if the spirit of capitalism and other ethos of modernity have not penetrated contemporary Africa. I understand the need and emotion behind the intense or exclusive focus on communitarianism, but it does not warrant playing fast and loose with historical records or the contemporary situation on the continent. The ethic of communitarianism is not the melanin-gene of African social ethics; it is not the only source of everything distinct about African social values; it is not the unchanging, eternal pigmentation of the color of African ethics.

I Love My Mama

Do not get me wrong. I know that a lot of Africans harbor communitarian values. I do also. But if you ask me to choose between my mother and my community, I will choose my mother. There are many Africans who believe in their communities or in communitarianism, but, like Albert Camus, they will defend their mothers before they will defend justice or community.

You may doubt that there were such Africans in the precolonial times or before the encounter of many traditional African societies with capitalism. Your doubt does not diminish the gap or hole in our understanding of the ethic of communitarianism in precolonial Africa. At what point in the evolution of the moral fabric of precolonial Africa did genuine commitment to communitarianism give way to private life, pursuit of private interests, or degradation of communitarianism? Or are you ready to argue that at the height of your preferred exemplary society of African communitarianism there was no personal or private life? Are you saying that precolonial Africa had no private, personal, individual life? Was every person one with the community? Indeed, if you said yes, then it means you are implying that there were no persons, only community. I wish you good luck with such a philosophical stance.

Such a strict view of communitarianism amounts to the smuggling of Kantianism into the precolonial African social ethic. It was Kant who, in the name of the categorical imperative, ruled out of ethics any emotion, personal sympathy, and personal feeling. He regarded any move away from the universal imperative of duty as a pathological inclination. He would regard the choice of my mother over justice as a pathological inclination that interferes with reason as the supreme foundation of morality.

Was there an African community in which warmhearted feelings for one's mother were regarded as an obstacle to some universal moral law? It is only in the academy that I find an interpretation of communitarianism as a kind of Kantian universal moral law and the pursuit of private interest automatically interpreted as an obstacle to the realization of the moral ideas of communitarianism. It is high time we stopped this line of moral reasoning. Most of us who study African social ethics fall into this Kantian dream because we have not paid sufficient attention to the reality of the tension between particularity and universality (communitarianism) in African societies.

How many of us who champion communitarianism to the exclusion of other forms of ethics in Africa can say that there was (is) no unconditional call of the particular face, as Emmanuel Levinas argues? Precolonial Africa is not the graveyard for the "sovereignty" of particularity. By African communitarianism, do we mean that Africans obliterated all selfish interests in the pursuit of ideals or the paramount goals of their community? If not, then how have we addressed the inevitable tension between defending community and defending mother? How did Africans negotiate the tension either when the two imperatives (mother and community) coincide or when they diverge?

The thorny issue that I see in African social ethics is that often well-meaning scholars prematurely dissolve the tension between particular interests and the communitarian call for group flourishing or universal justice in the community. Communitarian ethicists need to educate us on how Africans on a continual basis resolve the tension between the particular and the universal, the private and the public. Social ethics everywhere harbor a tension between the particular and the communitarian (or universal). The nonsense is to believe that Africans as moral animals are somewhat different. The Africans that I know are like other human beings who are dealing every day with the tensions of the universal and the claims of their mothers or other loved ones.

My protest against the current overemphasis on communitarianism in the study of African social ethics is that its proponents have, ultimately and a priori, dissolved the tension by elevating the universal (communal) above the particular. Of course, I am also aware that to prioritize the particular is also to settle the tension prematurely. Africans, especially today, are caught in the gap between the particular and the universal, between individualism (individuality) and communitarianism. So every form of social ethics that wants to be faithful to the everyday moral behavior of Africans must acknowledge the inevitable tension between particularity and universality in their moral fabric. The unconditional call to responsibility to the singular/beloved must be balanced against the valorization of the community's call for its paramount goal.

As a son of my eighty-seven-year-old mother, I feel myself placed under infinite responsibility for her. When I was a helpless baby, she had the same infinite responsibility toward me. To say all this is not to argue that my mother and I were autonomous moral subjects that rationally entered into a mutually beneficial contract. Given her maternal instincts and the ethos of her Kalabari community, she loved me as a baby without concerning herself with profits from the mother–child relationship. She loved me without a concern that I would love her. Today, I care for her, without equivocation, not with a sense of an abstract universal duty I must perform, not because communitarianism runs in my blood, but because of my "pathological inclinations." More importantly, neither my mother nor I considered the movement toward the other as self-negation or self-inflation. We do not feel that heeding to the unconditional call of the other person in the relationship amounts to negating ourselves. We do not feel that either of us is going beyond what is human to extend ourselves to the other. And we are not practically committing ourselves to love everyone in our community equally.

Did the particular loving focus of my mother on me as a baby cut her off from the communitarian stream of compassion in her community? The particular focus of my mother on me, her inability to love all children in her community equally at the same time, was never a form of turning away from communitarianism. Within her limited abilities and well-grounded understanding of the ethos of her community, she worked for and hoped for every child to have a loving home so he could grow up to actualize his potentialities and be a blessing to the community. Thus, my mother's love for me was ultimately not at the expense of other children in her community.

In this way of understanding communitarianism neither my mother nor I was commended to take a degree of responsibility that only God or the gods could bear. One act of hubris of the proponents of free-ranging communitarianism in Africa is that they portray Africans as capable of loving as God loves or capable of realizing the ideals of communion as God. The proponents' notion of communitarianism has no a priori limits and in its light Africans are mistaken for divine beings. The kind of responsibility, commitment, and communion demanded by the communitarian ethic amount to denying the humanity of Africans as it calls upon them to be Godlike.

Without intending to do so, the communitarian ethic almost sounds like the death of God theology. The ethic of communitarianism as it is often propagated is unequivocally inclined toward divine responsibility. Never mind that in it there is a lot of focus on gods and deities. Human beings, that is, Africans, are perfect gods who are perfectly committed to the ideals of communion; who are in some sort of perichoretic relationship with their neighbors. This does not make sense. The communitarian ethic must not burden finite, contingent Africans, past or present, with the divine task of assuming the infinite and absolute responsibility for building and sustaining perfect interpersonal or community-wide relationalities.

From Communitarianism to Agonistic Communitarianism

Nor does it make sense to present (traditional) Africans as incapable of ignoring the common interest for their own interests or welfare. The advocates of African communitarianism assume that the traditional African is consistently selfless. Traditional Africans, adherents of African traditional religion (ATR), like Christians, are not "always" able to be selfless, to consider the community and its welfare before their own. Such advocates of African communitarianism are as wrong as the Christian ethicists who hold that the arc of the ethos of Christianity inviolably bends toward communitarianism. Reinhold Niebuhr argues against ethicists who advocate ideas similar to African communitarianism in Christianity with these words:

> The . . . error consists in defining a Christian in terms which assume that consistent selflessness is possible. No Christian, even the most perfect, is able "always" to consider the common interest before his own. At least he is not able to do it without looking at the common interest with eyes colored by his own ambitions. If complete selflessness were a simple possibility, political justice could be quickly transmuted into perfect love; and all the frictions, tensions, partial cooperations, and overt and covert conflicts could be eliminated. If complete selflessness without an admixture of egoism were possible, many now irrelevant sermons and church resolutions would become relevant. Unfortunately there is no such possibility for individual men; and perfect disinterestedness for groups and nations is even more impossible.[16]

The key question before us is this: Is self-interest absent from communitarianism (in its past or present form), or is self-interest antithetical to the welfare of community? To answer this question, we need to ask more questions. What is the community? Is it my compound, village, town, ethnic group, or nation? If my town is confronted by another town and I support mine, are we (I and my town members) not guilty of collective self-interest? Is it too difficult to imagine that the values and norms that I was raised with as a Kalabari person, that habituated me into the community's moral life and taught me to prefer my town to other towns, can also prepare me—at least—to prefer my family to my town? In choosing my family (typically an extended one) over my town, am I not subjecting myself to the common interest? What is the common interest?[17] Is what is common telos to my family members not common interest? To answer the key question at the top of this paragraph, I would say that communitarianism does not dismiss self-interest, but must necessarily entertain it even as it resists it, that is, resists its illegitimate expressions.[18] Communitarianism does not consider it illegitimate when I execute what I owe to my family or town.

I will illustrate this point with a Kalabari proverb that is often misunderstood as advocating absolute communitarianism or teaching that community unarguably surpasses the individual: *Ama bebe buru ngeribo buru pakiri*, meaning "only the community is tantamount to a whole yam, the individual is always but a piece of it," or "the whole community constitutes the full yam and the individual is half a yam." There is something philosophically intriguing about this proverb in terms of the argumentative thrust of this essay. There are five ways to interpret the proverb with the central item of yam in mind.

First, it suggests that there are two yams. For if the town owns a full or whole yam, the piece that individual is said to possess must have come from another yam. It brings up the idea that the confrontation is between a full yam and a piece from another yam, suggesting that the whole (collective interest) is likely to overcome the part. Nonetheless, we do not see here the nonexistence of self-interest in the Kalabari version of communitarianism, but an indication of an agonistic struggle between two types of interest.

Second, whether the individual has a piece of the yam that the town claims to own or hers is a piece from a different yam, she nonetheless has a piece of yam. She is allowed her part, and, if you like, her self-interest, and she is given a space to make her decision whether to participate with the whole or to die in one corner with her piece of yam as her banner of resistance.

Third, while the proverb makes a subtle allusion to individuality or respect for self-interest, the whole framing of its logic suggests that the parts that individuals possess might (can) not add up to a whole yam even when they are added together. Note that the town is always credited with a whole yam and individuals only hold parts of a yam. There is the logic of zerosumness and non-zerosumness embedded in the proverb. Individualism without a bent toward cooperation leads to zerosumness, but when individuals act in concert and cooperate to achieve a common purpose, they create the benefits of non-zerosumness. The yam that is owned by the town (the signifier of cooperation) always works as a whole that is increasing because of the logic of non-zerosumness. The pieces of yam owned by individuals would not add to a whole, not to speak of a whole that is always increasing because the pieces themselves lack the feature of non-zerosumness. The point to note here is that communitarianism, at least in the Kalabari version, does not deny self-interest but acknowledges it even as it points it to the benefit of cooperativeness, inclusion, and non-zerosumness.[19] The idea of communitarianism embedded in this proverb, as I am interpreting it, points to the relentless search for non-zerosumness in relations, the benefits of interdependence, internal coordination, and cooperation. Communitarianism (cooperative intimacy) is an inherent process or ethos of not leaving anything or person outside the benefits of its relationality. Such an ethos, no doubt, accents increasing communality and the upbuilding of communal structures, but it does not deny self-interest or competitive intimacy.[20]

This last point brings us to the final interpretation of the Kalabari proverb. The communal yam in question is divisible: individuals are said to own pieces of it. Given the logic of the third interpretation, the community may not have begun with two yams as the first interpretation makes us to believe. From the outset it might be one yam, and when the dissenting individual takes her share of the whole, the incomplete yam that is left for the community grows back into a whole yam, and even a bigger one; the incomplete yam remakes itself because of synthesis and the cooperativeness of non-zerosumness. (This should not be construed to mean that individualism, which, in the Kalabari context, is competitive intimacy, does not or cannot create non-zerosumness in all circumstances.)

There is another interpretation of the proverb that occurs to the mind when its rumination is not directed by the central item of the yam but by the organizing principle of interests in the community. *Ama bebe buru ngeribo buru pakiri* suggests to me that the love for one's community or the community's paramount goal is the *ultimate concern* that unconditionally orders, prearranges, preapproves all other concerns and loyalties; and all other such loves, goals, and loyalties are partial, fragmentary, and incomplete. On second thought, the interpretation of the proverb in terms of ultimate concern does not require us to move away from the central idea of a yam. The yam may be interpreted as a metaphor for ultimate concern. *Buru* can also be translated as food or sustenance in general. In this sense, the proverb alludes to the paramount goal of the community as always the indivisible, comprehensive moral vision of the community, and personal goals are always partial and incomplete. The interpretations suggest that the proverb is not about the denial of self-interest, but a call for its right, proper ordering.

In the light of the preceding fivefold interpretation, the key difference between communitarianism and individualism is not the absence of self-interest, but how self-interest is coordinated to create the kind of communal structures and communality that each ethological system prefers. So it is an overreach on the part of some supporters of communitarianism to quarrel with me because I prefer my mother to the community. Once again, if you ask me to choose between my mother and my community, I will choose my mother. My decision is not a turning away from communitarianism, and my Kalabari people never burden me with the divine task of absolute responsibility toward upbuilding communal structures or community-wide relationalities.

My endeavor here to point out the overreach of a communitarian ethic should not be counted as a failure on my part to recognize that the traditional African social ethic calls upon an individual to consider her call to responsibility as extending beyond her immediate family context. I am only arguing that without the proper delimitation of the kind of absolute responsibility to the community demanded by distorted communitarianism, communitarian ethics is strictly impossible. The kernel of my critique is to point us to an approach to African social ethics that accents the simultaneous necessity of the spheres of the universal (community) and the particular, the community and my mother. My mother, in loving her child, the person whose face she saw, also paid attention to those who were not in a face-to-face relationship with her; she acknowledged her primordial ethical obligation to them as members of her community. Love and justice (social justice), love for her own child and love for other children, justice for her son and justice for her community, are compatible in this conception of the African communal ethic. This interplay or "mutual" recognition of love and social justice points us to the deeper play between community and individual in the traditional African social ethics. Communitarianism in Africa is an interplay of self-becoming and the community's telos or common social goals. It is not a strict opposition between collective obligation and free individual actions; not a war between the self and the social. My mother's "free" personal action, her love for her son, was located in a process of structuration. None of her behavior was totally or inviolably personal or individualistic; yet nothing was permanently an outcome of a *given* collective structure, or fixed beyond her interactions with others or outside the daily grind of interactions between persons.

On a different note—perhaps at a less concrete philosophical level—communitarians loathe individualism because they think that in the divide or tension between justice (meritism) and mercy (charity), individualism is on the side of the former. They reason that when it comes to helping the needy or poor, individualism insists on giving people only what they deserve, and often the poor or those who need help are deemed undeserving. But they will argue that communitarianism is always on the side of mercy; that the poor should get undeserved gifts from other members of their communities. As I shall demonstrate later, the contextual individualism in precolonial Kalabari society required the unity of justice and mercy. Kalabari individualism requires or habituates the well-off to make sacrifices that reconcile justice with mercy, as per the original name of the Kalabari people: *Perebo-kalakeibari*, "let the well-endowed give me a little of his resources, wealth." Kalabari individualism works with a moral spirit that the communal ethos supplies and even strengthens. The bread of individualism was leavened by the eros toward the community's constitutive goods.[21] Yet the community and the individual were not one; they were in constitutive relationships.

Neither individualism nor communitarianism was allowed to run "amok" in Kalabari society. Communitarianism had its place in the precolonial competitive Kalabari society, which emphasized individualism because of its trading culture and the *canoe-house system* of wealth accumulation.[22] In the colonial and postcolonial eras of the society's engagement with more robust capitalism and Western-induced individualism, communitarianism still has its place. The Kalabari notion of individualism starts with the definition or an understanding of the paramount goal, the telos of the community, and the moral law instituted by members of the community. Only after the citizens have arrived at an understanding that defines or elucidates their obligations, rights, and freedom can they work out the practices (or conceptions) of individualism that are compatible with it (telos). The self in this individualistic view is not abstracted from communal identities and inheritances or cut off from the stories of the community that claim it, and the self is deemed deformed if cut off from the narrative that gives it quest for life coherence or moral particularity.[23] Individualism was a continuous process of individual self-realization and movement toward increasing, uniting relationality. The separation that arose in each individual dynamic actualization was overcome or limited by its realization within the society as a whole and by virtue of mutual participation in one another's lives.[24]

As we can discern, the key idea in *Perebo-kalakeibari* does not accent communitarianism at a total disregard for individualism. It actually lauds the coexistence of both individualism and communitarianism. The ethos or principle of *Perebo-kalakeibari* encourages those who are talented or gifted to develop their skills and reap rewards with the understanding that their endowments, rewards, or winnings will be shared with the community, to give a little part of their rewards or winnings to improve the situation of other members of the community: "let him or her give me a little of his or hers." However, this expectation or obligation of generosity does not mean that in the traditional Kalabari society an individual's assets, endowments, or rewards belong to the whole community as common assets.

In the light of my foregoing interpretation of the original name of the Kalabari people, we may interpret Kalabari "communitarianism" as individualism with a powerful vision of equality. It is individualism that improves the lot of the community or the least fortunate members of it. It is not a communitarianism of leveling equality that stifles the kind of individualism (competitive intimacy) that ultimately helps the least advantaged.

Perebo-kalakeibari and *Ama bebe buru ngeribo buru pakiri* are two expressions important to the argument I am making in this chapter. When the two face each other, and when they flow into each other, we get the philosophy of *agonistic communitarianism*. In Kalabari the strong hand of communitarianism culturally formed a contextual variant of individualism—one might say communitarianism birthing and defending individualism. Agonistic communitarianism is an attitude and a position that speaks, on the one hand, to the intense and relentless struggle of individualism with the weight of communitarianism, and, on the other, to the struggle of communitarianism against the fires of individualism that want to melt and erode the established structures of the community. Agonistic communitarianism is individualism's artful irruption into communitarianism. It is a term of ethics, signifying not the ethos of transcending (idealistic) communion, but the practices of transimmanent egalitarianism under the weight of competitive entrepreneurism and creative destruction engendered by centuries of long-distance trade, investment risk-taking, and struggles for political power.[25]

Agonistic communitarianism (a combination of sense of self-interest and norm-grounded conception of the common good) as worked out or evolved in precolonial Kalabari was structured around what the culture considered as the three integral parts of the whole human person (*tombo*) and their ethical orientations. These are body (*oju*), heart (*biogbo*), and spirit, soul (*teme*). The soul is oriented toward righteousness, morality, justice. The heart, the seat of desire, yearns for fellowship, togetherness (*gboloma*, being-with), connection with others. When the heart is bad it turns away from this desire or yearning. The body is the fount of deeds, material gains; the ego-self striving for its success, the realization of its destiny. Communitarianism in the Kalabari context engendered or brewed a combination of the impulse of innovative deeds of the body, the energy of connectivity, the other-centeredness of the heart, and the power of shared common values and sense of mutual belonging that the soul embodies. In the competitive world of long-distance trade that the Kalabari inhabited in the precolonial era and in much of the colonial period, these triune roots of agonistic communitarianism brought about a quest for economic, entrepreneurial accomplishments, the upbuilding of communal structures and welfare, and the moral formation or virtuous habits of the individuals.

This Kalabari world of artful mix of cooperation and conflict (that is, competition) reminds us of the central dynamic of Akan communal relations that Kwame Gyekye illustrates with the art motif of the two-headed crocodile with one stomach. He argues that in Akan social thought communality and individuality coexist.[26] As he puts it:

> The symbol of the crossed crocodiles with two heads and a common stomach has great significance for Akan social thought. While it suggests the rational underpinnings of the concept of communalism, it does not do so to the detriment of individuality. The concept of communalism, as it is understood in Akan thought, therefore does not overlook individual rights, interests, desires, and responsibilities, nor does it imply the absorption of the individual will into the "communal will," or seek to eliminate individual responsibility and accountability. Akan social thought attempts to establish a delicate balance between concepts of communality and individuality. . . . Akan social philosophy tries to steer clear of the Scylla of exaggerated individualism and the Charybdis of exaggerated communalism (= communism). It seeks to avoid the excesses of the two exaggerated systems, while allowing for a meaningful, albeit uneasy, interaction between the individual and the society.[27]

In all these, communitarianism gives cover, aid, and comfort to individualism to flourish even as it holds up a two-way mirror to individualism to show it the paucity of its own social imaginary or logic of zerosumness. Everyday practical men and women who are not slaves to some defunct intellectual influence see through the same mirror that individualism is not limping after communitarianism. It is illuminating or gaslighting communitarianism by displaying its future or manipulating its fragility. The time for pure communitarianism in Africa—if there ever was such a period—was, perhaps, in the pre-twentieth-century era. It is far too late now. Our individualism-inflected culture, agonistic communitarianism, "not only exists, it thrives. The question is whether it thrives as a virus or as a bountiful harvest of possibilities."[28]

Agony and Antagonism of Divided Consciousness

With the foregoing arguments I hope I have succeeded in convincing my brothers and sisters who champion unbridled communitarianism as the true ethical foundation of Africans that scholars like me who disagree with them deserved to be heard, if not embraced for our "un-African" stance. Let me say that I am afraid that communitarian ethicists may still demand for my raw hide to be flayed in the hot tropical African sun. I am not sure if I have persuaded them to wake up from their dogmatic slumber. But I can still count on their love. The true ethical step for them under the canopy of the communitarian ethic is to throw away my "stupid talk" and embrace me as a brother. By embracing me, have they not suspended the ethos of communitarian universality; that is, have they not chosen against their communal ideals under the hammer of my particularity; have they not chosen to honor my face as the singular other? In so choosing, have they not acknowledged that there are Africans like me who emphasize particularity under certain circumstances and that we need to be protected? Compelled to choose between communitarianism and particularity, between justice and love, between their all-embracing position and me, have they not chosen me, affirmed my right to exist, my right to go contrary to their communal ideals? Have they not demonstrated some equivocation? Do they think their African ancestors did not show similar equivocation? What kind of equivocation was this? This was an equivocation between universality and particularity that did not give way to the ultimate prioritizing of the private sphere or individualism. Nonetheless, there was particularism or individualism. This is the slight adjustment of thought I am pleading for in this chapter.

We must not view African social ethics as monolithic. We should endeavor to capture the tensions in African stories and not try to smoothen its edges for the touristic and voyeuristic academic audience. Africa is not a single narrative that we can package and market to conference attendees in Western cities who are usually impatient with the complex and multilayered African reality. Africa is rich with multiple experimentations of social existence and organization. Africa is not a simple place and its ethics is not simplistically one-sided.

I am not simple either. I harbor tensions within me as I try to find the proper balance between the "community" and the "individual" in my scholarship and in my personal orientation to life such that the community is granted its right authority in all my endeavors. Many Africans today are stirred and wracked by layers of double consciousness: (a) mother, as the matrix of individual inclinations, warring against community, as the ammunition against such inclinations, which I have described in the preceding paragraphs; and (b) a twoness that is one crucial impact of colonialism and Christianity on African personhood: a received (precolonial) *being-with* and a modernist (European-capitalist) consciousness; "two unreconciled strivings; two warring ideals in one dark body, whose dogged strength alone keeps it from being torn asunder."[29] The dialectic of African personhood oscillates between subjectivity fashioned by an African sense of communion and individualistic orientation, being African yet feeling Western, and yearning for native Africanness but grasping for alien European cosmopolitanism. Africans labor under the weight of a crisis of personhood, self-identity, split self that is precipitated by Christianity, colonialism, and Westernization/globalization.[30]

The cumulative effect of the weight of racism, domination, and the oppression Africans suffered under colonialism and the various attempts by the colonial state and colonial Christian missions to transform African personhood to fit the Western-styled autonomous, self-focused individual have weakened the bond between individuals and their societies. In the 1970s Ekeh wrote an insightful essay on the existence of two publics: communal (primordial) and civic. In his thinking the communal or ethnic public is considered moral and beloved. The other is amoral, hostile, and largely hated. In the primordial one, because it recognizes the worth of his personhood and citizenship, the individual feels a sense of citizenship and membership in the community. The individual is morally linked to the society and she sees her duties as moral obligations to benefit and sustain a community of which she is a member. On the other hand, the civic public, primarily imposed by colonialism and its apparatus of coercion that refused to recognize the worth or citizenship of the individual, has no moral link with the individual. The individual steadily under attack from the colonial and postcolonial state is alienated from the state, and her attention is focused more on the primordial public, such as kin and ethnic groups, that is independent of the state. Unlike the attitude of cooperation in the primordial realm, the attitude toward the civic realm is purely materialistic and exploitative, and the individual experiences no moral urge to give back to the civic realm in return for its benefits. In fact, the individual is obliged to draw resources from the civic public for the benefit of the primordial community.[31]

For those Africans today who are more comfortable, for whatever reason, with the individualistic rather than the communal ethos of life, there is also a struggle within themselves not to slide into what I have elsewhere called the *lotus-self*.[32] This is the vexing disposition of Africa's political leaders and elites "enjoying" themselves amid the physical and metaphorical filth and decadence of African communities. Like the lotus flower, leaders and elites now strive, luxuriate, and "flourish" amid dirt, decay, and death. There is a frightening *withdrawal of self* from the public space and public concerns that is marked, defined, and even energized by a "banality of evil." There is a certain thoughtlessness about committing evil, a ubiquity of evil that is now the quiddity of living, and a senselessness of it all that is destructive of social existence, thwarting life itself. It is important to realize that this withdrawal of the self from the public is not such that the self has absolutely no relation to the public, specifically the state and its treasures. On the contrary, what is excluded in the lotus-self maintains itself in relation to state resources in the form of stealing state resources. The lotus-self is a kind of exclusion that is inclusive. In withdrawing from the public, the lotus-self takes the state resources outside of public control and rule. The lotus flower (the lotus-self) does not subtract itself from its environment (state); rather, the environment, suspending its rule of touching everything in it (the state ruling over all citizens equally), gives rise to the withdrawal (don't-touch-me stance) and, keeping itself in relation to the flower (self), first constitutes itself as a withdrawal (the state abdicating its reach). This is the nature of the paradoxical zone of indistinction between the lotus-self of deadly politicians and the privatized postcolonial state, which "maintains itself in its own privation," to govern in no longer governing.[33] The withdrawal of the lotus-self is thus not the withdrawal of political leaders from the chaos of primitive accumulation that precedes rational, market-based accumulation, but rather the condition that results from the suspension of rationality and the center in which the state finds its *raison d'être*, the coming to light of a "free and juridically empty space" unbounded by law that haunts the colonial-postcolonial state and functions as if it considers the state already dissolved.[34] This is at once anarchy of self-interest and banality of evil as the center of the political scene of twenty-first-century Africa. This is a grave moral problem. It is no longer the mere case of a decision-maker split between mother and community, but the shaking of the moral foundations of African communities.

Concluding Remarks

The function of moral philosophy in a situation like this is that of analyzing the import of communitarianism, individualism, or agonistic communitarianism for the liberation and human flourishing of the African people. All three are in play in contemporary Africa societies and it does no one any substantial good to insist that the authentic African social ethic is communitarianism.

My efforts to set the debate among these three forms in terms of mother versus community underlines my understanding that as an ethicist I am called to make a tragic choice between them. It is tragic in the sense that I am called to choose among three good options, and by opting for one I have turned away from the singular goods of the others. I am losing something. But in choosing agonistic communitarianism I am trying to minimize the "loss." I take as the core of African communitarianism other-centeredness, the summons to make what is outside the self, the care for others rather than the self, as the ultimate appeal of the human person. Agonistic communitarianism carries forward this summons, this worthy ideal as *mattered* by twenty-first-century sensibility and individual creativity, as *enfleshed* by individual agency. Agonistic communitarianism, as I am using the term here, is individualism (not selfishness) that is framed within communitarianism that undergirds and propels it. Individualism (an inadequate word chosen for a lack of a better term) in the context of agonistic communitarianism is not set as an opposite or rejection of communitarianism. It is an exfoliation of the abiding care and concern for individuality in African communitarianism, the individual-in-communion given an ample space better to actualize her potentiality for the flourishing of the self and what transcends it. Individualism here is covenantal individualism rather than expressive individualism. Individualism here is only a capstone of the community's relationships and not their keystone; it is not what forms and disciplines the societal relationships but what is fixed on top of them as symbol of unemasculated individual creativity.

Thus, the real task for social ethicists who aspire to bring African communal ethics to face the challenges of the twenty-first century's socio-economic development and civilizational shifts is to figure out how to create sturdy social structures, institutions, and policies that will promote fellowship as well as entrepreneurial innovativeness and self-transcending individualism—in other words, promote agonistic communitarianism.

2. Agonistic Competition and Excellence[35]

Having related excellence (the creative realization of human potentialities) to the agonistic theory of communitarianism in the introduction to this chapter, the primary task of this section is to show how the exercise of excellence as a paradigmatic virtue may lead to human flourishing. Excellence encompasses creativity, and that excellence is the principle of creativity. If excellence is essentially the drive toward actualization of potentialities for all human beings, it follows that creativity of human beings is the form that is adequate for that movement. Here I am not conceptualizing excellence as the virtue of doing something well or the mean of two extremes. Instead, excellence is understood as the *clearing* that allows human creativity to manifest and for persons to creatively resist obstacles to human flourishing in all forms of sociality. The concept of excellence is thus liberated from the excessive concern with order and good citizenry to serve as a liberatory principle for interrogating all present social organizations in the name of a better future. This has implications for how we interpret the human self. Here the human self is not interpreted as *maker*, as *citizen* or the *responsible self*, but as the *excellent self*. How do I live a full, amazing life? How do I come to the creative realization of my vital potentials at the highest possible level? The *excellent self* believes that something of a great moral, spiritual, or cultural significance can become manifest in it and, hence, it is an embodiment and revelation of possibilities.

The entry point into Kalabari-Ijo understanding of the excellent self is in their particular conception of God (*Tamuno/So*). As we discussed in chapter 1, in the traditional conception, God has two dimensions, parts, or selves: *Teme-órú* and *So*. *Teme-órú* is regarded as the female creative modality. *So* is the dynamic directing agency, the aspect of divinity that orders the created outcome, the neuter or male counterpart. The *Teme-órú* part is concerned with creation, existence, destruction (wrath). *So* is concerned with the destiny and behavior of people, groups, animals, and institutions. The shaping of destiny is done by or rather understood via the possibilities that *So* makes available to each person, group, or institution. *So* when applied to individuals is called *so*, to households it is *wariteme-so*, and to communities *amateme-so*.

We will soon learn how an individual comes to have his or her own *so*. Let us call *So* as applied to individuals, households, and communities as lowercase *so* and to the deity as uppercase *So*. Capital-S *So* is the universe of possibilities from which some are defined as available to persons and institutions and others remain either unfulfilled or simply the set of possibilities excluded to them at any given time. Uppercase *So* is the ultimate source of possibilities and the principle of limitation or selection.[36] Lowercase *so* is the ideal that the individual receives from God and that the person works out within history, that is, achieves its actualization, by the way he or she unifies its efficient causes. The person transforms the pure possibilities given to him or her into possibilities realizable under the conditions of the world.

The idea of God's directing activity being present in each person or collection of persons—as indicated by the attachment of lowercase *so* to person or groups—suggests that every person or group incarnates some degree of God's purpose in the world. The excellent self is the one who has (almost) fully realized his or her particular divine aim with little or no distortion or is in search of the maximum potential in his or her historical circumstances. The particular divine aims have been decisively realized in the lives of few individuals in history, and they became *gods* or *community heroes* (*amaoru*). The heroes, human-gods, became the embodiments of divine creative purposes, the specific divine addresses (speeches, *bibi*) to the community at a specific time, and a sort of transparent medium through which the people could read (comprehend and prehend) *So*'s aim for the community. The men and women who had so realized themselves became effective concrete lures for both individual and collective actions. They served also for personal and corporate self-understanding at a given historical juncture and what stood beyond them. Such men and women, in actualizing *So*'s particular ideals for themselves, expressed *So*'s general aim for their entire community, and it was received by all members of the community.

The interpretation of the work of *community heroes* and their reception is not timeless. When the historical situations that brought their works into collective consciousness and sustained them changed, their valuation also altered. Thus with the coming of Christianity and the expansion of the communicative reaches of the community, new excellent selves embedded in religiously relevant historical situations were sought. Anthropologist

Robin Horton argues that as the Kalabari horizon expanded owing to the increasing spheres of commerce, transportation and communication networks, and long-distance trade, the heroes they revered also changed or tended to change.[37] In the cosmological adjustment that ensued, many of the symbols and understandings of the old worldview were carried over.

When one considers the concept of Jesus of Nazareth as the Christ and as the second person of the Trinity, some resemblance with the Kalabari conception of *So* and community heroes can be discerned. Now, I am not saying that the Kalabari community in the nineteenth century, when they began to convert to Christianity in large numbers, consciously worked out the similarities between their concept of *So* and the Christian concept of Jesus as the *logos*. But for our limited purpose in this study, the similarities are worth noting for the purpose of enriching the Christian theology of excellence being developed in this work.

According to Christian theologian Lewis S. Ford, the *logos* is the totality of possibilities God envisages for the world or the totality of creative possibilities inherent in the nature of God. Jesus Christ is seen as an incarnation of the *logos*, the creative Word addressed to humankind.[38] In Paul Tillich's thought, the Christ-event is taken to be the emergence of a new humanity, a *New Being* who represents the closing of the chasm between potentialities and actualization. In the man Jesus of Nazareth, the "excellent self" has been realized, and thus there are radically new and creative possibilities for the transformation of humankind and history. Such "unique" actualization of potentialities, according to Tillich, is of universal significance and must lead to the creative transformation of historical existence.[39] The indigenous Kalabari understanding of *So* and excellent self is remarkably anticipatory of these received Christian theologians' conceptions of *logos* and *New Being*. We will return to the Christian idea of Jesus as *logos* and community hero in a short while. For now, let us continue our discussion of lowercase *so*.

How is *so* generated for each person in Kalabari? The individual is believed to have a two-part personality. The component parts of this personality act as separate "persons." One is conscious, the other unconscious. The unconscious part (the soul) before the birth of the person decides the destiny (*so* or *fiyeteboye*), the life-course of the whole person on earth. When a soul (spirit) is about to come on earth, the would-be soul of the person goes before *Teme-órú* and decides on a set of possibilities for the life of the individual it is going to inhabit. The other part (the conscious), the physical embodiment of the soul, works to actualize this chosen set of possibilities in history. If a person does not like the course of his or her life on earth, she goes to a diviner to change her *so* or *fiyeteboye*. The process of changing destiny is called *bibibari*, as we discussed in chapter 1.

Horton writes that in existence, that is, in history, the incarnating soul lives a split life. People are split from their real or deepest selves. The essential self (the set of pledged possibilities) is separated from the historical (earthly) self. Often they may even be in contention, going in opposite directions. When the chasm (alienation) between them becomes unbearable, a person undertakes *bibibari* (the recanting of speech) to recalibrate the balance between them, to close the gap. The uppercase *So* offers a new chance to each person's becoming if the earlier set of possibilities is not suitable for what the person wants to be. The importance of securing *bibibari* in the Kalabari concept of the excellent self cannot be overstated. It addresses the chasm between potentialities and actualization. Let us not forget the Kalabari concept of excellent life. It is a life where a person works out his or her potentialities, the given divine gifts. Thus, in a sense, life is a movement from separation into (impossible) union. This yearning force of being is the driving force behind the unfolding dynamics of potentialities.

Let us take a closer look at *fiyeteboye*, the remote antecedent of *bibibari*. Every person, the pre-born in some realm of essences or pure possibilities, some "heavenly realm" (*so-bio*), is obligated to see itself, to see what it might become on earth before it makes the nine-month journey into history. The spirit before the birth of the person on earth is to imagine itself in history. It says before God, "I imagine myself in this way . . ." The pre-born before the dawn of its existence is standing before God—before adorning its earthly garb—and with permission says, "I will be what I will be." The spirit takes on flesh only after this obligatory imagination. So with boldness we can say that the earthly body of the spirit is imagination. The spirit emerges from "heaven" to live a life of imagination. So in Kalabari imagination is at the core, the essence of who humans beings are. Imagination is ontological. Long before the person can alter Mbiti's "I am because we are," the person has altered "I imagine, therefore I am."

The spirit that said, "I will be what I will be" cannot be everything. The moment a decision is made, a cut is made into pure, infinite possibility. And "what I will be" is immediately a "fall," departure, or slice from the infinite possibility. Historical existence, as we have already noted, involves self-affirmation of these potentialities, the courage or eros to work them out under various existential constraints and to participate in this primordial imagination. So when people imagine their situation, when they see beyond what is given, when they see an alternative, they are expressing existentially their ontological humanization.

The *fiyeteboye*, this *speech*[40] before God is creative; the moment of its utterance is a moment for structuring the range of possibilities within which one's life will rhythmically move. This initial aim that the person sets for him or herself becomes an enlivening lure though the person is largely unconscious of it during life on earth. *Fiyeteboye* is singular, never used as plural. Yet the possibility (the divine gift of the possible) is not just one, "not a *simple* but rather a multiple one."[41] The multiplicities of possibilities are folded together—the complexity that is both all too human and all too representative of life—and about to unfurl. With *fiyeteboye* the person emerges on earth with a space of becoming and is enabled to be. The person is "let be." This letting be is a call to actualize the possibilities for the lineage and the community. It is to embody in his or her flesh, to incarnate, to make a carnal reality a set of possibilities in the midst of others. For every child born into the community there is celebration of a new possibility of shared flourishing. The anticipation of co-flourishing is also borne—at least in part—on another dimension of *So*, the collective set of possibilities. Every individual comes into the community with the call to actualize his or her possibilities, but the pieces of each of their limited efforts are gathered, extended, and shared in the community by the *amatemeso*. The coexistence or relationality of these two distinguishable but inseparable dimensions of *So* are the attraction and reception, intensity and width, disparity and beauty of the divine transformative power *within* the process of interaction.

Excellence is an erotic expression of the person's deep essential nature, the set of possibilities and potentialities that define the person's unique *name* (*ere*[42]) on earth. In this sense, excellence is ethics—the expression of a person's or community's deep self, a person's *so* or the community's *so* (*amatemeso*). In Kalabari, the crucial focus of ethics is on enabling a person to be all that he or she can be: that is, to support a person's ability to live out his or her *verbal script*,[43] to respond to the call of the voice, the speech, the imagination that preceded his or her journey to earth. The community is a symphony of the voices. Each unique sound contributes to the creativity of the ensemble to produce a melodious communal life. In this symphony each note is allowed to sound, but not at the expense of other notes. Ethics is thus about supporting a person's essential being and organizing the pursuit of each person's possibilities in such a way that will avoid violations of others' possibilities. The word "ethics" that comes from "ethos" even in its original Greek meaning carries the connotation of a stable that guards members of a society and also of the special nature of the persons within it or the whole community.[44]

In my 2008 book *The Depth and Destiny of Work*, I highlight certain aspects of Kalabari social ethics, drawing attention to the accent put on the preservation of communal well-being, personhood (as person-in-communion), and communion with gods. All these and many more are ways the Kalabari community uses to bring persons and community (the bonded collection of persons) to express the potentialities in their *So*. There is no necessary conflict between individual self-fulfillment and community well-being—they are aspects of the same fundamental process. They are different sides of naming the same state of being, that of realization of divine gifts (*so* and *amatemeso*) in the community and mature relatedness. Community norms, laws, and injunctions are not considered heteronomous or contradictory to human nature. The community's laws are to show each person his or her "essential nature," his or her true relationship with the gods, ancestors, other members, and him- or herself. The laws are to help each person's and each community's true nature to manifest, for the divine gifts (*so* or *amatemeso*) to show forth. Though a community member can alter his or her *so*, it stands (before it is altered) against his or her existence, supposedly commanding and judging it to bring about an undistorted manifestation of his or her potentials under the conditions of existence.

The divine gift that captures the person's essential being—lowercase *so*—is also an expression of the divine in the midst of history insofar as each set of possibility is a subset of the inexhaustible vessel of possibilities, uppercase *So*. Each person is a bearer of divinity. To the extent that each person carries a piece of the same thing (*So*), it should provoke an *eros* to communal belonging and fellowship. This *eros* in Kalabari is called *gboloma*. Excellence and, for that matter, ethics that is not rooted in *gboloma* will ultimately fail. Excellence that is not guided by the lowercase *so* is not deep, and *gboloma* (*eros*) will not enter into the inwardness of the person's spirit (*teme*) to move the person to fulfill his or her potential. This is why I stated above that excellence in Kalabari is an erotic expression of a person's essential nature, the set of possibilities given to him or her before physical existence.

Let us examine the concept of *gboloma*, the Kalabari notion of eros.[45] The word *gboloma* points to different dimensions of human relationality. First, in one sense, it points to something being inside another thing, getting involved, experientially being engaged in an activity, or participation. Second, it means the interconnectivity of all being, inclusiveness, social solidarity, fellowship, communion, merging, or interpenetration. Third, it means being fully engaged, present in an activity or in a person's life. So when someone shows lack of concern or an "I don't care" attitude to an activity or goings-on, a Kalabari person will say, *ani o gbolomaa*.[46] Fourth, the word is also used for intense desire, yearning, the ecstatic movement toward the other, longing that can culminate in or be modeled by sex. Finally, it is also used for a union or unity that is the community.[47] Thus, *gboloma*, *eros*, captures not only the urge/energy to realize one's potential but also the connection-making power within life. It is what animates and shapes community life. Without this creative energy for communal belonging, the necessary relations crucial for the community to support the self-fulfillment of the individual or for the individual to become what he or she potentially is cannot be sustained. Essentially, *gboloma* is what draws people to go beyond themselves into communion and participation for the creative unfolding of possibilities. It is the inner dynamics of both individual and communal life.

We have examined linkages between four Kalabari concepts—*So*, *fiyeteboye*, *bibibari*, and *gboloma*—to demonstrate the existential margin that the human being has to conquer to achieve excellence. The purpose is to understand what it is the Kalabari people understand by excellence in existential living and later to investigate how this foundational sense is linked to virtues and flourishing life. The four Kalabari concepts hide as much as they reveal. They reveal the divine gift of possibility to each person, but they hide the fact that often persons do not fully realize their gifts. The gift is often an ideal that resists any sense of final realization. *Bibibari*, precisely, alludes to this. It points to the lived experience that no one has ever so realized his or her gift as to become one with it. This is not only a Kalabari problem. In many other cultures and religions there is a diremption between potentialities and actualities. The pursuit of excellence holds out the possibility of permanently closing the gap, a search whose goal is elusive, and yet, as in Kalabari and Christian communities, there are figures who have been identified to have closed the gap between essence and existence and hence stand as models and lures for others' becoming. In Kalabari we have the *community heroes* and in Christianity we have Jesus Christ.

To demonstrate how the social-ethical framework of excellence I am proposing in this study can help move the discourse on economic underdevelopment, a well-known hindrance to human flourishing and excellence, I also engage the development theory of Nobel Prize–winning economist Amartya Sen.[48] I extend his theory of *development as freedom* in new directions so as to locate it both in the doctrine of human nature (beings who have the "future in their essential being"[49]) and in the construct of excellence. Consequently, in chapter 5 I put forward a new philosophical perspective on economic development—that of *development as excellence.* Excellence as a *clearing* allows economic development to manifest itself, and it is what is behind the search for economic *freedoms* as human capability development.

The history of the human race is a story of the expansion of human capabilities, the enhancement of the quality of life, and increasing interconnections between persons and people. No doubt this process has been thwarted in multiple places and at several times, but by and large this has been the trend of development. The central part of the exercise of this development, as Sen argues, has been the overcoming of problems, the removal of "unfreedoms" that thwart human flourishing.

The very view of development that makes a discursive space for the overcoming of obstacles to human freedom includes, by definition, an *eros* to freedom, a strong attachment of human beings to freedom. It begs for a conceptual-analytical endeavor to investigate and clarify the energy (force) behind the attachment or the principle of such an *eros.* While I find Sen's insights about development as *freedom* both provocative and relevant, I still think that his failure to relate this eros toward what it means to be human in the first place leaves room for the kind of study undertaken in chapter 5. It can indeed be argued that a proper understanding of what human flourishing and development are—their content and force—requires an analysis of the endowment and possibilities of human nature. The attraction of endowment and possibilities to higher forms of realization is behind the human drive to overcome all *unfreedoms.*

The self does not strive for human flourishing with something it does not have, an object besides itself. Human nature—and, by extension, human sociality—preserves and transcends itself by participation in excellence. Excellence is the self's power to actualize itself by overcoming obstacles in life that negate life. Excellence is also the self's power over itself. It is an expression of the essential act of human beings. It is not a contingent aspect of being and it makes a human what he or she is. Thus, to strive for human flourishing—the development of capabilities and opportunities—is to act according to human nature. In a positive twist of a familiar idea of Spinoza, I will argue that excellence is the power of acting according to one's true nature. And the degree of excellence is the degree to which somebody is striving for and able to affirm increasing levels of human flourishing.[50] Excellence in this light is the ontological foundation of human flourishing. Excellence is a virtue; the highest and most prior virtue is living, acting, and doing according to one's true nature.[51] As the Kalabari put it, *tombo tombo so*: let a person become a person.

Chapter 5

Pursuit of Excellence and Economic Development

Introduction

This chapter interprets the notion of excellence (*arete*) as the actualization of human potentialities, which is one form of overcoming obstacles to economic development, a way of removing "unfreedoms" that thwart human flourishing, as Amartya Sen might argue.[1] In this chapter, I pick up and expand the definition of economic development given in chapter 1. There I defined economic development as the creation of special and novel possibilities in an economy. This definition suggests that a nation has developed the capacity to shift toward producing more goods and services and creating possibilities (within reasonable and protective limits of ecological justice) of increasing the levels of human flourishing for all its citizens.

As I have done in the preceding chapters, I will approach the philosophical analysis of economic development through the notions of destiny, desire, temporality, and human flourishing as planted and nurtured within the intellectual soil of Kalabari traditional religion. Destiny is an "aesthetic capacity to recognize appropriately" the possibilities received from *Tamuno*, the creative ultimate.[2] Desire is not a longing for something lost; rather, it is a response to the possibilities offered by *Tamuno* (Heaven, *So*) and a recognition of the good in these possibilities for a person's and her society's flourishing. Human flourishing is the act of appropriately responding to these possibilities for all in society, advancing to a new and different set or contour of possibilities, and appropriately integrating the old and the new set of possibilities within the tincture of time. Time is not only a continuum that moves; it is also a dimension of the sacred as the universe of possibilities. Time as a dimension of *So* (the sacred, *Tamuno*, the ontological creative act) is the dynamic succession, incompleteness, and split nature of possibilities of determinate, created beings.

This is a book on economic philosophy that mobilizes these four key concepts (destiny, desire, temporality, and human flourishing) from Kalabari traditional religion to shed light on the principle of economic development. The philosophy that informs the book derives from African traditional religion, but its orientation is open to continental philosophy. In other words, I create an intersection of ideas about temporality, destiny, and desire from African traditional religion with cutting-edge discourses in continental philosophy (split, cracks, fractures, and irruptions in being, order of being, time or reality) to craft a philosophy for human flourishing—that is, economic development—in Africa.

The Split Time: Economic Philosophy for Human Flourishing in African Perspective is a systematic attempt to think the principle of economic development into the whole encyclopedia of Kalabari traditional religion. It explores and elucidates economic development, broadly defined as human flourishing, within the intellectual figuration of an African religion, plotting its significance for philosophical discourse. In this chapter I rethink the Kalabari notion of destiny, which I have earlier interpreted as the actualization of potentialities, and connect it to the idea of economic development as excellence (*arete*), an actualization of potentialities. Excellence is the flourishing life; it is what it means for a person to live well. Excellence involves the removal of various types of resistance, that is, obstacles or difficulties, that block the unfolding of being, the actualization of human potentialities. If this proposition is accepted, the reach of the philosophical and social-ethical analysis of this chapter inheres in establishing a coherent and adequate perspective of excellence, actualization of potentialities, as a means of understanding the role of economic development in making adequate provision for a future that starts today.[3]

Economy is the making of provision for the future. This involves the dismantling of unfreedoms and the consumption of freedoms. Within the restrictions of limited resources, the generation and consumption of freedoms is the art and science of actualization of human potentialities, the source of genuine creativity. From the logic of capitalism and some earlier civilizations, we can see that "making provision for the future" is split. One part harnesses the genuine human capacity for creativity in consonance with nature to create a sustainable environment for human flourishing. Another type of provision "eats" the future through unsustainable environment and social practices.[4] "Devoid of the capacity for genuine creativity, which would require higher degrees of self-criticism, global capital promotes an addictive logic that creates hunger where it most feeds, thus erecting the entropy of Lack to the level of a Law that wraps us up in persistent anxiety about the future."[5]

This chapter is divided into two sections. Section 1 is concerned with enacting or performing a new temporality of economic development. It embarks on a philosophic search for an organizing temporal/developmental logic that would allow Nigeria to embark upon a more successful and egalitarian trajectory of development and economic change. The arguments of this section, which heavily draw insights from continental philosophy, are about conceptualizing a new kind of temporality and new kind of subject that might transform the ethical malaise and problems of governance that constitute a formidable obstacle to economic development in Nigeria. I argue that any serious consideration of the prospects of development in Nigeria must involve fresh thinking about how to achieve freedom from the "time" of the postcolonial state, to construct another "time," a time of freedom within the state's practice of development as unfreedoms and poverty. Section 2 picks up this concern and lays out a social-ethical framework for organizing economic development as a pursuit of excellence, the actualization of human potentialities for the sake of human flourishing.

1. The Place of Time in Economic Development[6]

Here I offer a relatively inspirational account of temporality that differs from the Nigerian postcolonial state's inhuman understanding of time, which stifles the potential for development. I conceptualize time as a set of possibilities, as a counter-logic that enables change-makers to discover novel capacities for framing our present. We live not in a single homogenous time but in convergences and divergences of time with different frames for our present. For instance, there is the time of the state and the ruling class, which, as the French philosopher Jacques Rancière argues, is "the dominant description of the state of the things that constructs the frame of our present."[7] But there is always an alternative interpretation of time that offers a different account of the set of possibilities and impossibilities in the state of things. "Every description of a 'state of things' gives priority to time," and economic development is not only about the description of the state of things in a given society, but also about the possibility of changing the state of things in it.[8] Economic development, in a crucial sense, is about the construction of a set of relations between time and time, between the "empirical idea of time as a succession of movements" and "the idea of time as a set of possibility," that is, as creating a time (disruption) within time as a horizon of emancipation.[9] Every idea, project, practice, or mechanism of development gives priority to time; it tells us what is possible and what is not and puts forward its own interpretation of the state of things as objectively given.

Since the Nigerian state and its backers in the global capitalist regime have failed to deliver development to the masses of Nigerians, any economic theory of development in Nigeria must now be concerned with resisting and countering the time of the postcolonial state, the "time in which we live" that determines what is possible and impossible in the nation's state of things. We have lived in the time of the state and its sense of development for over fifty years, and we are still far away from the dreams that became possible for our nation when it achieved independence from Britain on October 1, 1960. So for us to consider seriously the prospects of development in Nigeria, we have to start afresh, we must start thinking about how to free ourselves from the postcolonial state's time, to construct another time, a time of freedom within the state's practice of development as unfreedoms and poverty. Let me describe the kind of place that the time of the postcolonial state has created in our nation: Nigerians live in a place of tension between two forces, neither of which is good for its citizens.

Nigeria in the Portraits of Time

Nigeria presents two portraits (not images) of time.[10] Nigeria draws, extracts, and projects before our faces a certain intimacy with the meaninglessness and destructive forces of time. This nation is like a woman giving birth astride an open and deep grave—just as Samuel Becket evoked in his *Waiting for Godot*. The nation is also standing as the "angel of history." Like Walter Benjamin's angel of history (Paul Klee's *Angelus Novus*), the people have their backs turned to the future, facing the ruin, the wreckage of history. Our past catalog of promises that routinely pass from the darkness of the womb to the darkness of the tomb is traveling toward us every day. It is not going away. As Moses says in the Bible, our sins do not travel into the past but are actually traveling from the past to find us where we are today (Num. 32:23). Our future is also traveling to us as the wreckage of history. Micaiah saw the future, the fate of King Ahab and his army, as a future set in the past and coming to the present as a wreckage of history (1 Kings 22:17).

But I *see* another two figures. There is another angel who is standing by the side, flapping his wings, ready to replace the angel of history. This time, to continue our metaphor, the angel is the angel of the future (Simone Martini, *Angel of Annunciation*) gazing at the coming age of abundance and glory. And now the negativity of history, suffering, wreckage is behind us. But this angel is largely invisible. He is invisible not because he is not as substantial as the other angel or the woman giving birth. He is invisible not because he is the ghost of British colonialism that still haunts the country. He is invisible because we refuse to see him; we have no place in time to stand in order to see him. We have allowed ourselves to be caught and twisted by the time of the state instead of cutting into time ourselves to create a space for development. Amid our demonic twisting and contradictions, there is also another figure: the *Nigerian subject*—note, not the Nigerian citizen.

There is a huge difference between being citizens and subjects. The subject is a kind of transformed citizen. Subject, or subjectivation as I am using here (drawing from Alain Badiou's philosophy), is about commitment or fidelity to a past and/or coming event. Citizens are Nigerians who have made peace with the current state of things, whereas those I call subjects are Nigerians who are committed to creating a radically new space and time for emancipation and development, seeking to overthrow the current state of things. The citizen is conditioned and circumscribed by the *time* of the state and its politics; he or she has bought into the present order of things. The subject, on the other hand, breaks or attempts to break with this *time* and the dominant ordering principles that hold the past, present, and future in thralldom and in a stable relationship between oppression and underdevelopment.

I regard the citizen as a subject not only in the sense of an *actor*, as Hannah Arendt argues, but also in Alain Badiou's sense as one who shows fidelity to the coming event.[11] For too long, development has been confused with marking time in the old spaces of oppression and injustice. Development has been mistaken for obedience, and suppression of freedom from conformity to "time-tested" technical theories of socioeconomic management, rather than as constant preparation for entering a new mode of life.

Those who are familiar with the typical literature on time might have already concluded that my analysis of time and its metaphors do not make good sense. You are thinking that my attempt to link the topic of economic development and time with the political theory of subjectivation is not what you expected to hear. So far you cannot categorize my approach in terms of the commonly inherited framework of time and temporal orientation and their relationships with economic development. This is because the inherited categories are not very useful when it comes to thinking about Nigeria's economic development as an event or as the creation of subjects who are faithful to the *event* of development as a horizon of hope. As I argued in chapter 3, we have to conceptualize or philosophize economic development as the founding of a temporal gap in the continuum of time so as to make the world of the average Nigerian—which is always fleeting, short, and harsh—more durable and fulfilling through human action. Every day in Nigeria thousands die without actualizing their potential and without overcoming what Amartya Sen calls the "unfreedoms" of development. Such people die with their distinctive gifts and potentials unrealized, without having contributed to Nigeria's socioeconomic development. Their "time" never came for them. This is why we must consider economic development as the liberatory praxis of founding a new temporality by which citizens insert themselves between the infinite past and the infinite future of their country in order to exercise their uniquely and supremely human capacity to begin something anew and display the distinctiveness ("the who") of each individual. This requires subjects who are willing to navigate the present time and politics of the state that encompass them and the time that is to come in order to create a new temporality for development.

Time and Economic Development: Temporal Orientation as Political Praxis

The task of creating a new temporality for development, which is set within the tension of time, is not something others have not encountered before. In the third chapter of Philippians, Paul gives a glimpse of this tension. He had left his "rubbish" behind him, and he was pressing forward, moving into history, reaching for the messianic power, the power of resurrection

(Phil. 3:8–14). Paul transcended this tension when he cut into time. Paul was able to turn his face to the future of promise because he was able to cut into time, as Giorgio Agamben informs us in his book *The Time that Remains*. Paul breaks into the coherence and continuity of the normal flow of time in order to find the "time of the now," the time before the time's end, the time between salvation and the end, the time that remains between the event of the resurrection and the Parousia, the coming of the messiah. This time that remains is time within the present time where and when a subject appears who is faithful to the event of resurrection and who hastens to fulfill the promise, the messianic promise.

To find this time that remains is what I mean by the "place of time" in Nigeria's economic development. The history of economic development leading up to this moment has been a story of a place, a people in a place that is struggling and competing to catch up with another place, the West. This concern with place is not really about spatiality but a contest of places and for place. It is about being like the West and the privileges that come with a hierarchical place to dominate fellow citizens. The proposal of this chapter is to ask for a time of development, for a people to prevail over time and in time. In this chapter we do not conceive of time as an empty and homogeneous flux of being. Time is *a* house of beings (persons) who are existentially present and *ex-posed* to one another. The place of time is about genuine spatiality, the co-presence of citizens with one another.

This conception of time of place in economic development calls for subjects who are faithful to the event of development. Such *subjects*—not citizens—are urgently needed to construct a "present space" between the past and the future for the coming of the age of human flourishing. To create this space requires a monumental struggle, the creative imagination to cut into time and to hold back, with our hands, the forces of the past and the future. The effort requires us to slide between the womb and the grave to rescue our children, the fount of possibilities. We need to grab forcefully the angel of history and the violent storm caught in his wings and turn him around to face the future of our paradise. Once we turn his face around, transforming him into the angel of annunciation, the baby in the womb of the woman will leap for joy, for she will hear the sound of the bearers of hope.

We cannot confront and transform the angel of history into the angel of annunciation by standing in the totality or space of time called past, present, or future. We require a new *cut* in time, the general space of time transformed into our own specific place of time, into a *home*. If we are to reach the glorious heights of development, it is necessary for us to create this place, to build this abode, to create a radically new space for development that up until now does not exist.

This cut is a zone of time that is neither past nor future but subtracted from the present and that remains as a cut, a breach of pure praxis. This cut is not only subtracted from the present; it also does not coincide with the already and not-yet. It is not exterior to them either, "but divides the division itself."[12] The division of division engenders a tension within time itself. With the subjectivized cut into time, it is no longer possible for any part of the earlier divisions to coincide with itself or with any other.[13] Time seems to have transformatively contracted (shortened itself) into a concentration and the emergence of economic development is expected at any instant.

The effort to grab or force the angel of history is not only about relating to the world as it *is*, but also *as it can be*, given a particular vision of unexplored possibilities. In this venture of mediating the worlds of "is" and "as," the subject inserts himself or herself between the past and future of the time spectrum. From here the subject seeks to break with social institutions and shared human existence and force them toward a new horizon of possibilities. Suspended between (or subtracted from) the "no more" (or no longer acceptable) and the "not-yet," the Nigerian subject faces two antagonists, as in Franz Kafka's parable of the *He*.

> He has two antagonists: the first presses him from behind, from the origin. The second blocks the road ahead. He gives battle to both. To be sure, the first supports him in his fight with the second, and he wants to push him forward, and in the same way the second supports him in his fight with the first, since he drives him back. But it is only theoretically so. For it is not only the two antagonists who are there, but he himself as well, and who really knows his intentions? His dream, though, is that some time in an unguarded moment—and this would require a night darker than any night has been yet—he will jump out of the fighting line and be promoted, on account of his experience in fighting, to the position of umpire over his antagonists in their fight with each other.[14]

Kafka's *He* has the dream of jumping out of the struggle. But this is not possible for the Nigerian subject. The "place of time" is our unavoidable site of struggle against the dark forces of past and future. No nation can afford to elude this battle if it wants to create a flourishing economy. At a deeper level the parable is about human beings stepping into the continuum of time to create a gap between the past and future in which they change the meaning of the past and stop or redirect its perceived evil trajectory in order to help life flourish better.

Hannah Arendt also interprets this parable as revealing something about time. She says the two antagonists are past and future. Thus interpreted, the parable indicates that human beings are not just borne along in the flux of time but insert themselves in the battle between the past and the future in order to create a space where freedom can appear. She writes that

> seen from the viewpoint of man, who always lives in the interval between past and future, time is not a continuum, a flow of uninterrupted succession; it is broken in the middle, at the point where "he" stands; and "his" standpoint is not the present as we usually understand it but rather a gap in time which "his" constant fighting, "his" making a stand against the past and future, keeps in existence. Only because man is inserted into time and only to the extent that he stands his ground does the flow of indifferent time break up into tenses; it is this insertion—the beginning of a beginning, to put it into Augustinian terms—which splits up the time continuum into forces which then, because they are focused on the particle or body that gives them their direction, begin fighting with each other and acting upon man in the way Kafka describes.[15]

This middle, this gap is the space (place of time) where Nigerian subjects need to insert themselves into the process of development and into the time of the state "without being forced to jump out of human time altogether."[16] In this gap humans do not wait for the future as such to come to them but, rather, create it. For the citizen as the subject is marked by fidelity to the discerning of possibilities visible from a particular context or place of time. Subjectivation is basically a process of pushing the boundaries of the world further outward, creating and actualizing possibilities, which refashions social coexistence for the sake of human flourishing. This refashioning or world-making requires a different conceptualization of temporal orientation or a fresh understanding of the connection between economic development and temporalities. How do citizens incarnate this split in time and keep it perpetually open to economic development or emerge as citizens who initiate social transformation?

Finding the Subject in Time for Economic Development

Subjects always live between two events. "They are never simply confronted with the opposition between the events and the situation but are in a situation upon which events of the recent or distant past still have an impact. The political subject is, then, the interval between the past event and the coming event."[17] This interval is not generic. There is no universal place of time that is not internal to a given space, socio-space, context, or situation. The place of time is always a common ethical space immanent to a given situation. Thus, the norms that must be applied to it are, first of all, norms that are specific to it, its concept of the good. When Nigeria achieved independence from British colonialism in October 1960, the good that was demanded was, simply, human flourishing—the development of Nigerians to their full human capabilities. Put differently, the supreme economic good was creative emergence and actualization of human potentialities for higher levels of flourishing. It did not take long before it became obvious to almost all the citizens that this good was an impossible demand. The then-current state of things, the *time* of the state, did not consider human flourishing for all Nigerians to be compatible with its own narrow interests. But now we need to demand the impossible from the system. This is the only way to save Nigeria.

As I have argued, the place of time is about the subject, who stands in the rupture between the past and the future, between events of the past and the coming event (the emergence of Nigeria as an economic superpower), and aware of the good or the idea of development. The interval, the gap that the Nigerian inhabits to summon the impossible, to beckon to another possibility that is forbidden, excluded, or delegitimized by the prevailing situation, is the place of time. The place of time is a moral source of new possibilities, the locus of subjective activity disposed to welcoming the event, open to prophetic criticism of the system of oppression, inclined to declare possibilities, and enthusiastic about creating organs of resistance in anticipation of the event and for making a radical break with the system.

The place of time is not about abandoning belief in time as a flow or sociocultural preference for one of its traditional segments, but is about resistance to structures and supports, guarantees and fantasies—supposedly authenticated and legitimated by the passage of time—that hold people back from the difficult challenge of altering their social existence. For too long the "place of time in development" has been mistaken for obedience—suppression of freedom against conformity—to time-tested technical theories of socioeconomic management, rather than regarded as constant preparation for entering a new mode of life, into an intensification and beautification of life, into becoming and new creation.[18] The place of time promises this new mode of living that can transform human coexistence into sources of possibilities. The time of place is human existence cutting into time. It is social space cutting into time for a new place-time fabric that supports human flourishing and protects Nigerians' fragile dignity.

The place of time is also the place of preparedness, the inward awareness of the subject as he or she anticipates the event. It is not a place where those who are committed to the event of Nigeria wait to expect a miracle. As French philosopher Alain Badiou informs us,

> "To be prepared for an event" means being subjectively disposed to recognizing new possibilities. Since the event is necessarily unforeseeable given that it doesn't fall under the law of prevailing possibilities, preparing for the event consists in being disposed to welcome it. It's being convinced that the state of things does not set down the most important possibilities, those that open onto the construction of new truths. Being prepared for an event consists in being in a state of mind where one is aware that the order of the world or the prevailing powers don't have absolute control of the possibilities.[19]

Placing yourself in the place of time or subjectivizing your citizenship as a Nigerian means preparing consciously for the coming event of economic liberation of the country. In addition, it means becoming a symbol of the interval between the past of corruption, poverty, underdevelopment, and human indignity and the coming event of economic development and human flourishing. It means embodying the possibility of development and having the courage to pass it to other citizens. What is this possibility? It is the idea that every Nigerian has a right to become all that he or she can be. You ask that the state create an environment "for every individual to bring out the best and most elevated in themselves."[20]

At this point, the reader may argue that the political subject of development as defined above is an exceptional human being, a superman or -woman. This is far from the truth. In all of us there is both the exceptional (the subject) and the ordinary (just being the human animal). Fabien Tarby puts it well when he writes,

> The two tendencies exist in each of us: the ponderousness of the human animal that is satisfied with what there is, and the possible grace of the subject that opens itself up to *something else*, to the [the possibility of development]. We are permanently caught in this body and this mind that are ours, and yet we are, at the same time, disposed towards the best, but also the most exigent. . . . No one is an exception to this; everyone lugs their existence from one to the other, from the human animal to the subject that is possible. Each human being [each Nigerian] is potentially a subject, [a political subject of development].[21]

In the next section I discuss the vision of the economy that puts maximum emphasis on the actualization of human potentialities in the name of the possibility of economic development. It lays out a social-ethical framework for organizing economic development as the pursuit of excellence, the actualization of human potentialities for the sake of human flourishing.

2. Excellence and Economic Development[22]

The pursuit of economic development, which has often been characterized by fits and starts, rides on a basic creative propensity in human nature and, arguably, the most important virtue in human coexistence. The concern about economic development is a question about human existence. Economists respond to questions about human existence with answers that point to differences in the wealth of nations and disparities of wealth in various eras in human economic existence. They develop their answer unaware that economic existence itself is the question. Such answers typically presume modern economic behavior for human nature: the enhancement of human capability for self-transcendence and economic strides for human excellence, while any gap between them is overlooked. Philosophically, if we stick to this reasoning, it means that we can only explain excellence as the product of human economic self-realization in the progressive process of economic history. This is a wrong path to take. For if the economists are correct, then all who are estranged right now from the lofty economic achievements of the advanced nations may be lacking excellence.

Excellence is not a creation of economic self-realization; rather, it is the ontological drive of human life to exceed forms and to be directed toward the infinite. In and through economic creations and progress, the urge of excellence can actualize itself; it can become manifest. Economic progress is a medium, a bearer pointing beyond itself. Economic development is not itself excellence; it is a process whereby the regime of possibility that structures an economy, a regime of excellence, is modified. It is an active transformation of excellence, a moving of the boundaries of excellence. Its ultimate goal consists in making possible precisely that level of human flourishing which, from within the extant regime of possibility, is declared impossible. Economic development is, therefore, of interest philosophically not from the point of view of increase in gross national product or even economic welfare (though all these are important), but from the point of view of its power to express aspects of excellence in and through the drive to exceed forms insofar as such drive conditions our "being."

The purpose here is to analyze how an understanding of the concept of excellence will impact our thinking about economic development. What kind of light will be shed on the Nobel Prize–winning economist Sen's notion of development as *freedom*? He has argued that economic development is not just about quantitative increases in gross national product, but principally about giving people the freedom, the *capability* to become both the means (agents) and the end (goals and recipients) of their own economic development. Bringing this about, he argues, involves deliberate successive removal and vigilant resistance to *unfreedoms*.

Particularly, Sen has famously described economic development as *freedom*. By this he means the continuous and calculated attempt to remove *unfreedoms*, endowing people with capabilities so that they will become both the agents (means) and the end of their process of economic development. I find two major shortcomings in his analysis. First, the idea of development as freedom is not philosophically linked to humans who have the "future in their being." Humans are by nature future-oriented, and we need to know how the constant struggle to eliminate unfreedoms is related to their basic nature. Second, there is no discussion of the basic ontological foundation of freedom. Is the human struggle to create and sustain freedom—of which economic development is just one major aspect—basic to what it means to be human? What is there about human beings that may possibly undergird the search for freedom? In this section, I argue that what undergirds economic development and its aim of freedom is excellence. Excellence is the matrix from which freedoms come forth. So I will argue for a new perspective in economic development: *development as excellence*. This is not to say that economic development and excellence are identical. And I am not positing that we should think of excellence only in terms of economic development, only within the territory of developed countries, or even only in terms of scientific-technological breakthrough. I believe that material economic development can never be the ground and essence of excellence, but the latter can manifest itself during the process of development or scientific-technological breakthrough.

As noted above, Sen has made a fine distinction between economic development as increase in total output and economic development as *freedom*. He writes about development as *freedom*; development is presented as release from *unfreedoms*, as the veritable engine (agent or cause) of development. I interpret this notion of freedom as the dynamic quality of human existence. Freedom as an agent of development points beyond itself, demanding its completion in further development. Development (rising gross national product) itself points beyond itself, also demanding more development, more unshackling from unfreedoms. But the nature of the demand for completion is different in each case. When economic development points beyond itself to demand completion, it is about the filling in of what is lacking in human well-being. We add what we consider to be lacking to our basic well-being. Electricity, education, and medical services, for example, are added to complete the incomplete life of dehumanizing (incomplete) existence. "Such is the case, for example, with the restoration of a mutilated statue, of a partially destroyed painting. We see the need for completion, see too in what general direction it points; by supplying what has been missing, we make the incomplete complete."[23]

But when economic development as freedom demands completion, when it points beyond itself, it is not about filling or adding, but is strictly about replacing. The demand for completion of every gain of freedom "is not only toward the appearance of something that is not yet [more freedoms], but at the same time toward the disappearance of what is now present."[24] For example, the state of incompleteness, the inadequacy of an illiterate village woman's ability to properly weigh and trade agricultural produce, expresses itself in the demand for education. The demand for education will not be satisfied—in other words, the woman's inability to weigh properly will not go away if a government measuring agency is simply provided to her. The appearance of the proper skills of measurement requires the disappearance of illiteracy. For the education to realize complete freedom, literacy must disappear. What is lacking must appear in the place of what is given. In economic development as quantitative increment, what was lacking now appears along with the lack, but in development as freedom, what was lacking succeeds to replace the lack. As Victor Zuckerkandl put it in his comparison of visual incompleteness and auditory incompleteness in music, "the demand for completion on the part of a tone is a demand to cease being and to let something else, something that is not yet, appear."[25]

What is common to both cases (freedom and material quantitative development) is the "something dynamic, the pointing beyond itself, a demand for completion,"[26] and this common basis is excellence. Excellence is the dynamic that undergirds economic development either as an addition to the current level of well-being or as the generator of freedoms that must necessarily displace unfreedoms. This common basis needs to be investigated and properly understood by economists, but it has been largely ignored. I find the neglect of this basic human dynamic in the general debate toward defining economic development unacceptable. This chapter is an attempt to respond to this neglect.

Economists have interpreted economic development with the purpose of delivering it. With a few notable exceptions, this concern has been limited to making—that is, creating or engineering—development rather than understanding it. To offer a rough analogy: the problems of economists are the problems of composition rather than music. What they have mainly said is all about the difficult technique of producing development. There is nothing much to hang on to when it comes to understanding development itself, its nature, its essence. Development must be properly related to human nature in all of its physical, social, and spiritual dimensions via excellence. All this is intended not as blame or reproach, but to point out that the inner core of development must be understood. In other words, to use Victor Zuckerkandl's analogy, how can economic ethics, philosophy, or theology of development focus on the problems of electricity rather than on the problems of the electrician?[27] In this section I want to address the questions that are internal to the development phenomenon.

Neither economists nor ethicists appear to be focused on the inner core of development. Some of them need to play the role of the nineteenth-century English physicist Michael Faraday to understand the "electricity" of economic development, and others need to play the role of Hollywood technicians who set up the neon lights to dazzle people. But this is not happening. Economists and ethicists are arguing against each other from the same side of the fence. A third voice is needed to both enrich the flow of the debate and nudge it away from the eddy in which it is trapped. Economists say that development—no matter how it is sliced and diced—conveys the sense of a series of gains in well-being, in flourishing. Ethicists say: It is the positive changes in well-being that make a series of steps in innovations, inventions, and transformation meaningful. This writer argues: Series of innovations or increases in gross domestic product will no more constitute the essence of development than successions of tones will make a melody. "A melody is a series of tones that makes sense."[28] Strictly speaking, melody and rhythm happens in between the tones.[29] It happens in the "margin," and this is useful knowledge to have. Excellence happens in the margin too.

At first blush, it may appear that ethicists and neoclassical economists differ greatly on the idea of economic development. The debate between neoclassical economists and ethicists is not about the succession of progress that marks development but about the *meaning* in the progress. Yet, neither meaning nor succession is at the inner core of development. What is it, then, that inheres in a succession of progress? Or what inheres in the changes in meaning of the series of material and immaterial gains that is at the core of what it means to be developing in general? In all these there is a pointing toward—every movement is dictating a direction, placing itself in a direction, wanting to pass beyond itself, and does not want itself.[30] This is in the nature of all succession, and every take on development consciously or unconsciously presupposes it. Thus no series of progress, no amount of change in ethical meaning or interpretation of economic progress, is capable of reaching a satisfactory conclusion. The dynamic quality that characterizes human existence is the inner core of development. It is this inner core that encompasses and transcends every form of economic development.

This dynamic quality is, properly speaking, the human quality of development. It is a universal quality of the finite being, the concrete actuality of being called human. It is a universal dimension of human existence. This dynamic quality is, in a certain sense, what makes us human and undergirds the development process. This demand to proceed, this unfinishedness or incompleteness of every step that accrues to every activity, every meaning in the context of existence is integral to what it means to be human. It is a process in which a human becomes a person and ceases to be a "thing."[31]

It is the original fact and act of all self-creativity and self-transcendence. The dynamic self-realization or self-affirmation is a fundamental character of the human life. It gives validity to every development and it is present in all development or progress. In every instance of progress, innovation, invention, or transformation the human personhood actualizes itself. This dynamic quality of human existence can be analyzed philosophically or theologically: philosophically, only if we examine it just as it is, but theologically if we also affirm it as a manifestation of the infinite or show how it can penetrate through the finite to its infinite ground. Christian theology, in particular, will further interpret it as belonging to the created goodness of humanity.

Once we understand economic development or *freedoms* as embedded in, empowered by, and released by excellence as *clearing*, the task of inducing and sustaining economic growth and development becomes the task of creating and maintaining a healthy vibrant *clearing*. Development is no longer only about quantitative increases in national output or acquisition of capabilities for freedom as it moves beyond *development as freedom* to fundamentally *development as excellence.*

This *excellentist* philosophy is the philosophy of economic development that leads us beyond economic development itself. Development as freedom is a particular perspective that reveals merely the context of an opposition to the current paradigm of economic development but not the development of humanity itself. The holistic perspective is this: It is in knowing the human in her self-transcendence to grasp the be-ing in which freedoms proper to the enhancement of capability flow, and by that she achieves development and thus realizes herself, and there she goes beyond herself.

Her ability *to be* and to seize her own possibilities is the primitive and primary freedom to participate in this process of self-enactment that is economic development. She acts economically or developmentally as she has being (ability to be) and is in her being. Economic development is one of the freedoms to participate fully in the process of transcendence, and it is itself embedded in this process.

Development as excellence asks not about a particular paradigm of economic development, but about human development as such, about human nature, the human impulse toward the future, and human self-transcendence that are presupposed in any encounter with economic reality.

It is also about the philosophical-theological character of every economic action that is in it insofar as it is. Economic development is a category of human excellence and has its basis in it. Economic growth or development presupposes a human subject and an object (for example, human flourishing) about which it is directed that, in turn, presupposes beings actualizing their potentialities. The philosophy of excellence is the system of ideas in terms of which every form of economic achievement can be interpreted and that ultimately expresses the general principles requisite to the ethical analysis of any paradigm of economic development whatsoever.

Excellence is the depth of economic development and is manifest through it—and both point to the ground of existence. Economic development keeps endlessly transcending the finite realities of forms of economic organization, production and distribution, and freedoms, and yet it remains bound to excellence, which bears it along. In this way of putting the matter the theological character of every form, phase, and era of economic development is easy to discern. The power of transcendence points to a subject (man, woman) whose mind is directed to experience its own unlimited potentialities and who belongs to that which lies beyond the *margin* of the achieved and not-yet-achieved, beyond nothing, beyond nonbeing—to being-itself. As Tillich puts it,

> The fact that man never is satisfied with any stage of his finite development, the fact that nothing finite can hold him, although finitude is his destiny, indicates the indissoluble relation of everything finite to being-itself. Being-itself is not infinity; it is that which lies beyond the polarity of finitude and infinite self-transcendence. Being-itself manifests itself to finite being in the infinite drive of the finite beyond itself.[32]

In light of these points, the ethical framework developed in the previous chapters becomes the basis not only of ideas for forging a suitable social ethics or philosophy of excellence, but also of ideas that speak directly to the design and dynamics of economic development—and indeed to the philosophy of African economic development.

Modeling Excellence on Factors of Economic Development

So far I have tried to understand economic development in terms of excellence as a clearing. Here I will try to deepen our understanding of economic development by casting excellence in economic language. Albert Einstein showed us long ago that if two things are related, it may make sense to examine one in terms of the other and vice versa. His famous equation for mass-energy equivalence, $E = mc^2$, "energy equals mass times the speed of light squared," states that mass and energy are the same thing, interchangeable at the most fundamental level. Now I will not be bold enough to state that economic development and excellence are interchangeable. For they are not! But I will venture to assemble some key factors familiar to development economists to show that what they already know about development can be recast in the now familiar language of excellence. I will use only two factors—population and the speed of information flow—and a playful allusion to Einstein's famous equation here and there to make my case. The point of this exercise is not to convince anyone that physics or economic modeling can substitute for rigorous ethical thinking, but to show that some kind of analogical thinking may shed a light or two in a different field of inquiry.

I have described excellence as a moving force immanently present in history. I also presented it as a human phenomenon and not as something mysteriously infused into history from elsewhere—though it is open toward the infinite. In order to understand this immanent, in-history, in-finite dynamics I am inspired to think of it as a kind of social energy. I now consider it as a power for the actualization of possibilities that arises from and is sustained by the combinatorial and multiplicative implications of population size and the speed of information flow (that is, the speed of connectivity, cooperativeness, social integration, communion). The argument linking excellence to population density (mass) and the speed of information flow is not very difficult to conceive. One only has to accept that there is some close connection between the striving for excellence and the collective rate of innovation in any given society. The two factors of population and speed of information flow behind technical innovations, cultural evolution, and cultural complexification have long been accepted by economists and other social analysts.[33] Besides, we have already noted that excellence is the clearing that allows innovative products and ideas to materialize.

Let us return to Einstein's equation. The equation enables us to see the same thing in two perspectives: a pen is either a mass or a bundle of energy. A tiny piece of mass, like a nut, is seen in its potentialities as a bundle of almost limitless energy. A human being is simultaneously a person and a source of excellence, a site of the energy for excellence, a clearing for the manifestation of innovative ideas or potentialities of the whole of humanity. This site, this clearing is always a part of and a location within the intersubjective sphere of human existence.

I will now manipulate Einstein's equation to help us see excellence not only as a bundle of energy but also as an alternative way of speaking about persons as beings-in-communion. The degree of manifested excellence at any given time can be considered as a product of the mass of people in a given community and a possible three-dimensional communion among them. It is the power unleashable in the interaction of human beings, the social energy stored up in relationality or communion. Excellence is not only a power coming into existence at the interactions of a mass of related persons; it is also the in-between of persons. Not only does excellence create this space within which it functions and within which persons encounter one another, but such a space constitutes a clearing for the transformative, shaping power of creativity in an intersubjective context.

Excellence equals population (M) times the speed of information flow or *connectance* (C) raised to at least the third power ($E = MC^3$) for reasons that I will shortly explain. (This is not an equation requiring the reader to get his or her pencil and paper out to work out some hard numbers. It is an "equation" to stimulate thinking, to nudge the reader's attention—especially those ethicists who are mathematically challenged—to some key issues of economic development.) The power or energy implied in the product of population and the multiplicity of interactivity between the subjects in the population gestures to the power of unfolding life in history—the process of intensification of life and actualization of potentialities in history. And history here is the communication among persons, the relationship and exchange that is shared by all and surrounds all. It is the common sphere within which life happens simultaneously and connectively for all persons. Excellence is the *configuration of processes* that allow and give economic agents the means to express their potentialities, the opportunity to shape their own sphere of history and deepen their connectivity to being. The earmark of the presence of life as explained by biologist Robert E. Ulanowicz is the drive "toward ever more organized and coherent configuration of processes" that occur because of "autocatalysis," "increasing ascendency," and "centripetality" in the face of tendencies toward disorder, disintegration, and "overhead."[34]

Why do we have to multiply the population by the speed of information flow to suggest how much capacity exists for excellence in a given society? Before answering this question directly, let us first try to understand the importance of information exchanges in the growth and development of societies. It was Fernand Braudel who long ago told us that "All thought draws life from contacts and exchanges."[35] History has shown that innovation, the emergence of new ideas, is most rapid in societies in which people have come together to constitute a social information-processing system. This allows for social cooperation, integration, and non-zero-sum gains. Social scientist Robert Wright likened human society to a social brain and had this to say:

> Its neutrons are people. The more neutrons there are in regular and easy contact, the better the brain works—the more finely it can divide economic labor, the more diverse the resulting products. And, not incidentally, the more rapidly technological *innovations* take shape and spread. As economists who espouse "new growth theory" have stressed, it takes only one person to invent something that the whole group can then adopt (since information is a "non-rival" good). So the more possible inventors—that is, the larger the group—the higher its collective rate of innovation.[36]

Now we can formulate an answer to the question: Why do we have to multiply the population by the speed of information flow three times over to estimate how much potential capacity exists for excellence in a given society? The reason is that if a person is to affect the collective rate of innovation in his or her society or what we may call the overall clearing for innovative ideas and thoughts, if she is to "convert" her *be-ing* into energy that will fuel collective excellence, the resulting idea (*excelleme*) has to spread, by definition, at the existing speed of information flow in the society.

Why, then, do we say that communion among people in a community has to be at least three-dimensional? I will first present a biological argument and quickly move on to the more familiar social theory argument. The biologist Ulanowicz, using information theory to understand connections in an ecosystem, has worked out some kind of upper limit of connections per node. According to him, the greatest number of connections per node in a stable system is in the range of three.[37] Human society can be considered a certain kind of ecosystem.

Another reason for saying that the speed of information must be considered in three dimensions has to do with the nature of information-*ing* and our understanding of excellence as the font of possibilities. Information-ing is the process in which potential direction (unformed social life) becomes actual direction (formed social life) in the participatory movements of life. There are possibly three dimensions to this forming process, and all of them appear to be happening at the same time as possibilities are evaluated, validated, and designed for actions. First, there is depth to the relationality that is the basis of information exchange. This depth is the matrix of possibilities, the inexhaustible source from which every decision is a cutting away of some. Second, the possibilities chosen have to be organized, shaped, and molded to fit the ideal and futural character of human existence. This second aspect we shall call form and meaning of relationality. The third dimension is fulfillment; their ecstatic transformation. It is the actualization of the structural elements of the forming or decision-making process in their unity and in their tension. It is the union of the earlier two dimensions; the principle of unity within the relationality and by which the process finds its fulfillment. It is a way of currents that carries the two elements to the fulfillment of the telos of life. And life, as Tillich reminded us decades ago, "is the process in which potential being becomes actual being."[38]

In my 2008 book *The Depth and Destiny of Work*, I identified three crucial features of divine creativity as it courses through forms of human sociality.[39] I named three features of the dynamics of the working of divine creativity that are akin to the three aspects of relationality that we have mentioned above. Using medieval theological concepts, I named these features *complicatio*, *explicatio*, and *implicatio*.[40] *Complicatio* is the folding together of possibilities, the matrix of possibilities. It is what contains all—all pathways and opportunities before any decision or cutting is made. (*Decision* comes from the Latin *de* plus *caedere* [to cut] and points to the practice of mentally cutting away alternatives or possibilities to decide on one.) The possibilities are realized or unfold (*explicatio*) as each entity "*divines* and *actualizes*" its possibilities in participatory movements. *Explicatio* points to the going out of the self and returning to the self (in a process Paul Tillich calls individuation and participation) and thus to the unoriginative originating set of possibilities. In participation each penetrates the other in a way that defines being and becoming. All human creativity or actions are in possibility, and possibilities are in all actions. All actions or human creativity begin in relations and are continually in relations. "And that relation, 'the relation of relations,' may be called by *implication*"[41] the human community. This brings the two (possibilities and participation) together in interdependence. All three are rooted in the spirit, the font of and groundless ground of relations. Here the notion of spirit I have in mind is akin to that of Jürgen Moltmann as laid out in his work *God in Creation*. It is the common sphere (that is "elevated above the requirements of necessity") in which human beings act and live out their lives and that binds and weaves them into a higher life with one another. In this book, he described the spirit in these terms:

> As long as people can distinguish past and future, and can recognize in the temporal dimension of the future the open scope of the possibilities ahead of them, we shall be able to interpret the anticipatory structure of their organism and their social organization as "spirit" . . . Since we have described the *anticipatory* structure of the human constitution as "spirit," we have to interpret its complementary structure of *communication* as spirit too. Human life is dependent on natural and social communication and only exists in such communication. Life is relationship. Life is exchange. . . . This exchange creates community and is only possible in community. . . . It is communication in communion. Human life is what happens *between* individuals.[42]

We can get another perspective on the three-dimensional nature of communion by examining Michael Hardt and Antonio Negri's conception of the constituent power of the *multitude* in *empire*. In their 2004 book *Multitude*, they examined the dynamic relationship between communication, collaboration, and cooperation and the *multitude* that is capable of releasing the energy (the necessary dynamism) to configure and transform *empire*. Their argument could be summed up in two steps. First, they reasoned that the *multitude* as a "multiplicity of singularities" must first produce the *common* (clearing in our language) that allows them to communicate and act together.[43] "[The] communication, collaboration, and cooperation are only based on the common, but they in turn produce the common in an expanding spiral relationship."[44] Second, they argued that the energy (*constituent motor*, *virtual power*) that sustains, transforms, and moves the *common* is a function of the *multitude* and its attendant fusion power of communication, collaboration, and cooperation.[45]

From the above discussions about life, relationality, and communication, the idea of modeling excellence as somewhat equivalent to the product of population and the various dimensions of ongoing communication amid them should not be construed as pointing us to some inanimate abstractions or a mathematical identity, but to the dynamics of social life. The elements in the equation are to be considered as symbols of the answer to the question of actualization of potentials implied in the "common sphere" of human existence. The elements are symbols of the analogy between the basic structure and dynamics of human coexistence and the energy in the universe (as revealed by Einstein) that undergirds human life. I hope that this analogy provides us with the potential for new thinking on how people and the relationships they form can be transformed into sites for excellence for human flourishing.

This promise notwithstanding, I would like to add that we should not set great store on the "excellence equation." For the equation does not provide precise information as does Einstein's equation; it is only a heuristic device to stimulate thinking; it is to simplify a difficult economic argument for philosophers. There are a couple of reasons why we cannot at this point go beyond using it as heuristic device to organize thinking about excellence. When dealing with electrons, one is dealing largely with perfectly homogenous sets whose behavior can be determined by laws. But when we are dealing with social systems or persons-in-communion we are dealing with heterogeneous groupings whose dynamics are fixed not by laws but by processes.[46] There is also the problem that there has been no reliable and generally acceptable constant, as the speed of light, worked out for the speed of information flow in modern globalizing societies. In fact, there need not be a constant for the speed of information.[47] As new innovations come on stream, as *excellemes* pile on *excellemes*, the speed of interaction between economic agents changes, making it unreasonable to fix the speed of information flow for all times.[48] The speed not only affects the pace of excellence—it is itself also a function of the advance of excellence.

Instead of focusing on precise numbers for the speed of information flow and the mass, the import of the equation is on how it points us to two crucial areas of managing economic development. The "mass" in the equation calls attention to human capability development, human capital. The higher the quality of human capital in each subject in the population base, the higher the potential energy that can be released for economic development. The speed of information flow can be accelerated by focusing on, among other factors, raising social capital (intensification of relationality among economic agents), social trust, participatory democracy, urban-rural articulation, and physical infrastructures that will ease the burden of interaction at all levels in the community. This kind of approach will trigger economic development as an inevitable outcome of the increasing of the range of the clearing we have named excellence, the power of unfolding life in history.

Excellence and Money

Excellence in this study has been portrayed as a "being" that is eternally becoming (or "coming"), as if trapped in a web of eschatological expectation of a better future, to echo British philosopher and theologian Philip Goodchild. Money is also a being that is always becoming, trapped in a similar web. This raises some hope that if some perspicacious mind can connect both forces together, align them to work for the benefit of human flourishing, we can move the poor out of poverty much more quickly. Below I will attempt to think through how eros of money could be unleashed to function within the clearing that is excellence.

Nowhere is the force of perpetual becoming more discernible than in the "eschatological structuring" that is imbedded in the *discounted cashflow model* of security valuation used by economists. Under this methodology, the value of an asset is based on its expected (projected) cash flow. An analyst will forecast the future net cashflow or income stream from given assets and then discount them by the appropriate discount (interest, return) rate to arrive at the *net present value* of assets. Money—the value of assets and liabilities—is deemed "eschatological in its structuring," because "the present is created from the future."[49] Economists and bankers calculate the value of assets or liabilities by evaluating anticipated flows of income, anticipated returns, promises of expansion in an imagined better future. Managers make asset allocation decisions (deployment or withdrawal from the market) by also looking at projections about value and income flows from assets in the future. Yet when this imagined future arrives, the value of the asset would still be based on the next expectations of what it will be in a further imagined future. Capital is trapped in a web of eschatological expectation of a better future—a being that is eternally becoming or "coming."[50] According to Goodchild,

> Capital is not merely a flow because it is always an anticipation of an imagined future—whether we are concerned with speculation or credit, it is always an anticipated rate of return

> that determines how much there will be. What there is now is dependent upon what we believe there will be.[51]

To be precise, valuation is always about the future, the redemptive eternity the economists call "the long run."[52] It is also about totality. The depiction of value in modern neoclassical economic thought, far from opening the object (the item so valued) to the rest of the world, traps it within its own dynamics and trajectory. Valuation aspires to a kind of totality, that is, an integrated perspective that subordinates everything, every dynamic in the entire economy and environment, to the common principle expressive of the value of the object. There is a question being asked and answered in the discounted cash flow model used for valuation: How does the whole set of dynamics in an economy, and indeed in the global marketplace, impact the future cash stream of the asset?

The totalizing orientation of valuation gives the impression of being open to the future, but what is actually happening is that the future is imagined and created, and it is mysteriously birthed, appropriated, and consumed in the present. What is happening is that the vitalities (or potentialities) of the future are divided and appropriated even before they are born. The data or information about the asset is projected into the future as series of potential flows and then pulled back or down by the mathematics of discounting and cajoled, conjured, and "shaved" to appear in the present as what is euphemistically called *net present value*. The name "present value" is a misnomer. What has been calculated and tagged "net present value" has no present being. It is a "value" between values. The asset or security that was evaluated had a past record of cashflows that were known and has a future value that is only expected. By calling it "present value" the economists assume that the future is the present. This *presentized* future is then sold and bought in the marketplace. In valuation the unborn children of time are sold and consumed; time, like an ever-rolling stream, is not allowed to bear its children away. There is a profound ambiguity in all this. From one angle of vision, it appears that capitalist investors are open to the future, ready to risk the future, but actually they are afraid of the future. So the future is discounted and heavily depreciated—this is why the method of valuation is called *discounted cash flow method* (DCF). The bigger the fear, the higher the discount factor (interest rate) and the lower the growth rate applied to the current earnings that donate their possibilities to the future stream of income.

It is important to mention that the possibilities that are being calibrated and calculated are not the same as possibilities that noneconomic scholars such as theologian Jürgen Moltmann and philosopher Ernst Bloch call the "Real-Possible."[53] The economists' notion of possibilities as discernible in the valuation model is "objectively Possible." The reality from which economists discern possibilities for the working of their model is not expected to produce the startlingly new. For it is reality surrounded by the cycle of what has already become and is largely conditioned by the parameters of the model, the theories behind the model, and the present circumstances of the asset. In the case of the neoclassical economic model, there is a certain *givenness* to the possibilities; in the Bloch-Moltmannian theological model there is a *processive openness* to them. Frankly, economists are focused on trend rather than on possibilities.

Thus, although economists may be concerned with the redemptive long run as this study of excellence is, they are laden with different sensibilities and orientations. The philosopher of excellence looks into the future with hope, eschatological hope. This is not so for the economists. As was stated earlier, in calculating the value of an exchangeable item (an asset), the analyst's thoughts are drawn toward the horizon of the future, and what she focuses on as she peers into the future is not hope but assurance—not latent possibilities she cannot conceive, but palpable possibilities that are carefully conceived, calibrated, and calculated (*trend-mentality*). Assurance tries to eliminate the risk of disappointments, but hope embraces the risk of disappointment. It is with such a hope that is open to the future—the *Real-Possible*—that I am going to make an attempt to provide a basic framework for monetary policy that will fit with the philosophy of excellence ventured here. I will construct an alternative perspective from which the world of monetary policy is to be seen. The major issue in doing this is to show how monetary policy should be thought about and crafted to identify the true potentials of an economy, region, sector, or market situation and enable them to be realized. In doing all this I will rely on my skill as both a social ethicist and a former investment banker on Wall Street. This imaginative framework is important to develop even if political and economic realities block its immediate implementation. The alternative thinking provided by this framework exposes, at the minimum, the values of the current monetary policy regime that are threatening the moral order of many a nation, and thus it serves as a critique of the current monetary thought that dominates development thinking. I will discuss the monetary policy issues together with work because the primary goal of monetary policy is to order work aright in any economy. If money—in the forms of credit economy, exchange, and capital—is the condition of possibility for work, what should function as the condition of possibility for money itself?

Economic Development: The Role of Work and Monetary Policy

Here I want to discuss the conceptions of work and monetary policy that are likely going to promote economic development as a manifestation of the clearing that we have named *excellence*. What is work? And what is monetary policy?

Work is the unfurling of humanity toward a wholeness in which all selves and others are inextricably linked.[54] Work is the daily means (involving body, mind, and spirit) of humanity to begin, to undertake (Old English *beginnan*) the iterative dynamic of becoming itself that we have named *excellence*. That a fresh beginning be made in the fluid dynamics of transcending humanity work is done. Working is fundamentally the communication and exchange of that by which a human being is in dynamism of positing a new possible world.[55] The *that* that is communicated is the set of possibilities (potentials) for forward movement. Work is that by which the human being "stands in" and "stands out" of excellence, the processive openness toward the not-yet. Excellence is working on working.

The importance of monetary policy in producing the right environment for "excellent selves" to triumph and prosper in their work cannot be overstated. Monetary policy is what orders work in any modern economy. Monetary policy is the mobilization of an economy's monetary and financial resources for the preservation, promotion, and ordering of its work. Productive and reproductive work—organization and distribution of rewards thereof—maintain the structure of mutuality of life through which a people shape their lives and cope with their day-to-day problems. The control of the money supply in any economy affects which work prospers and which work weakens in it; and thus is determined "who shall benefit and who shall sacrifice"[56] in the production and reproduction processes of life.

Every organization of a monetary system and, for that matter, work is coded with its own peculiar set of principles, motivations, and information for either supporting or thwarting (even if unwittingly) the *clearing* that is excellence. It is, therefore, important for us to spend some time reflecting on the approach to monetary policy that will foster economic development as an opportunity for and a process and product of increasing the range of the *clearing*.

Everywhere, monetary policy shapes the landscape of economic and social lives. How it does this is dependent on a philosophical-ethical understanding of the role of monetary policy in modern economies. Is monetary policy simply a technical adjustment of quantities of money in an economy or a sophistic manipulation of interest rates with no connections to deep national aspirations? Or is it, rather, suffused with discernment of entrepreneurial passions and highly ethical judgments as to what is of value and importance to the development of a national economy? I will argue that there can be no adequate ethical perspective on monetary policy without an adequate understanding of what I will call the *eros* of money.

The crucial role of monetary policy is to tap the wellspring of vital energies in the socioeconomic phenomenon that is money for economic growth and development. A good and development-oriented national monetary policy should offer the experience of both the fulfillment and the endless awakening of the creative force and yearning for mutuality in the national economy. There is a connection-making power of money that a good monetary policy is meant to unleash. A monetary policy is good, among other considerations, when it expresses possibilities for wider integration, cooperation, and transformation at both the personal and transpersonal levels in an economy. It is good when it can positively shape communal relationships. Additionally, from a nationalistic point of view it is good when citizens can see their own "spirit," values, ideals, and hopes incarnated in it.

Some neoclassical economists may consider the above ethical stance on monetary policy "strange." But the stance came after reflection on the received neoclassical economic wisdom on money and the need to transcend the limited perspective it offers. Those of us who are interested in liberating the poor from "unfreedoms" should learn to think new thoughts even as we think the thoughts of Milton Friedman and his cohorts. I am offering a "strange" perspective on monetary policy not out of a desire to stand outside the ballpark of mainstream monetary thinking but to *un-conceal* a new vista in monetary policy thinking. It is my hope that this vista may give us an opening for new possibilities in poor economies, to enable them to move from lower levels of performance to the highest possible levels.

It does no good to focus only on the quantity of money in monetary policy decisions as this is generally done in the leading central banks of the world. Money is not a mere quantitative thing. It is something that has the vitality to grow and expand, to connect and nourish all those persons and sectors it touches. It has the power to transform and deepen relationships between economic actors and their economy if properly handled.[57] It is this vitality, energy, impulse that I have named as the *eros* of money. *Eros* is the power of creativity, the impulse to move from a lower standing to a higher dimension, the transition from brokenness to wholeness—approaching but never quite reaching it. It is a power in human sociality to secure that which is salient and essential to its well-being and greater flourishing.

It was Plato in his *Symposium* who put out the argument that there is an impulse in all beings to move from incompleteness to wholeness, to desire that which will complete them. This movement, the transitions to higher levels of fulfillment, he named as *eros*. The purpose of the movement or desire is not just for the sake of coming together but to release the power of creativity in humanity for the sake of a flourishing life. *Eros*, he argued, is a power that underlies all of human creativity, from procreation to the love of philosophical wisdom. *Eros* is a life-giving power and the driving force in all human coexistence, including economic togetherness and cultural creativity. *Eros* is both an awareness and a movement in the direction of greater flourishing. It is about a painful awareness of a gap and the desire to close that separateness, a demand to possess that which the person does not wholly possess. The sheer separateness from that which could make one whole releases one's vitality for the pursuit of wholeness and greatness necessary for happiness or *eudaimonia*.

The peculiar kinds of destructive separateness and incompleteness that have been undermining economic development in the Nigerian economy are not hard to discern. What has been hard to notice is a deliberate attempt to release the kind of *creative eros* that can raise it beyond poverty and underdevelopment. Destructive incompleteness in the Nigerian economy is revealed in its dependency, decades of failure to raise living standards, monetary systems that are not geared to the development of internal resources, crippling urban and rural disarticulation, and massive income inequality that eviscerates the well-being of the poor. For too long, Nigeria has been separated from the flourishing economy it should have. Everywhere her people look, they experience the *pathos* of separation and poverty in their midst.

Monetary policy, then, should be both a paradigm and a series of steps that aim to bring their crushing longing and incompleteness to an end. The Nigerian central bank should be aiming at releasing the creative and animating force that is in money so that it can exert positive influence in all spheres of their economies, connecting regions and sectors. Those charged with making the nation's monetary policies need to make all good efforts to understand the "essential nature of money," not simply its twisted expressions under the conditions of underdevelopment, neocolonialism, and empire as we currently find all over Africa, Asia, and Latin America. The "essence" of money is its *creative eros*. The *telos* of the Nigerian central bank should be to remove the cleavage between the "essence" of money and its twisted and ambiguous expressions in its territory; to overcome the chasm between the nation's potentialities and current levels of achievement, to encourage every economic agent to strive and yearn to raise himself or herself toward higher levels. Monetary policy should be a source of movement of the citizens toward integrated, internally powered development.

In order for us to understand how monetary policy can become a source of movement toward a well-articulated economy, we need to decipher the elements of *eros* and lift them up as norms of monetary policy. The hope is that the pursuit of these norms in decision-making by central banks will fruitfully enable the Nigerian economy to resist underdevelopment (a kind of *nonbeing*) and preserve and promote development (*being*).

Following Paul Tillich, I interpret *eros* as the umbrella Greek word for love with four components: *epithymia*, *philia*, *eros*, *agape*.[58] *Epithymia* (longing) names the desire to fulfill need. Simply, it is the recognition of a need and the movement to satisfy the need. *Philia* is the movement toward union between equals. The part within *eros* that bears its name points to a movement of that which is lower in a scale of value toward that which is higher. *Agape* is the part of love that affirms the other unconditionally; it affirms not because the other is higher or lower, pleasant or unpleasant, desirable or undesirable. The only interest is to draw the other into a union. When *agape* is present in a relationship, it can transform and purify the other components of love and move them to their pure forms as dynamic movements of the separated to (re)union.

The Platonic-Greek philosophical idea of love as *eros* is not about pleasurable feeling; it is about a creative, dynamic, primal power that moves the world toward fulfillment and deepens relationships. It is the connection-making power in human life and the whole of the universe.

Money is a form of *eros* in any modern economy because it is the moving power of economic life. Money is not a mere tool of exchange; it is a force (a form of *social relation*[59]) that calls persons, regions, and sectors beyond themselves and draws them from separation, detachment, and disarticulation into integration, articulation, and participation in the unfolding creative processes of an economy.

Money is actually a two-edged sword. Money connects, money separates. It cuts and it attaches. Money looks inward and outward. It is both constructive and destructive. The *creative eros* of money reveals the constructive power of money over its negation. Money embraces within itself destructive forces that are opposed to its *creative eros*. When we speak of the *creative eros* of money, it is only with an affirmation of money's positive constructive force in recognition of its destructive potential. Monetary policy is, simply, an affirmation of money's creative forces while resisting its destructive tendencies. The real expertise in central banking is to acquire and preserve the power to affirm the creative forces of money despite the destructive ones over and over again.

This is one of the ways central bankers can affirm the *creative eros* of money through policy. They set and abide by some basic norms that can induce and sustain relationality, mutuality, and transition to higher levels of economic performance and human flourishing in their economies. The norms come from adapting and transforming Tillich's elements of love into a set of ethical canons for monetary policy. First, the criterion of *stimulation* (*epithymia*) is the capacity of monetary policy to drive economic agents into more and more intercourse and interdependence, to stimulate the movement of the less vibrant, less efficient sectors and agents toward sectors, areas, and resource centers that fulfill them. In order to promote economic interdependence and eliminate all forms of insidious economic duality, monetary policies most encourage the movement of the deficit (that is, needful, less vibrant, less efficient, less articulated) industries toward the sectors and resource centers that will help to liberate their potentials and fulfill them.

The second norm is about the criterion of *integration* (*philia*). Monetary policy should not only stimulate intersectoral intercourse but also encourage and sustain movement toward better integration and union within each sector and region. While *stimulation* is an external movement of sectors, *integration* is about internal movement within sectors and regions. Monetary and fiscal policies must encourage movement toward better integration and union within each sector and region. In terms of persons, this involves providing equality of access to present and accumulated economic and social resources so that most persons will have equal opportunity to develop their capabilities and fully participate in the preservation and promotion of their community well-being.

The third norm is *transformative*; monetary policy should promote right relationship, pushing or pulling all sectors, industries, regions, and persons from levels lower in cooperativeness and potential toward their highest forms. The fourth norm is that of *promotion of sociality* inherent in the social practice of work. The issue is how to know whether or not a certain monetary policy regime is structured to include all groups and classes to participate fully in the economy so as to create flourishing lives for themselves. Does it foster participation and communion, human mutuality, and reciprocity? The right monetary policy that fosters participation and communion points to an *eros* quality in every interpersonal and intersectoral relation in the economy. Mutuality is the key category for understanding the reality of money, work, and monetary policy. It is also the central symbol as well as the source of norms. Mutuality emphasizes comprehensive inclusiveness; that is, it includes all groups, classes, sectors, and regions to participate fully in the economy so as to create flourishing lives for themselves.

The knowledge of how to generate and sustain the *creative eros* of money is the mother of all forms of monetary knowledge. This knowledge is about initiating and sustaining collective capacity, knowing how to integrate sectors, discerning how to harness the dispersed energies of the citizens to achieve national flourishing, how to marshal individual economic resources to act for the common good, and how to orient all men and women toward excellence.

Concluding Remarks

Economic development lives and moves in the tension that arises from the synthesis of immanence and transcendence; that is, the *form* of excellence and the inexhaustibility of excellence. To grasp this point is to understand economic development as deeply multidimensional. Every economic progress or development, and thus every actualization of a people's economic potentiality, comprises three dimensions. First, it is an interconnection and articulation of improvements. Individual improvements or sectoral advancements are never fully apprehended in isolation, but always from within the context of the whole economy. Economic development and its interpretation and apprehension always presuppose a synthesis. This synthesis, from which particular sectoral advancement or regional growth makes sense, is human flourishing. Yet human flourishing does not represent the source of *import*[60] of the particular improvement or progress. The source is the second dimension, which we have named *human self-actualization*, and it resides—or rather, is embedded—in any particular improvement. But it transcends every particular improvement too. It is the living power that stands over, above, and beyond every particular form of improvement. This explains the fact that no level of economic development can be satisfied in itself; it cannot be self-enclosed. Self-actualization as a living power is *form-bursting*; it demands that every level, stage, phase, or range of societal development positively annuls itself so it can preserve itself in a higher synthesis. This is the way to elevating and transforming human flourishing in a positive way, moving it toward increasing interconnections of being and meaning. The process of economic development is a dialectical tension experienced as actualization of potential and as a *demand*, as an "ought to be." This demand is the third dimension of economic development. By this I mean that the actualization of any people's potential for economic development presupposes an awareness of this demand, the demand for excellence as a clearing, the demand to fulfill humanity.

All this suggests that economic development is a spiritual process, for through it the human spirit fulfills its being with meaning and points beyond itself. As Tillich insisted long ago, all particular human forms of meaning point beyond themselves and need to be connected, transparent, or open to the unconditional meaning that resides in and transcends every particular meaning.

The *metalogical*[61] method to economic development, as indicated in this chapter, does not argue for the formalism of development about which economics makes statements; rather, it provides a critical analysis of the dynamics of development with respect to its *power* and through this analysis finds its transcending quality. It is doubly pointing beyond its current form or manifestation. The task of the philosophical analysis of economic development is to grasp the inner dynamism of form in the extant form (phase, level, stage) of economic development and show how it can be prophetically geared to a *higher synthesis* and also how it can be guided toward human flourishing for all Africans.

Chapter 6

Naija-Dialectics

Theory and Methodology

Introduction

It is usual for scholarly authors to say that their works fill gaps in the literature. This work does not fill any gaps; rather, it opens up gaps in our understanding of a subject matter. It perforates our comprehension of temporality, destiny, and desire in traditional African communities. It creates "wounds" and dehiscence in our inherited framework of interpretation of indigenous (communal) philosophy in Africa. The rupture of stilt frames makes it possible to elevate everyday, ordinary, religious ideas to the dignity of deconstructible philosophical notions.

If wounds and dehiscence are the only things we gain from this book, we are of all readers most miserable—channeling Saint Paul here. We should be pitied more than anyone. No, the book grafts its wild, disruptive knowledge onto economic philosophies to become a partaker with them of the root and riches of the African "development olive tree" that is about to grow big and blossom. Based on the historical data of the Kalabari-Ijo of the Niger Delta in Nigeria, our thesis of split time led us into the theory of agonistic communitarian framework—not simply communitarianism—as the best open, unfinishable frame for interpreting one of Africa's economic philosophies in the nineteenth century. Agonistic communitarianism is an economic philosophy that combines communalism and individualism. It is a system that encourages an abiding tension—agonism—between cooperation and competition to allow an economy to create and distribute wealth in ways that promote human flourishing. The insights from this theory were quickly extended into the quest for an economic philosophy of development based on the actualization of human potentialities.

Since the book does not close gaps, bind wounds in the subject matter before us, or provide any medicine for readers longing for healing from diseased thoughts, it has multiple orifices into which a reader can plug to suck its juices, its seminal fluids both tonic and poisonous, for their own creativity. For the ocean of production, reproduction, destruction, and development of knowledge in whose foaming wake I traffic, this book, owing to its unyielding pursuit of the Moby Dick of human flourishing for all Africans, deserves to be taken down into the abyss as Ahab and the whale.

The last time I checked I got the joyful feeling that it was better for my book to go down into the abyss than for me to do so. The Ijaw (Ijo) people that I have written about can also send a man and his book (his lover) into the abyss for disagreeing with them. This is the picture Gabriel Okara paints of the Ijaw in his pathbreaking novel, *The Voice.*[1] The characters Okolo and Tuere challenged the consensus knowledge, the received wisdom of their community, and for this they were hogtied, were put in a small canoe to drift far offshore—and were eventually sucked into the abyss of the sea. "Down they floated from one bank of the river to the other like debris, carried by the current. Then the canoe was drawn into a whirlpool. It spun round and round and was slowly drawn into the core and finally disappeared. And the water rolled over the top and the river flowed smoothly over it as if nothing had happened."[2]

Let me boldly declare to you that the ideas in this book cannot be drawn into the deep. I did not manufacture them out of my hoary head. I only excavated them from the hidden, *tehomic* depths of my Kalabari-Ijo community. These ideas have lived for centuries in the abyss, and now that they have come up to see the sunlight, no one can take them back into the dungeons. The ideas of *fiyeteboye* (destiny), *bibibari* (recanting of spoken words), split time, and desire directed to immanent living-on have arisen to shine, their light has come, and the glory of economic philosophy shines over them. The close interplay or foreplay that this book stages between Kalabari religious (secular) ideas and economics raises the possibility that each of them can shed light, shed its grace on the other. Kalabari religio-secular ideas crown the good of economics with six gifts, growing from strength to strength. These are the six areas that Kalabari notions of temporality, desire, destiny, and human flourishing have elevated to the honor of rigorous economic philosophy even as they illuminate it.

The book is specifically devoted to developing a socioeconomic theory of development in the light of the philosophical ideas embedded in African traditional religions (ATR). The ideas, practices, and institutions that were retrieved from historical Kalabari indigenous sources, and then the body of thought that went into explaining, defending, and applying them to Nigeria's present quest to overcome its economic predicament, constitute a notable contribution of ATR to development studies. African traditional religion, instead of Christianity or Islam, is used to undergird the economic-philosophical constructive tasks in this book. I made the deliberate choice to formulate the critical-theoretical discourse of economic development in this book only through the perspective of African traditional religions, subjecting socioeconomic theory to a specifically ATR reformulation. This was a conscious effort to develop an economic philosophy or craft socioeconomic theory under the rubric of ATR. I demonstrate in this book that there is a proper conceptualization of ATR that makes it indispensable to a rigorous analysis of religious and philosophical ideas as they intersect with economic development studies in Nigeria.

Second, African traditional religion engages, confronts, or critiques economic philosophy or neoclassical economics. The book, deeply informed by indigenous philosophy and history, is an inquiry into what social transformation would be required for Nigeria's national economy to thrive. Here "to thrive" carries the meaning of how the nation's economic time, talent, and treasure can be worked out to coexist most rewardingly, to enable Nigerians to live with one another to promote their common good. The meaning of "thrive" goes beyond economic growth to include human flourishing, and in this way it challenges the focus of neoclassical economic thought and its emphasis on mere technical processes of growth. The book points to the ethical, ethological dimension of the economic processes of national life.

Third, I have systematically accounted for these key elements in Kalabari philosophy: time, destiny, desire, community, individualism, and human flourishing. Essentially, this book offers a radical economic interpretation of history, worldview, and philosophy that generates fresh insights into the developmental potential of Nigerian precolonial cultural institutions. Its method is based on the rediscovery of the practices and principles of emancipatory economics and a retrieval of fundamental orientations to human coexistence that go to the core of the functioning of economies bent toward human flourishing. This study builds up economic philosophy from a place of indigeneity.

Fourth, every human society must deal with the questions of temporality, desire, destiny, and human flourishing. Each society develops discourses to offer a framework (narrative) that connects time, possibility of fulfillment of desire, and pursuit of happiness (eudaimonia). These questions and their integrative or contradictory narrative play a fundamental role in society's economic philosophy. Desires—the fundamental stimulus for human striving—are by nature time driven, and their movement or destination is evaluated in the light of a society's understanding of human flourishing. The motion and telos (if any) of any desire are often connected to a source that defines its origin, character, tensions, pleasure/pain, and the distance it has to travel to its fulfillment or satisfaction. The provenance and its proprietary features are what destiny (or freedom) is about. Economic philosophy is a set of discourses and ideologies that respond to questions concerning temporality, desire, destiny and human flourishing in ways that legitimize the extant organization of society for its production and distribution of wealth. It works because people believe in it, and it often serves to justify inequality. According to the economist Thomas Piketty, economic philosophy is neither economic nor rational; it is religious and ideological.[3] This book has, among other accomplishments, demonstrated this view of economic philosophy as a discursive framework. But the version here has a deep orientation to human flourishing and does not justify inequality.

Fifth, this book demonstrates that beliefs of African traditional religion (in this case, Kalabari-Ijo traditional religion) have the capacity to shape economic behavior, provide psychological sanctions for development policy regimes, and shape citizens' orientations toward themselves and others. What citizens believe about the religio-philosophical presuppositions of their society in great part influences what they consider as reasonable courses of actions in their economic conducts and how they relate to themselves and others. The combined impact of all these points us to an economic ethic. The notions of destiny, desire, and split time in Kalabari philosophy are structured to induce individuals to exert themselves to actualize their potentialities, to deploy their personal capacities for efficient work and self-advancement. These notions, especially destiny, reject fatalism in favor of dynamic self-improvement, the capacity to initiate something new amid ongoing social processes, the capacity to begin. The psychological impact of the beliefs in destiny and desire conduces to active commitment to living a finite, temporal life and to agonistic progress in human flourishing.

Finally, this book contains an implicit new approach to the study of African traditional religion that is worth making explicit at this juncture. I have approached the study of destiny (*fiyeteboye*), recanting (*bibibari*), desire, and time as (some kind of Deleuzian) *flows* that are variously coded or decoded by society. I departed, for instance, from defining the features or properties of destiny or desire to focus instead on how they are produced. They are results of ongoing sets of social processes, coded and decoded flows. Destiny and desires are ways of assessing and assigning values to flow and appropriating and possessing values of flows—in some instances, coding flows. Human flourishing is about how these flows encounter one another and coalesce and conjugate to promote socioeconomic development, or about how the Kalabari traditional society codes and decodes these flows for the advancement of its agnostic communitarianism. The flows of the impulses, drives, and affects relating to destiny, desire, and time are the subjective essence of economic development. These flows (libidinal economy) are an integral part of the economic infrastructure of any economy. Every economy presupposes the presence, continuity, and vibrancy of these flows. Indeed, an economy is a complex of abstract and concrete, subjective and objective flows. This book constitutes an attempt to theorize, to philosophize subjective flows within the context of the traditional Kalabari-Ijo society. It portrays Kalabari persons as interceptors of flows, both as destinations of multiple flows and producers of numerous new flows, constantly breaking and capturing flow. Even their notion of the sacred is ultimately conceptualized as a flow: the flow, coding and decoding, of possibilities. Destiny or desire are forms of breaking and capturing possibilities and the production of possibilities. Hopefully, there is a lesson here for economists who "think" the production, coding and decoding, and consumption of subjective and objective flows or possibilities in the Nigerian economy.

Now we have reached the explicatory plan that I mentioned in the introductory chapter. Chapter 1 bears the whole of the book's arguments in a nutshell. Chapter 2 represents itself and presents the arguments of chapters 3–5 *in nuce*; this pattern is carried forward to chapter 5, the last chapter. This concluding chapter presents the book's collective arguments as a retrospective (retroactive) gesture or refolds the major theoretical moves of the book. Each chapter, including this conclusion, is a "signature" (in the Agambenean sense) of the contents and method of the whole book, even as fresh arguments of every chapter unfold, refold, enfold, and energize ideas of its preceding chapters while carrying forward the whole book in a sort of relay race.[4]

Next, I will reveal that there are also underlying railroad tracks that carried the freight train of *signatures* throughout the book. Without these tracks, I could not have made these signatures run smoothly from one to another and point us to our ultimate direction, from thesis to transfinite thesis. The metaphor of railroad tracks applies to the study's methodology, which is based on the style of elucidation and dialectics of the jokes by a Nigerian comedian with the stage name MC Edo Pikin (Mr. Gbadamasi Agbonjor Jonathan is his real name). As we shall soon see, I have (retroactively) taken his comedic style and elevated it to the dignity of a philosophical template for analyzing the contemporary social situation in Nigeria.

I can only now reflect on and articulate my method after its practical application in the preceding five chapters. As I proceed to articulate the methodology of the book based on MC Edo Pikin's comedic style, let me quickly state a philosophical problem that I encountered. It is not enough simply to state that one is using his dialectics to retroactively articulate one's methodology; one must clarify how his style was transformed into a philosophical discourse. By virtue of what operations, what conditions of transition was one able to close the gap between his work and the sequence of concepts, ideas, and analyses in the preceding pages of this book? One is able to close this gap by viewing the chapters of this book as the signatures of comedic dialectics. According to Agamben, a signature makes it possible for us to grasp the internal logic, the distinguishing mark of a situation (or thing, being, world). It is a process of transference that allows us to move knowledge (concept or discourse) from one domain to another. Signature makes the sign of situation (being, thing, world) intelligible, allowing meaning to happen.[5] The chapters of this book not only manifest the hidden virtues of MC Edo Pikin's narrative style but also make it intelligible in a philosophical discourse. Let me quickly add that the ideas, concepts, and discourses of the preceding chapters of the book are neither the essence of MC Edo Pikin's dialectics nor something foreign to it. My work only disperses it "toward revelation and knowability" by brushing it against the rigors and systematicity of a philosophical discourse.[6] As Walter Benjamin might put it, this book is an image wherein MC Edo Pikin's (preexisting) dialectics come together in a flash with the now of my philosophical ruminations to form a constellation.[7] In other words, the book is a signature or constitutes a set of signatures of MC Edo Pikin's remarkable dialectics of cultural criticism.

The Comedy of MC Edo Pikin

Comedian Gbadamasi Agbonjor Jonathan (stage name MC Edo Pikin) was born on January 2, 1990, in Edo State, Nigeria. He obtained his first degree in theatre and media arts from Ambrose Ali University, Ekpoma, Nigeria. His comedy caught my interest because of its structural dialectics, its comparative definitions. He has a series in which the whole comedy is about comparative definitions of everyday terms, events, and reality in Nigerian society, and in this way he forces into active awareness what others have not noticed or have simply ignored. In each of the series he offers hilarious definitions of three related terms, functions, or offices that portray the actions of his fellow Nigerians. His comparative definitions are always in response to the question, "What's is the difference between X, Y, and Z?" The first definition focuses on *deeds in themselves*. He defines for his audience what Nigerians in a particular function, office, or status usually do (the "X"). The second definition emphasizes *deeds for themselves* (the "Y"). He explores how the people understand their actions, their engagement in functions, in the practice of their statuses, or in the performance of their deeds. Finally, he comes down to the *idea of the deed* (the office, function, or reality; the "Z"). He would say the "Z" does not exist or live in Nigeria. The idea of the deed is about the practices and commitments of the deed (office, reality, event, function) that make it transhistorical; that is, make it applicable and meaningful in all historical epochs. Transhistorical here does not mean beyond history. When he says the Z does not exist in Nigeria, I take it to mean not that he is saying the idea is too abstract or beyond concrete application in the Nigerian polity, but that it is not yet embodied in material, social, and institutional practices in the country. His well-crafted comparative definitions are held together by a tripartite movement of an original dialectic, which I am naming here as thesis, antithesis, and transfinite thesis (novo-thesis).

As the four examples of his comedy that I have transcribed from his YouTube collections will demonstrate, the movement from thesis to transfinite is "predictable" by the infractions of conventional, descriptive syntax.[8] In a Cubist manner the descriptive contours of each definition are distorted. This is done so well that each figure (symbol, subject matter) being defined is conceptually obliterated through a deliberate distortion of our background (taken-for-granted understanding of it). In this way, a figure (new conceptualization) emerges within the distorted spaces around the definition (defined figure) and coincides and clashes with spaces around it. Shifting and displacing shapes of definitions or subject matter, suddenly all these movements appear in new contours, new relations, and new figures. This new, emergent figure appears to take a further step, breaking out of the frame of the criticism (logic) of the thesis and antithesis as the boy in the painting of Pere Borrell del Caso, *Escaping Criticism* (1874), who is stepping out of the painting with eyes wide open in wonder.

Let me illustrate this point with his 2019 skit on the voter's card.

> **Question:** Please, what is the difference between a voter's card and PVC?
>
> **MC Edo Pikin:** . . . Voter's card is an ordinary PVC. PVC is a very powerful voter's card. PVC is a permanent voter's card, a powerful voter's card. The one that cannot be bought by any political party. Voter's card is the one where you stand under the sun for weeks to struggle to get it. After getting it, you now go on the day of election to sell it for 2,500 naira. How much is the subscription? How can you say voter's card that is your right and you go across the road to buy akpu and egusi soup [local delicacy]? Some people will sell their voter's card to buy igbo [marijuana]. Will you be high for four years? The most shameful thing [is that] you will see your voter's card and you will go and carry ashawo and buy condoms. Will you have sex for the next four years?
>
> Ogakpakpata [the supreme chief] of them all is your conscience. Conscience is the general overseer. Conscience is the one that will tell you to vote for the individual but not the political party. Conscience is the one that will tell you to vote for competency, competency that cannot be sacrificed on the altar of mediocricy, weakness, and failure. The problem I have with this country, the people that are voting, they don't have conscience. The people that we are voting for, they don't have conscience. The people that are counting the vote, they don't have conscience. In fact, conscience does not live in

> Nigeria. In 2019, we need to go and borrow a conscience to vote. Make sure you don't sell your conscience. In 2019 vote your conscience, thank you.[9]

His definitions interrupt, challenge, and shake up the discursive stability of the words or concepts and thus raise the possibility of an alternative, enlarged understanding. The result is that the third word is shot through with the meaning of resistance to the prevailing ethos or status quo and has the impulse of forward movement into the not-yet. The moral weight of the third word is not all about maintaining order, but about disrupting and interrogating order in the name of a new and better Nigeria.

The third figure (the transfinite thesis) always bursts from nowhere, so to speak. At the beginning, he is comparing only two items, but suddenly, as if moved by the powerful logic of his comparative analysis, a figure or idea that was not in the cards jumps out. (Did you notice how conscience jumped out, seemingly from nowhere, when the two initial comparative terms only related to forms of the voter's card?) A figure that is neither part of the "was" nor of the "is," but is that which is to come. It is not the new that flows from the trajectory of the past and the present. It is the new that asks for, creates, and sustains the alternative possibilities, the unexpected path.[10]

Below is one of his sets of triune comparative definitions that also clearly brings this point out:

> **Question:** Please, what's the difference between an artiste and a musician?
>
> **MC Edo Pikin:** The difference is very clear. . . . A musician is a responsible artiste. An artiste is an irresponsible musician. A musician is the one that gets their inspiration from God, but an artiste gets his inspiration from igbo [marijuana]. A musician is the one that sings for the love of the people, that sings what the people can understand, but an artiste sings for yansh [buttocks], breast; an artiste sings just for women to twerk. A musician is the one that sings what people will go home and think about. An artiste sings to make money. A musician sings for the love of music. . . . A musician is the one that can perform with a live band, but the artiste runs away from a live band.

> But the ogakpatakpata of them all are legends. Legends are the ones that understand the rudiments of music. They sing for the people and the world. They sing to highlight the ills in the society. They sing against maladministration or bad governance. Legends, when they die, their music is passed from generation to generation. Some of the legends are like prophets, they sing to tell you what will happen in the nearest future. Like Bob Nesta Marley, like Fela Anikulapo Kuti, like Lucky Dube, like Michael Jackson. In fact, legend does not live in Nigeria; we only have few legends in Nigeria and one of them is 2Face Innocent Idibia. He is the ogakpatakpata of them all. His music will live on from generation to generation.[11]

Given the way the joke is structured, the movement starts from the artiste (1), moves to the musician (2), and ends or points toward the legend (3). MC Edo Pikin clearly establishes a formal relationship between the first two parts and the third one. The properties or objective features of musician and artiste are combined in contingent ways relative to the perception and intent of the agent (in this case, the comedian) or the needs of the (Nigerian) symbolic network in which the features are embedded. The movement from (1) to (2) is not a matter of the etymology of (1) and (2), nor of their functions, designs, or regnant practices. The dynamic he sets in motion or the logic he presents is not about the unfolding of inherent potentials. It all depends (not in any way deterministic) on the perceiving and acting agent's interaction with, interpretation, and ethical assessment of his or her situation or the particularities of her surroundings. All these afford him or her the capacity or opportunity to discover the path from point A (1 and 2) to point B (what in the introductory chapter I call the *novothesis*).[12] The connection between points A and B, the movement from A to B is one way of showing how the features of thesis (artiste) and antithesis (musician) might be combined in a distinctive way to envision a site that exceeds ordinary synthesis, a site that mimics what happens in an *emergent process*. Novothesis (an *ideal*) shows how the features or properties of an existing system, institution, or object can be taken up and elaborated, improvised, critiqued, etiolated, or exceeded within shifting paradigms.

This novothesis involves each of the two definitions' (1 and 2) relationships to each other and to an ideal one that evaluates, critiques, or disturbs them. In a definitional triangle, the comedian (interlocutor) brings two functions (capacities, roles, offices) together with respect to similarities and incongruencies and points them toward an ideal to which they are also positioned as failed performances and thus subject to transformation. This is a highly stylized and dramatic style of interlocution in which the ordinary articulations of "what a thing is" are saturated with ethical descriptions and evaluations.

Occasionally the ethical evaluations can be burdened by an archaic view of women that borders on misogyny. Take, for instance, this episode of girl, babe, and lady that highlights not only his distorted views about the role of women in modern Nigerian society but also the triangular formation of his skits:

> **Question:** What is the difference between girl and babe?
>
> **MC Edo Pikin:** The difference is very, very clear. A girl is a responsible babe. And a babe is an irresponsible girl. A girl is the one that still gets excuse [permission] from her parents before she leaves the house. A babe is the one that is outside for a long time and even her parents are begging her to come back home. A girl is the one that goes to church, weekly services and every Sunday. A babe is the one that waits for Shiloh [yearly anointing service] until she now goes to church. A girl can quote all the verses in the Bible, but a babe can quote all the wines in the bar and their alcoholic percent. A girl can cook four different soups in a day, but a babe can visit four different clubs in the night. Even some boys learned how to smoke and drink from their babes.
>
> But the ogakpatakpata [the supreme chief] of them all, the general overseer of them all, is a lady. A lady is the girl who makes a madman feels like a gentleman. A lady has got the tenacity to work. A lady believes that responsibility in a relationship is for both sides, not 100 percent on the boyfriend. A lady is a mentor to other girls. A lady is a decent woman with the fear of God. A lady is a well-cultured woman who carries the parental upbringing of her parents to the husband's house. A lady works so hard that she even puts men on the payroll. In fact, ladies put to bed [give birth to children], while

> babes have abortions. Ladies end up getting married, while babes end up getting frustrated. . . . Do we still have ladies in Nigeria? Ladies do not live in Nigeria.[13]

This episode of girl, babe, and lady illustrates the "triangle" that animates his comparative definitions and the hilarity of his comedy. The top of the triangle harbors his third thesis, the transfinite thesis. The triangle appears to point beyond itself, beyond reality. The third thesis ("lady" in this case) is not an immutable Platonic standard, not an infinite object that Nigerians are seeking to grasp. It is a directing principle and not a constituting concept. It asks what lies beyond the finite, corrupt substandard form of living that Nigerians celebrate or have attained. And in this way it directs them to the quest for the unlimited potentialities of their minds and sociality. As MC Edo Pikin directs the minds of Nigerians to experience their own potentialities, his listeners feel a tension in his definitions.

There is a tension between internal transcendence and external transcendence in his conceptualization of the third term. If it does not exist in Nigeria, does this imply that it does not exist in history? Does it exist only in that peculiar Nigerian sense of only God can do it or save us? He settles this tension or forestalls anyone taking the external, extrahuman notion of transcendence when, in the episode of gentleman or preacher/teacher, he points to actually existing Nigerians that fit the transcendence of the third term.

> **Question:** What is the difference between a preacher and a teacher?
>
> **MC Edo Pikin:** The difference is very clear. A preacher is one that will tell you about knowledge, while a teacher will impart knowledge into you. A preacher is one that will tell you about the kingdom of God, while a teacher will show you to the kingdom of God. A preacher is the one that will tell you that money is the root of all evil, while a teacher will tell you the blessings of God make rich and add no sorrow. . . . Preachers are always close to the rich members in the church, while teachers are close to the poor members, so that they can make them rich. . . .
>
> But the ogakpatakpata of them all . . . is Pastor Kingsley Okonkwo. Pastor Kingsley Okonkwo is a great servant in the

> vineyard of God Almighty. . . . Pastor Kingsley Okonkwo, the general overseer, the ogakpatakpata them all, of DCC, David Christian Center . . . you don't live in Nigeria, you live in DCC, David Christian Center, Lagos.[14]

Here MC Edo Pikin says Pastor Okonkwo does not live in Nigeria when DCC is clearly in Lagos, Nigeria. This is an interesting revelation of the dialectics or the philosophical depth of the comedian. Pastor Okonkwo lives in DCC, a stand-in for the ideal site or thought. This ideal place might be physically located in Nigeria, but it does not really *belong* to the situation of Nigeria. DCC belongs to the Nigerian situation as a set but does not belong to any part of the situation. It is an excluded part that does not fit normally or properly into the Nigerian situation; it is unrepresentable. In the language of French philosopher Alain Badiou, DCC is akin to a singularity, a void that bears potential for a revolution in a situation. DCC, in this case, is the generic name for the disruptive element from which an event, Nigeria's transformation, can emerge. DCC is the ideal, the consistent multiplicity that can disrupt or interrupt the order of things.

We were led to the episode of preachers and teachers because we observed a tension between internal transcendence and external transcendence in his conceptualization of the third term. We stated that the episode of gentleman or preacher/teacher demonstrates that his notion of transcendence is not something from beyond history. Yet his various episodes occasionally play at the boundary between internal and external transcendence. This does not necessarily represent a deficiency of his philosophical thought or a display of the vexing Nigerian tendency to look beyond the immanent realm for social transformation of their nation. The line between the two forms of transcendence is not always clear-cut in social analysis. What the American philosopher Martha Nussbaum says about sorting out the lines of demarcation between the two forms of transcendence is apt:

> The line between the appropriate (internal) sort of transcending and the other sort (external, extrahuman) is not and can never be a sharp one. For human striving for excellence involves pushing, in many ways, against the limits that constrain human life. It is perfectly reasonable, within the human point of view, to want oneself and others not to be hungry, not to be ill, not

> to be without shelter, not to be betrayed or bereaved, not to lose any of one's faculties—and to strive as hard as one possibly can to bring all that about in life. In fact, one of the merits of focusing on the internal sort of transcendence is that it tells us that such things really matter, that these jobs are there for human beings to do, for politics to do. . . . What is recommended is a delicate and always flexible balancing act between the claims of excellence, which lead us to push outward, and the necessity of the human context, which pushes us back in. It is not easy . . . to say where the line is drawn.[15]

From Format of Comedian's Joke to Philosophical Methodology

In this section, I want to capture the philosophical format of MC Edo Pikin's comedy to show how I can view it as methodology that illuminates what I have done in this book. MC Edo Pikin's first thesis (definition) states the "what is" of a situation. The antithesis is the opposite of what is. It is more powerful than the thesis; the opposite arises because its inherent nature is to exceed or defeat the performance or the glory of the thesis condition. Finally, we have novo-thesis (that is, a new thesis, that which exceeds the synthesis of the thesis and antithesis, hence it is a transfinite thesis). It is not a synthesis, a higher combination of the previous two or the realization that the antithesis has always been part of or embedded in the thesis, but an ideal that transcends the positivity of both the thesis and the antithesis and is not subject to their antagonism. This is the sense of novothesis as "beyond." It is a paradigm shift.

The juxtaposition of the two theses forces the mind to conceive that which is beyond them—the new thing, the *novum*; hence the *novothesis*. The commonplace definition of synthesis of Hegelian dialectics presents it as a combination of thesis and antithesis. An alternative interpretation, which also emphasizes combination, offers a twist. It says the combination is always already present—in the thesis. The synthesis, or rather the idea that harmonizes the thesis and antithesis, is already in the thesis and emerges only by recognition of what is already there. Novo-thesis is not a combination of the thesis and antithesis, but a paradigm shift. It is about that which is to come. That which is when it is present moves along with its antagonistic opposite to a new site in Being.

This new site has some similarity with the "abandoned" (superseded) site(s) such that the reader can see the new site as being a plausible reality of the future. They see it as a not-yet. Let us quickly add that the envisaged new site is never a reified, dehumanized world. It is in history. Novothesis employs the logic of cognitive estrangement. It encourages new ways of thinking about the thesis and antithesis that not only offer an alternative way of thinking of the theses individually or collectively, but also subversively undermine the ground (spatial, temporal, and social), status quo, paradigm, or framing that undergirds or nurtures both the thesis and antithesis.[16] The aim is to estrange the reader or the listener from the familiar reality and help her look toward an alternative form of social existence.

The ethos of cognitive estrangement informs how MC Edo Pikin even describes or explains both the thesis and the antithesis. They are presented in ways that jar their commonplace, assumed meaning. Their very definitions immediately begin to destabilize, to cognitively disturb the configuration of concept (word) and its normal ground. They seem to harbor an *event*.

Novothesis is a kind of a "jump" from obvious reality. It comes off as an *event*. You cannot predict it from the thesis and antithesis. The engine for the jump here is like emergence. By emergence I mean novel properties, traits that arise from a given set of matter in the right sort of organized complexity. The properties are novel because they not only cannot be found at lower levels of complexity but are also unpredictable phenomena produced by the interactions between preexisting elements or parts. Emergence names the process whereby "the underivable"[17] can be birthed amid many derivable conditions.

We can examine the novothesis from another angle, in terms of affirming or negating a predicate. The novothesis (the idea that comes after the thesis and antithesis) does not negate a predicate but affirms a non-predicate. Let us take an example from a simple format of philosophical argument to clarify this point. "The soul is mortal" is a positive judgment. This statement can be negated in two ways: (a) "The soul is not mortal," and (b) "the soul is non-mortal." In the first instance, the predicate ("mortal") is negated, but in the second case, a non-predicate is asserted. "The indefinite judgment [as per Kant] opens up a third domain which undermines the underlying distinction."[18] This occurs in the same vein when we say a "person is inhuman" instead of "he is not human," a new space beyond humanity and its negation is opened up. "'He is not human' means simply that he is external to humanity, animal or divine, while 'he is inhuman' means something thoroughly different, namely that he is neither human nor not-human, but marked by a terrifying excess which, although negating what we understand as 'humanity,' is inherent to being human."[19] Novothesis is neither thesis nor antithesis, but marked by a terrifying (not-terrifying) excess that, although negating what we know as thesis/antithesis, is inherent to being a thesis of the situation. It is always about a state of condition that is unlike the ones that came before it yet does not escape or transcends them.

The insights of novothesis structured this book, especially as it is very discernible in chapter 5. A farmer's income is limited because of illiteracy. The typical "antithesis" in development programs is to provide to the farmer what is missing, an extension officer to help him measure and prepare his harvest for sale, so he would get a better price in the market. But the novothesis will demand that we take a different approach. This approach is not about aiding the farmer but about changing the unfreedom that thwarts his human flourishing. The different approach demands that we should not just provide the illiterate farmer with a field extension worker to help him properly weigh and trade agricultural produce, but that we also make his illiteracy go away by educating him. This is the ethical thing to do in order to ensure that he is an agent and beneficiary of economic development, that she fosters her own flourishing.

Embedded in the dynamics of the movement from thesis to transfinite thesis there is always an articulated notion of what is just. MC Edo Pikin takes for granted a shared moral universe with his audience and a certain disposition of faith. In addition to the sheer joke and the connective of reason that reveals the incongruities of the simple but profound definitions of terms, there is also a capacity for faith for what Nigeria could become in the vision of the third (transfinite) thesis. Thus, the goals of ethical transformation run through the definition of the triangle, which speaks to human flourishing.

Thesis 3 (transfinite thesis) is what it means for the thesis and antithesis each to function well—to best express, authenticate, reveal its "essence" (that is, its central function). Transfinite thesis is thesis cutting into thesis to lift it up to a higher plane, just as *agape* is love cutting into love to lift all forms of love into a higher level, beyond the ambiguities of self-centeredness. According to Paul Tillich, "in the holy community the *agape* quality of love cuts into *libido*, *eros*, and *philia* qualities of love and elevates them beyond the ambiguities of their self-centeredness." In another place in the same book he writes, "*agape* is love cutting into love, just as revelation is reason cutting into reason and the Word of God is the Word cutting into all words."[20]

The third term or thesis gives us a glimpse of native psychoanalytic insights that MC Edo Pikin has about Nigerian citizens and their desire for economic development. According to the psychoanalytic literature, when a desire cannot be satisfied society or subject turns "the *inherent impossibility* of its satisfaction into a *prohibition*."[21] This way they convince themselves that they would have succeeded if only the rules of the social order were different. Nigerians seem to have convinced themselves that economic development, a corruption-free society, or corruption-free economic development are inaccessible. This is so because Nigerian leaders and elites deliberately refuse to seek means of accessing them. MC Edo Pikin subtly captures this refusal or the impasse constitutive of the desire for corruption-free economic development by the tripartite scheme of definitions. In this schema, that which will satisfy the desire of Nigerians for economic development or a corruption-free society is declared impossible, nonexistent in the country. His point—or, at least, my interpretation of his underlying theory—is that if not for the existence of the first and second definitions, which represent the current rules, norms, and practices of the social order and its *abjected* figures, the third definition, which represents the satisfaction of national desire, would be attainable. In MC Edo Pikin's comedic representation the symbolic order of the nation is split. And there is a celebration of failures of the two "figures" around the traumatic cut that represents the hindrance to the country's progress.

This book precisely considers economic development in the mood and mode of the transfinite thesis. I refuse to accept that economic development in Africa is impossible. I believe that we can retrieve ideas of human flourishing from African indigenous knowledge system and traditional religions.[22] As per what we stated in the introductory chapter, we can say that if *fiyeteboye* is what birth offers as thesis, then *bibibari* is the antithesis, and *after-bibibari* is the transfinite life. *After-bibibari* is about a person using her imaginative vision to create the future she wants, to craft an alternative world or plan of well-being for herself, believing that the future is not determined or lost. In the succeeding five chapters, this book has carefully unfolded the logic and dynamic, the nature and organizing principle of this vision for Nigeria's economic development and for the flourishing of her citizens.

This study drew its key insights for Nigeria's economic development through the examination Kalabari notions of destiny (*fiyeteboye*, *bibibari*, and *after-bibibari*), time, desire, and human flourishing as essential elements in a new matrix of development, and some readers might wonder why the same resources have not necessarily worked in favor of the Kalabari-Ijo themselves. As far as they know, the Kalabari-Ijo are not uniquely prosperous in an otherwise immiserated Nigerian ethnoscape. Why? What is going on here? In my previous work *The Mind of African Strategists: A Study of Kalabari Management Practice*, I demonstrated how Kalabari indigenous economic and corporate management ideas propelled them to become one of the most successful entrepreneurial groups in precolonial Africa.[23] After a thorough examination of the corporate management practices of precolonial entrepreneurial society of Kalabari, I deliberated on the issue of its failure to transition to a matrix of modern industrial corporations in the twentieth century.[24] Apart from the obvious and regular explanation of how Europe's rapacious imperialism and brutal colonialism underdeveloped Africa, I argued that Kalabari entrepreneurs' failure to invest in the development of meaningful managerial structures undermined their society's economic development in the twentieth century. I stated that "It is my argument that the failure of Kalabari entrepreneurs to develop and invest in managerial hierarchies, to separate ownership from management, was the most important cause of the decline and disappearance of that collective enterprise and entrepreneurism we have come to call Kalabari Inc. Their management style was destined to lead the corporation away from the tripartite investments in production, marketing, and management that ensured the growth and survival of the corporation in the western world."[25] Indeed, I dedicated a chapter, "Entrepreneurial Failure," to investigating why Kalabari businesses declined in the colonial era after doing so well for centuries.

Specific failures of the past should not deter Africans in the current generation from retrieving past indigenous ideas for their current economic development needs. The above question implies that because Africans today are not as successful as they should be in the project of economic development, there is nothing for them to retrieve from their past or current indigenous ideas. When America reached back into ancient Greek history to retrieve and improve upon the idea and practice of democracy, the modern Greeks themselves were not democratic. Today's Africans must also reach back and claim from the continent's past what they need to move forward in socioeconomic and political developments. They must know where the rain beat them so they can discern how and where to dry their bodies. As the great writer Chinua Achebe put it, "This is how I see the chaos in Africa today and the absence of logic in what we're doing.

Africa's postcolonial disposition is the result of a people who have lost the habit of ruling themselves, forgotten their traditional way of thinking, embracing and engaging the world without sufficient preparation. We have also had difficulty running the systems foisted upon us at the dawn of independence by our colonial masters. We are like the man in the Igbo proverb who does not know where the rain began to beat him and so cannot say where he dried his body."[26] I hope this book offers some of the preparation Achebe is talking about here—preparation for increased levels of human flourishing in Africa.

Notes

Introduction

1. I have borrowed this phrasing from Paul Samuelson. He wrote, "We would expect people in the marketplace, in pursuit of avid and intelligent self-interest, to take account of those elements of future events that in a probability sense may be discerned to be casting their shadows before them. (Because past events cast their shadows after them, future [coming] events can be said to cast their shadows before them)." See Paul Samuelson, "Proof that Properly Anticipated Prices Fluctuate Randomly," *Industrial Management Review* 6 (Spring 1965): 41–49; quote, 44.

2. Here I allude to Martin Heidegger's appropriation of Aristotle's philosophy. For a discussion of Aristotelian and Heideggerian thoughts as they relate to actualization of potencies, see Nimi Wariboko, *The Principle of Excellence: A Framework for Social Ethics* (Lanham, MD: Lexington Books, 2009), 51–53.

3. Nimi Wariboko, *The Split God: Pentecostalism and Critical Theory* (Albany: SUNY University Press, 2018), 99.

4. I have slightly expanded Fanon's thought to meet my requirements here. See Frantz Fanon, *The Wretched of the Earth* (New York: Grove, 1968), 40.

5. Another term we could use here is irruption or protest. The Kalabari views destiny as an irruption of being in her life. The Kalabari people believe that she can protest against an irruption or the series of irruptions that defines her life course here on earth. In fact, she can even change her prenatal wishes, which is what destiny is about in this culture.

6. Martin Hägglund, *Dying for Time: Proust, Woolf, Nabokov* (Cambridge, MA: Harvard University Press, 2012).

7. I have done a similar exercise with regard to political theory (continental philosophy). See Nimi Wariboko, *Ethics and Society in Nigeria: Identity, History, and Political Theory* (Rochester, NY: University of Rochester Press, 2019).

8. Karl Marx, *Capital: A Critique of Political Economy*, vol. 1, trans. Ben Fowkes (London: Penguin, 1976), 125. Marx states in the second volume of

Capital, "For capitalism is already essentially abolished once we assume that it is enjoyment that is the driving motive and not enrichment itself." Karl Marx, *Capital: A Critique of Political Economy*, vol. 2, trans. David Fernbach (New York: Penguin, 1981), 199.

9. This way of framing my thought was informed by Daniel Tutt, "The Object of Proximity: The Ethics of Psychoanalysis in Žižek and Santner via Lacan," San Francisco Society for Lacanian Studies, accessed August 25, 2020, lacan.org/tutt.

10. Samo Tomšič, *The Capitalist Unconscious: Marx and Lacan* (London: Verso, 2015), 173.

11. Tomšič, *Capitalist Unconscious,* 196.

12. Stephen C. Littlechild, "Three Types of Market Process," in *Economic as a Process: Essays in the New Institutional Economics* (New York: Cambridge University Press, 1986), 27–39; quote, 29.

13. Littlechild, "Three Types of Market Process," 30.

14. By this I do not mean to say that all other African communities have irrevocable destinies. There is a spectrum of conceptions of destinies in Africa that ranges from (a) irrevocable to (b) revocable, and to (c) radically revocable. I would categorize Kalabari understanding of destiny as falling into the category of the radically revocable. Theirs is very "fluid." For them if destiny is about "essence" then it is akin to something like "existence is essence" (Jean-Paul Sartre). For it is from the deeds, subpar accomplishments, or—more precisely—failures in life that they infer the destiny of a person. Precisely, it is presumed regularity of disappointments and failures that provoke the crisis of destiny, the search for one's prenatal wishes which can ultimately explain an individual's persistent failures in life. Success retroactively confirms *fiyeteboye*, destiny, but incessant, unrelenting failures force the person to go to the diviner to find out what his or her prenatal wishes are and to entreat the *Tamuno* (the Supreme Being, the Creatrix) to change them for good. Destiny as an explanation of the vicissitudes of life is an ultimate-level explanation of the course of individual existence; hence, it involves the ultimate being, only she can allow a person to renegotiate his or her prenatal wishes for an individual course of life on earth.

15. Littlechild, "Three Types of Market Process," 31.

16. Littlechild, "Three Types of Market Process," 38.

17. Martha Nussbaum, *Poetic Justice: The Literary Imagination and Public Life* (Boston: Beacon, 1995), 4.

18. Nussbaum, *Poetic Justice*, xix.

19. This way of putting it was influenced by Jacques Lacan, *Écrits: A Selection*, trans. Alan Sheridan (London: Tavistock Publications, 1977), 165–166.

20. Tomšič, *Capitalist Unconscious*, 188.

21. For the phenomenal "I," time is an internal relation.

22. This way of explaining the function of the "organization of chapters" was informed by Michael Franz, "Editor's Introduction," In Eric Voegelin, *The*

Collected Works of Eric Voegelin, vol. 17, *Order and History*, vol. 4, *The Ecumenic Age* (Columbia: University of Missouri Press, 2000), 1–28; quote, 3.

23. This thought was inspired Eric Voegelin, "Order and History," in Eric Voegelin, *The Collected Works of Eric Voegelin*, vol. 18, *Order and History*, vol. 5, *In Search of Order* (Columbia: University of Missouri Press, 2000), 17.

24. Remember, we said the prenatal wishes are forgotten at the birth of the human being.

25. Pardon the Hegelian turn of phrase here.

26. This paragraph was inspired by Athanasios Moulakis, "Editor's Introduction," in Eric Voegelin, *The Collected Works of Eric Voegelin*, vol. 15, *Order and History*, vol. 2, *The World of the Polis* (Columbia: University of Missouri Press, 2000), 1–48; quote, 16.

27. Giorgio Agamben, *Infancy and History: On the Destruction of Experience* (London: Verso, 2007), 155.

28. Franz Kafka, "He: Notes from the Year 1920," in Franz Kafka, *The Great Wall of China: Stories and Reflections*, trans. Willa Muir and Edwin Muir (New York: Schocken Books, 1946), 276–277, quoted in Hannah Arendt, *Between Past and Future* (New York: Penguin, 1968), 7. Arendt slightly amended the translation from German.

29. Nimi Wariboko, *The Split Economy: Saint Paul Goes to Wall Street* (Albany: State University of New York Press, 2020), 1–24.

30. Amartya Sen, *Development as Freedom* (New York: Random House, 1999).

31. G. O. M. Tasie, *Kali Kulu Kulu Kalika: A Check-List of Kalabari Drum Lore*, supplement to the *Journal of Niger Delta Studies* (Jos, Nigeria: Ehindero Nig. Ltd., 1999), 17–18. See also p. 24. Italics in the original.

Chapter 1

1. For a simple discussion of PPF, see Sean Masaki Flynn, *Economics for Dummies* (Hoboken, NJ: Wiley Publishing, 2005), 38–44.

2. It is important to add that points on the curve that are considered efficient by economists may not always be ethical, moral, or good for workers. Managers might have attained positions on the efficiency frontiers by paying very low wages or externalizing the cost of environmental pollution or ecological degradation.

3. Robert Cummings Neville, *Ultimates: Philosophical Theology*, vol. 1 (Albany: State University of New York Press, 2013), 197–198.

4. Neville, *Ultimates*, 236.

5. Neville, *Ultimates*, 237–238.

6. I am here deeply indebted to Robert Cummings Neville, *Eternity and Time's Flow* (Albany: State University of New York Press, 1993).

7. Nimi Wariboko, "Kalabari: A Study in Synthetic Ideal-Type," *Nordic Journal of African Studies* 8, no. 1 (1999): 80–93.

8. Slavoj Žižek, *Event: A Philosophical Journey through a Concept* (London: Penguin Books, 2014), 128.

9. For a fuller discussion of the sacred, see Nimi Wariboko, *The Split God: Pentecostalism and Critical Theory* (Albany: State University of New York Press, 2018), 83–110.

10. Mircea Eliade, *The Sacred and the Profane: The Nature of Religion* (New York: Harcourt, 1957).

11. For more detail on my theorization of the sacred, see Wariboko, *Split God*, 83–110.

12. Richard Fenn, "Sociology and Religion: Searching for the Sacred," in *The Oxford Handbook of Religion and Science*, ed. Philip Clayton and Zachary Simpson (Oxford: Oxford University Press, 2006), 256.

13. From here on I am going to adapt Fenn's theory of religion as elucidated in his "Sociology and Religion," 253–270.

14. Fenn, "Sociology and Religion," 258.

15. Fenn, "Sociology and Religion," 259.

16. Fenn, "Sociology and Religion," 257–258.

17. If a person does not like the course of her life on earth she goes to a diviner to change her *so* or *fiyeteboye*. The process of changing destiny is called *bibibari* (altering or nullifying the spoken word, recanting). The person visits a diviner to let *Teme-órú* (the supreme goddess) know that the person would like to change how he or she wants to live his or her life-course on earth. Once the change of destiny is effected, the new *so* (which becomes a new point of fixity) determines the whole course of the person.

18. Nwankwo T. Nwaezigwe, "Ikenga Cultic Symbol and Structural Representation of Igbo Enterprise," *Journal of Tourism and Heritage Studies* 2, no. 1 (2013): 2–13; see pp. 9–10 for relevant information. Nkiru Nzegwu, "Art and Community: A Social Conception of Beauty and Individuality," in *A Companion of African Philosophy*, ed. Kwasi Wirendu (Malden, MA: Blackwell, 2004), 415–424; see in particular 422–423.

19. Formally, as Neville puts it, "To be a thing is to be determinate, to be something rather than something else or nothing . . . to be determinate is to be a harmony of at least two kinds of components. The conditional components of a thing are those by virtue of which it is related to other things. Conditioned by them or conditioning them. The essential components are those by virtue of which the harmony integrates the conditional components so as to have its own-being" (Neville, *Ultimates*, 193).

20. "Essential and conditional components are both equally necessary for determinateness. 'Essential' should not be imply greater importance or necessity than 'conditional.' To say that things are *harmonies* of essential and conditional

components is to say that their components simply fit together. They are not components of some underlying substance, although some harmonies might have properties like substances. The harmony itself is the determinate entity. The fitting together of essential and conditional components in a harmony is not derived from a higher integrating principle, although some harmonies are possibly only because they exist within larger harmonies, like heart and lungs working together in a human body. The ontological reality of the harmony is just the fitting together of its components, which must include essential and conditional ones" (Neville, *Ultimates*, 195). We may need to differ from Neville on this point of the underlying principle of integration if we are to remain faithful to the Kalabari data. In Kalabari philosophy as we are laying it out here, telos, purpose, destiny integrates the parts of a harmony. There is also some sense of "spirit" (which may also mean "telos" considered differently) as a higher integrating principle.

21. Neville, *Eternity and Time's Flow*, 73.

22. Neville, *Eternity and Time's Flow*, 156.

23. Neville, *Ultimates*, 176.

24. Neville, *Ultimates*, 171.

25. Neville, *Eternity and Time's Flow*, 19–28, 89–90, 102–103, 168–170, 186–187.

26. Neville, *Ultimates*, 219.

27. When self-identity is properly understood and handled, it dovetails into self-esteem or sustenance of self-esteem and it bleeds into virtues, for people will value their self-identity only to the extent that they believe in the esteem they enjoy from such an identity. "For esteem will rule people's lives only so far as they can continue to believe in the possibility of estimable or virtuous behavior and only so far, therefore, as there are at least some individuals who offer persuasive examples of virtue." Geoffrey Brennan and Philip Pettit, *The Economy of Esteem: An Essay on Civil and Political Society* (Oxford: Oxford University Press, 2004), 7. Self-identity dovetails with or becomes tangential to esteem when the person seeking to act out of self-identity presupposes *reidentifiability* (wants a recognizable name) and desires the honor and approval of others. A pursuit of one's identity may also be the pursuit of esteem as positive esteem could be one of the most important values with which the rational person identifies when making decisions (Brennan and Pettit, *Esteem*, 2–3). A purposeful pursuit of self-identity in one's community can lead to attitude of esteem or disesteem from other members of the community.

28. Neville, *Eternity and Time's Flow*, 186.

29. Neville, *Eternity and Time's Flow*, 186.

30. Neville, *Eternity and Time's Flow*, 59; italics added.

31. Neville, *Eternity and Time's Flow*, 188.

32. Neville, *Eternity and Time's Flow*, 193–194.

33. Neville, *Eternity and Time's Flow*, 59.

34. Neville, *Eternity and Time's Flow*, 103.

35. The accountability I have in mind is not about subjecting oneself or one's identity to the imprisonment of tradition. It is a democratic principle that emphasizes the point that everyone is in dialogue with another person, and no one is superior or subordinate to the other. It is an accountability that recognizes the person of the other and cries for the remembrance of the deeds of the individual long after they has been done. Such a tradition of accountability is a sense of anchor. See Howard Thurman, *Essential Writings* (Maryknoll: Orbis Books, 2006), 157–158. His view of accountability squarely ties up with the Kalabari notion of legacy and identity (that is embedded in a community).

36. Neville, *Eternity and Time's Flow*, 166–167.

37. Neville, *Eternity and Time's Flow*, 134.

38. Robert Cummings Neville, *Existence: Philosophical Theology*, vol. 2 (Albany: State University of New York Press, 2014), 79.

39. Giorgio Agamben, *The Use of Bodies*, trans. Adam Kotsko (Stanford, CA: Stanford University Press, 2015), 81.

40. Walter Benjamin, "Notes Toward a Work on the Category of Justice," trans. Peter Fenves, in Peter Fenves, *The Messianic Reduction: Walter Benjamin and the Shape of Time* (Stanford, CA: Stanford University Press, 2011), 257, quoted in Agamben, *Use of Bodies*, 81.

41. Alasdair Macintyre, *Ethics in the Conflicts of Modernity: An Essay on Desire, Practical Reasoning, and Narrative* (Cambridge: Cambridge University Press, 2016), 53.

42. Nimi Wariboko, *The Depth and Destiny of Work: An African Theological Interpretation* (Trenton, NJ: African World Press, 2008), 87, 105, 119; Wariboko, *Principle of Excellence*, 87–88.

43. Neville, *Eternity and Time's Flow*, 59; italics added.

44. The terminology in this paragraph is indebted to Ben Vedder, "Heidegger on Desire," *Continental Philosophy Review* 31 (1998): 353–368.

45. Existence by itself is shapeless, without any structure, an inarticulate substratum of spirituality that can be subjected to desired forms. When the experience of struggle to cover the gap that is desire is added to it, existence acquires rhythm, structure. Structure here is not just a simple aggregation of the facts of life into an ensemble of meaning, creating a whole that has more meaning than the sum of the parts. Similarly, structure is not the "something else" that is added to an ensemble of life's facts and interpretations that makes the whole more than the sum of the parts and solidifies them into a unity. Thus, the thinking here about structure is not about a search for either "that which causes something to be what it is" or that ultimate, minimum irreducible element of the new life. It is about *form* that maintains existence in presence, puts it in its "proper station in presence" (Giorgio Agamben, *The Man without Content*, trans. Georgia Albert

[Stanford, CA: Stanford University Press, 1999], 98. Pp. 94–103 of this book inspire this section on temporal structure).

But what grants existence its proper place? Existence is an ongoing flow of activities, a pure flow in an infinite space-time continuum (or fabric, if you like). Social existence, in particular, appears as a perpetual movement of instants, the inexorable course of daily mortal life, running toward ruin, destruction, and death. This flow, when interrupted or interfered with, creates rhythm, introducing a split and stop in its relentless match. "Thus in a musical piece, although it is somehow in time, we perceive rhythm as something that escapes the incessant flight of instants and appears almost as the presence of an atemporal dimension of time" (*Man without Content*, 99). In the same way, when the Kalabari person has put herself in the mundane transformational context, "panel-beating" the self into a relevantly shaped vehicle of her lowercase *so*, a particular type of moral subject, she perceives a stop in time, "as though she is suddenly thrown into a more original time. There is a stop, an interruption in the incessant flow of instants that, coming from the future, sinks into the past, and this interruption, this stop, is precisely what gives and reveals the particular status," the mode of presence proper to her existence. The pursuit of her individual *so* appears to have broken the automatism, the inexorability of social existence and lets her find her present space between past and future (*Man without Content*, 99).

This split is enacted in the midst of a flow: in the flow of time, in the flow of social existence. While pursuit of her individual *so* reveals the proper place of existence, locates her in the presence proper to her as a work of *Temeso*'s hand, the flight of life's instants goes on that do not reveal their meaning and place fully as they move on. The split is thus an inside that is "also a being-outside, an *ek-stasis* in the more original dimension" (*Man without Content*, 99). The experience of the pursuit gives her the sense of her proper place (an ecstatic dwelling in it), but still retains her in the quotidian draw of existence.

So now we understand structure as rhythm, as what determines the proper ("original") place of existence. By opening to the Kalabari woman her perceived authentic spatial and temporal dimension of existence, the pursuit also "opens for him [her] the space of belonging to the world, only within which he can take the original measure of his dwelling on the earth and find again his present truth in the unstoppable flow of linear time [and inexorable course of daily to destruction and death]" (*Man without Content*, 101). It is in this authentic space in the world or temporal dimension that the Kalabari person sallies forth to recreate the self and the world, is able to put her being and the past and future at stake in order to achieve the transformation of her subjectivity and access the full promises of the born-again experience. This is why experience of working out *fiyeteboye* (lowercase *so*), that is desire, *tari*, is called "beginning," and is architectonic in the archaic sense of production of origin (*Man without Content*, 101).

In sum, the efforts to close the gap that we have named desire can be considered as a form of production of temporality, new temporality to fashion relevant subjectivity for the telos from *Temeso* and as a route to legacy. The mindfulness of desire, this consciousness that breaks the automatism of ongoing social processes, that interrupts the normal patterns of sights and rhythms of sounds of social existence to create the space for human existence, a space of appearance, renews (recreates) the person's sense of reality. The consciousness of one's destiny involves intentional acts of rupture, which lift off the crust of tradition and habitude over the common world, to offer a new time gap of existence.

46. Wariboko, *Principle of Excellence.*

47. Paul Tillich, *Morality and Beyond* (Louisville, KY: Westminster John Knox Press, 1963), 20.

48. Hannah Arendt, *The Human Condition* (Chicago: University of Chicago Press, 1958), 9, 177–178, 247.

Chapter 2

1. Paul Tillich, *Systematic Theology*, vol. 1 (Chicago: University of Chicago Press, 1951), 184–185; italics in the original.

2. Stathis Gourgouris, *Lessons in Secular Criticism* (New York: Fordham University Press, 2013), 45.

3. On the question of the killing of gods see Wariboko, *Ethics and Society in Nigeria*, 35–50.

4. Gourgouris, *Lessons in Secular Criticism*, 45.

5. Gourgouris, *Lessons in Secular Criticism*, 45.

6. This sentence was inspired by Pierre Dardot and Christian Laval, *The New Way of the World: On Neoliberal Society* (London: Verso, 2014), 34.

7. Tillich, *Systematic Theology*, vol. 1, 185.

8. This interpretation of Africa's notion of destiny was inspired by Keiji Nishitani, *Religion and Nothingness*, trans. and intr. by Jam Van Bragt (Berkeley: University of California Press, 1982), 3.

9. Nishitani, *Religion and Nothingness*, 3.

10. This way of expressing *fiyeteboye* was inspired by Christos Yannaras, *Person and Eros*, trans. Normal Russell (Brookline, MA: Holy Cross Orthodox Press, 2007), 161.

11. Yannaras, *Person and Eros*, 161; italics in the original.

12. Jean-Paul Sartre, *Being and Nothingness: A Phenomenological Essay on Ontology* (New York: Washington Square Press, 1943), 601–624.

13. For a discussion of social immortality as attained through the legacy of work, see Nimi Wariboko, *Depth and Destiny of Work*, 139–177.

14. Sartre, *Being and Nothingness*, 601–624. See also Kate Kirkpatrick, *Sartre on Sin: Between Being and Nothingness* (Oxford: Oxford University Press, 2017), 170–172, 174, 176, 207.

15. Søren Kierkegaard, *Either/Or*, vol. 2, trans. H. Hong and E. Hong (Princeton: Princeton University Press, 1987), 217.

16. Sartre, *Being and Nothingness*, 583.

17. Sartre, *Being and Nothingness*, 589.

18. In Kalabari thought we are condemned to being and cannot cease from being, whether before natality or after death. There is no limit for being except in Being-itself. There is no nothingness, and no space between being and nothingness. Nothingness is a metaphor, a descriptor of Being in other (non-Kalabari) worldviews.

19. Todd McGowan, *Capitalism and Desire: The Psychic Cost of Free Markets* (New York: Columbia University Press, 2016), 28.

20. McGowan, *Capitalism and Desire*, 28.

21. McGowan, *Capitalism and Desire*, 150

22. McGowan, *Capitalism and Desire*, 28.

23. This way of putting the matter was inspired by McGowan, *Capitalism and Desire*, 152. It is a sickness unto death because one is unable to forget (or to forget forgetfulness), even as there is no hope of ever remembering it; and this hopelessness cannot be healed even by death or reincarnation.

24. McGowan, *Capitalism and Desire*, 180.

25. Robin Horton, *Kalabari Sculpture* (Lagos: Department of Antiquities, Federal Republic of Nigeria 1965), 8.

26. "First and foremost, sculpture is an instrument for bringing the spirits into spatial confinement. Its efficacy derives from the fact that it is a 'name'—i.e., a collection of motifs which have been designated as the sign standing for a spirit. So long as these motifs are recognizably present, the piece will be effective." See Horton, *Kalabari Sculpture*, 23.

27. Horton, *Kalabari Sculpture*, 10; see also p. 38.

28. Wariboko, *Depth and Destiny of Work*, 37–39. See also Horton, *Kalabari Sculpture*, 6, 10, 29.

29. *Agu-nsi* is an Igbo word that has been adopted in Kalabari. The Kalabari word for carved or sculptured idol is *ẹkẹkẹ-tamụnọ*; and *ẹkẹkẹ* means stone, piece of stone or rock.

30. Robin Horton, *Kalabari Sculpture*, 8–9; see also Robin Horton, "The Kalabari Worldview: An Outline and Interpretation," *Africa* 32, no. 3 (1962): 204.

31. Horton, "Kalabari Worldview," 204. I have heard of at least two cases of gods that have been disrobed of their powers. One is the *Owu Akpana* (shark) cult and the other is *Ogboloma* (called *Kun-ma* in Okrika, also a Niger Delta community) cult.

32. Robin Horton, "A Hundred Years of Change in Kalabari Religion," in *Black Africa: Its People and Their Cultures Today*, ed. John Middleton (New York: Macmillan, 1971), 194–198.

33. John Caputo, *The Weakness of God: A Theology of Event* (Bloomington: Indiana University Press, 2006).

34. In the Kalabari-Ijo world, a community never appears without its *amatemeso*—the soul of the community. (For discussions of *amatemeso*, see Nimi Wariboko, *Ethics and Time: Ethos of Temporal Orientation in Politics and Religion of the Niger Delta* [Lanham, MD: Lexington Books, 2010].) The living community is its embodiment. A body, communal or individual, does not appear without its soul. The characteristic gesture, the principle of recognizability of the *amatemeso*, is indissoluble from what constitutes its body—and vice versa. Although the *amatemeso* cannot be said to exist apart from the people (its flesh), it nevertheless cannot be reduced to the group, the embodiment. The collective is not only the actuality of the *amatemeso*; the *amatemeso* is also the historically specific regulatory ideal under which the society is materialized. The *amatemeso* is "the normative and normalizing ideal according to which the [communal] body is trained, shaped, cultivated, and invested." See Judith Butler, *Bodies that Matter: On the Discursive Limits of "Sex"* (New York: Routledge, 2011), 9. I have borrowed Butler's words to use in a very different context.

35. Martin Hägglund, *This Life: Secular Faith and Spiritual Faith* (New York: Pantheon Books, 2019), 31; italics in the original.

36. Hägglund, *This Life,* 6–7; italics in the original.

37. Hägglund, *This Life,* 49; italics in the original.

38. Martin Hägglund, *Radical Atheism: Derrida and the Time of Life* (Stanford, CA: Stanford University Press, 2008), 137.

39. Hägglund, *Radical Atheism*, 109–111.

40. Hägglund, *Radical Atheism*, 111–117; quotation, p. 111.

41. Hägglund, *Radical Atheism*, 137; italics in the original.

42. Aristotle, *Metaphysics*, ed. Richard McKeon (New York: Random House, 1941), 1050b, 10. The quotation above uses the translation in Giorgio Agamben, *Homo Sacer: Sovereign Power and Bare Life*, trans. Daniel Heller-Roazen (Stanford, CA: Stanford University Press, 1998), p. 45.

43. Giorgio Agamben, *Potentialities: Collected Essays in Philosophy*, ed. and trans. Daniel Heller-Roazen (Stanford: Stanford University Press, 1999).

44. Slavoj Žižek, *Less than Nothing: Hegel and the Shadow of Dialectical Materialism* (London: Verso, 2012), 229–231.

45. Žižek, *Event*, 128.

46. Hägglund, *This Life,* 17–18; italics in the original.

47. Nimi Wariboko, *The Pentecostal Principle: Ethical Methodology in New Spirit* (Grand Rapids, MI: Eerdmans, 2012). This principle actually developed out of my analysis of Kalabari society in Wariboko, *Ethics and Time.*

48. Stéphane Mosès, *The Angel of History: Rosenzweig, Benjamin, and Scholem*, trans. Barbara Harshav (Stanford, CA: Stanford University Press, 2009), 132.

49. Mosès, *Angel of History*, 135–136.

50. Mosès, *Angel of History*, 111.

51. See Mosès, *Angel of History*, 1–8.

52. Franz Kafka, "The City Coat of Arms," in *The Great Wall of China: Stories and Reflections of Franz Kafka*, trans. Willa Muir and Edwin Muir (New York: Schocken Books, 1946), 245.

53. Kafka, "City Coat of Arms," 245–247.

54. See Mosès, *Angel of History*, 5.

55. Jorge Luis Borges, "The Secret Miracle," in *Ficciones*, trans. Anthony Kerrigan (New York: Grove Press, 1962), 147.

56. Borges, "Secret Miracle," 143–150.

57. See Mosès, *Angel of History*, 8.

58. F. W. J. Schelling, *Abyss of Freedom/Ages of the World* (Second Draft, 1813), trans. Judith Norman (Ann Arbor: University of Michigan Press, 1997).

Chapter 3

1. Hägglund, *This Life*. I am indebted to this book for inspiring the ideas in this paragraph.

2. Hägglund, *This Life*, 22; italics in the original. See also 295–297.

3. Jacques Lacan, *Seminar II: The Ego Freud's Theory and in the Technique of Psychoanalysis*. Ed. J. A. Miller, Trans. S. Tomaselli (New York: Norton, 1988), 223.

4. Hägglund, *Dying for Time*, 3–4; italics in the original.

5. Hägglund, *Dying for Time*, 5.

6. Hägglund, *Dying for Time*, 7.

7. Hägglund, *Dying for Time*, 8; italics in the original.

8. Hägglund, *Dying for Time*, 9.

9. Hägglund, *Dying for Time*, 7–8; quote, 8.

10. Wariboko, *Ethics and Society in Nigeria*, 35–50.

11. This interpretation was inspired by Hägglund, *Dying for Time*, 10–11.

12. Hägglund, *Dying for Time*, 13–14; quote, 14.

13. "Of course, even if you identify as religious you can still care intensely for the fate of our lives on Earth. My point, however, is that if you care for our forms of life *as an end in itself*, you are acting on the basis of secular faith, even if you claim to be religious. Religious faith can entail obedience to moral norms, but it cannot recognize that the ultimate purpose of what we do—the ultimate reason it matters how we treat one another and the Earth—is *our fragile life together*. From a religious perspective, the ultimate purpose of what we do is to serve God or attain salvation, rather than to care for our shared lives and the

future generations for which we are responsible. As soon as we acknowledge that our finite lives—and the generations that may carry on our finite legacy—are ends in themselves, we make explicit that our faith is secular rather than religious." Martin Hägglund, *This Life*, 9; italics in the original.

14. Hägglund, *Dying for Time*, 5; emphasis added,

15. This interpretation was inspired by Hägglund, *Dying for Time*, 126–127.

16. Slavoj Žižek and John Milbank, *The Monstrosity of Christ: Paradox or Dialectic?* (Cambridge, MA: MIT Press, 2009), 256.

17. John D. Caputo and Gianni Vattimo, *After the Death of God*, ed. Jeffrey W. Robbins (New York: Columbia University Press, 2007), 156.

18. Slavoj Žižek, *The Sublime Object of Ideology* (London: Verso, 2008), 142.

19. Marika Rose, *A Theology of Failure: Žižek against Christian Innocence* (New York: Fordham University Press, 2019), 138.

20. Hägglund, *Dying for Time*, 159.

21. Hägglund, *Dying for Time*, 145.

22. Hägglund, *Dying for Time*, 144.

23. Wariboko, *The Depth and Destiny of Work*.

24. Hägglund, *This Life*, 7; italics in the original.

25. Martin Hägglund, *Radical Atheism: Derrida and the Time of Life* (Stanford: Stanford University Press, 2008), 109, italics in the original.

26. Hägglund, *Dying for Time*, 14.

27. Hägglund, *Radical Atheism*, 41.

28. Hägglund, *Radical Atheism*, 40; see also 80–81, 97.

29. Bruce Fink, *The Lacanian Subject: Between Language and Jouissance* (Princeton: Princeton University Press, 1995), 46.

30. This paragraph is taken from Wariboko, *Split Economy*, 131.

31. Hägglund, *This Life*, 213; italics in the original.

32. Karl Marx, *Grundrisse*, trans. Martin Nicolaus (New York: Penguin Classics, 1973), 173.

33. Hägglund, *This Life*, 187; italics in the original.

34. Joan Copjec, *Imagine There's No Woman: Ethics and Sublimation* (Cambridge: MIT Press, 2002), 43.

35. This way of articulating my thought was influenced by Copjec, *Imagine There's No Woman*, 42.

36. Copjec, *Imagine There's No Woman*, 42.

37. This way of articulating my ideas is indebted to Copjec, *Imagine There's No Woman*, 45.

38. Copjec, *Imagine There's No Woman*, 172.

39. This section is drawn from Wariboko, *Ethics and Time*, 1–33.

40. Ronald Beiner, *Hannah Arendt: Lectures on Kant's Political Philosophy* (Chicago: University of Chicago Press, 1992), 155.

41. Hannah Arendt, *Human Condition*, 199.

42. Alain Badiou, *Logics of Worlds: Being and Event II*, translated by Alberto Toscano (London: Continuum International Publishing Group, 2009), 384.

43. Badiou, *Logics of Worlds*, 509.

44. Hannah Arendt, *The Life of the Mind*, vol. 1, *Thinking* (San Diego: Harcourt, 1978); see also Hannah Arendt, *The Life of the Mind*, vol. 2, *Willing* (San Diego: Harcourt, 1978).

45. Ole Fogh Kirkeby, *Management Philosophy: A Radical Normative Perspective* (Berlin: Springer, 2000), 26.

46. Jean-Luc Nancy, *Inoperative Community*, trans. Peter Connor, Lisa Garbus, Michael Holland, and Simona Sawhney (Minneapolis: University of Minnesota Press, 1991), 19.

47. Nancy, *Inoperative Community*, xxxvii; italics in the original.

48. I have here variously quoted and paraphrased Nancy, *Inoperative Community*, xxxvii–xxxviii.

49. Nancy, *Inoperative Community*, 58.

50. Nancy, *Inoperative Community*, 30.

51. Nancy, *Inoperative Community*, 33.

52. I was inspired to write this paragraph due to the influence of Nancy's thought: *Inoperative Community*, 127, 132.

53. Arendt, *Life of the Mind*, vol. 1, *Thinking*, 203–213.

54. Kirkeby, *Management Philosophy*, 185.

55. Kirkeby, *Management Philosophy*, 220n10.

56. In Kalabari diviners claim also to smell time. They claim to smell the presence of evil spirits in an area. Diviners smell not only evil, foul spirits that are currently present in a given location, but also, based on the newness or weakness of their odor, they can determine how long such spirits have been gone from a place. Diviners can also sniff approaching foul spirits from the air coming from the time or places ahead. Since the smell of foul spirits varies over time, the diviners' ability to detect the age of odor is a way of telling time.

57. Kirkeby, *Management Philosophy*, 25.

58. Alain Badiou also argues that it is the fidelity to truth and the choices that perpetuate it that render the past as an amplitude of the present. He says that "history does not exist. There are only disparate presents whose radiance is measured by their power to unfold a past worthy of them" (*Logics of Worlds*, 509).

59. For a brief review of ethics and time in Western philosophy see Joanna Hodge, "Ethics and Time: Levinas between Kant and Husserl," *Diacritics* 32, nos. 3–4 (2000): 107–134.

60. Watsuji Tetsurō, *Climate and Culture: A Philosophical Study*, trans. Geoffrey Bownas (Tokyo: Monbushō, 1961), 10, quoted in Graham Mayeda, *Time, Space and Ethics in the Philosophy of Watsuji Tetsurō, Kuki Shūzō, and Martin Heidegger* (New York: Routledge, 2006), 47.

61. Watsuji Tetsurō, *Climate and Culture*, 10.

62. Arendt, *The Life of the Mind*, vol. 1, 205.

63. The gap is infinite. It is an infinite that derives from infinities by means of limitation. It is a lacunary abstraction. As the gap absolves any obsession with omnipotence and omnipresence, infinity is no longer seen as an exception, an excess over the finite. Infinity, it seems, is dispersed into the ordinary existence of the finite and every situation in it presumably has infinite possibilities. The ethical pathos of such a subtractive finite is not toward death but toward the *we* as the infinite. The *we* is the people and their social institutions. The Japanese philosopher Watsuji Tetsurō recognized this once he rejected the Heideggerian enthrallment to death. My thinking of the gap as a space with dispersed infinity was inspired by Alain Badiou, *Conditions*, trans. Steven Corcoran (London: Continuum International Publishing Group, 2008).

64. Krzysztof Ziarek, "The Ethos of History," in *What Happens to History: The Renewal of Ethics in Contemporary Thought*, ed. Howard Marchitello (New York: Routledge, 2001), 67–93; quote, 75.

65. Ziarek, "Ethos of History," 75.

66. Quoted in Ziarek, "Ethos of History," 67.

67. This way of putting across my ideas was influenced by Hägglund, *Radical Atheism*, 190–191.

68. Copjec, *Imagine There's No Woman*, 37.

69. Hägglund, *Radical Atheism*, 194.

70. Hägglund, *Radical Atheism*, 203, inspired this paragraph.

Chapter 4

1. Hägglund, *This Life*, 11.

2. Hägglund, *This Life*, 13.

3. Laurenti Magesa, *African Religion: The Moral Traditions of Abundant Life* (Maryknoll, NY: Orbis Book, 1997).

4. Hägglund, *This Life*, 13.

5. Hägglund, *This Life*, 29; see also 57.

6. Hägglund, *This Life*, 300–304.

7. This thought was inspired by Hägglund, *This Life*, 309, 313.

8. For a detailed discussion of the philosophy of excellence and *arete* see Wariboko, *Principle of Excellence*.

9. Mihaly Csikszentmihalyi, *Flow: The Psychology of Optimal Experience* (New York: HarperCollins Publishers, 1990), 72–73.

10. Wariboko, *Principle of Excellence*, 8–9.

11. As I was completing this chapter, I came across the work of Moses E. Ochonu in which he basically agrees with the position I have taken. He argues that too much epistemic visibility has been given to the "incorrect notion of pre-

colonial Africa as a site of subsistent communalism, an undifferentiated societal continuum supposedly unspoiled by the twin capitalist evils of the profit motive and private wealth accumulation. . . . Evidence . . . indicates that a communitarian ethos underpinned and mediated the entrepreneurial pursuits of precolonial Africans. . . . Even the most communally organized precolonial societies and economies had enterprising members who improved their lives through entrepreneurial initiatives, indicating that neither communalism not subsistence, two hyperbolized and overgeneralized features of precolonial Africa, was incompatible with private property or the pursuit of individual wealth for self-improvement." See Moses E. Ochonu, "Introduction: Toward African Entrepreneurship and Business History," in *Entrepreneurship in Africa: A History Approach*, ed. Moses E. Ochonu (Bloomington: Indiana University Press, 2018), 1–27; quote, 16.

12. Robin Horton, "Social Psychologies: African and Western," in *Oedipus and Job in West Africa*, ed. M. Fortes and Robin Horton (Cambridge: Cambridge University Press, 1983), 41–82; here, 54.

13. Peter Ekeh, "The Public Realm and Public Finance in Africa," in *African Perspectives on Development*, ed. Ulf Himmelstrand, Kabiru Kinyanjui, and Edward Mburugu (London: James Currey, 1994), 234–248; Peter Ekeh, "Social Anthropology and the Two Contrasting Uses of Tribalism in Africa," *Comparative Studies in Society and History* 32, no. 4 (1990): 660–700; Peter Ekeh; "Colonialism and the Two Publics in Africa: A Theoretical Statement," *Comparative Studies in Society and History* 17, no. 1 (1975): 91–112.

14. This definition was inspired by Michael Onyebuchi Eze, "What is African Communitarianism? Against Consensus as a Regulative Ideal," *South African Journal of Philosophy* 27, no. 4 (2008): 386–399.

15. Marc Stier, "Reconciling Liberalism and Communitarianism," paper presented at the Annual Meeting of the *American Political Science Association*, Washington, DC, August 31–September 3, 2000. Note that my notion of agonistic communitarianism is quite different from his. Stier's notion is based on the usefulness of conflicts between different conception of goods and schemes of virtues, between liberalism and communitarianism. Mine, as I will latter demonstrate, is about the existence of the ethos of individualism within the framework of communitarianism in Kalabari ethical consciousness.

16. Reinhold Niebuhr, *Love and Justice* (quoted in George W. Forell, *Christian Social Teachings: A Reader in Christian Social Ethics From the Bible to the Present*, 2nd ed., rev. and ed. James M. Childs [Minneapolis: Fortress Press, 2013], 259).

17. Niebuhr, *Love and Justice* (quoted in Forell, *Christian Social Teachings*, 259).

18. Niebuhr, *Love and Justice* (quoted in Forell, *Christian Social Teachings*, 259).

19. Robert Wright, *Nonzero: The Logic of Human Destiny* (New York: Vintage Books, 2001).

20. The terms "cooperative intimacy" and "competitive intimacy" came from my Gambian friend, Mariama Khan. I have deployed them here in ways that differ somewhat from her usage.

21. J. Budziszewki, *The Revenge of Conscience: Politics and the Fall of Man* (Dallas: Spence Publishing Company, 1999), 121–124. This paragraph was inspired by these pages.

22. See Nimi Wariboko, *The Mind of African Strategists: A Study of Kalabari Management Practice* (Madison, NJ: Fairleigh Dickenson University Press, 1997).

23. Michael J. Sandel, *Justice: What Is the Right Thing to Do?* (New York: Farrar, Straus and Giroux, 2009) gave me the language to express my ideas here.

24. Paul Tillich, *Theology of Peace*, edited by Ronald Stone (Louisville: Westminster John Knox Press, 1990), 94; I have borrowed language from this book to articulate my understanding of individualism in precolonial Kalabari.

25. Advocates of African communitarianism have the dream of transcendence. This is the dream of transcendence of acting and thinking from a non-individual location, of an individual engagement with fellow community members without the original sin of self-interest, self-preference, partiality, that communitarians hold fast.

26. Kwame Gyekye, *An Essay on African Philosophical Thought: The Akan Conceptual Scheme* (Cambridge: Cambridge University Press, 1987), 145–146, 158–161.

27. Gyekye, *An Essay on African Philosophical Thought*, 160–161, 162.

28. Toni Morrison, *The Source of Self-Regard: Selected Essays, Speeches, and Meditations* (New York: Alfred A. Knopf, 2019), 335. I have implanted her words from a different context to make my point here.

29. W. E. B. Du Bois, *The Souls of Black Folks* (New York: Penguin, 1989), 5.

30. See Nimi Wariboko, "Colonialism, Christianity, and Personhood," in *Blackwell Companion to African History*, ed. Charles Ambler, William A. Worger, and Nwando Achebe (Hoboken, NJ: John Wiley and Sons, 2019): 59–76.

31. Ekeh, "Social Anthropology and the Two Contrasting Uses" and "Colonialism and the Two Publics."

32. Wariboko, *Ethics and Society in Nigeria*, 19–34.

33. Agamben, *Homo Sacer*, 28.

34. Carl Schmitt, *The Nomos of the Earth in International Law of the Jus Publicum Europaeum* (New York: Telos Press, 2003), 95.

35. This section is culled from Wariboko, *Principle of Excellence*, x, 82–88, 135, 181–182.

36. See Wariboko, *Depth and Destiny of Work*, 39–49.

37. Horton, "A Hundred Years of Change in Kalabari Religion," 192–211.

38. Ford, *The Lure of God*, 63–66, 71–79, 100–101.

39. Paul Tillich, *Systematic Theology*, vol. 2 (Chicago: University of Chicago Press, 1957), 80, 119, 133–137, 150–153.

40. *Fiyeteboye* can be likened to fate, though they are not exactly equivalent. The word *fate* derives from Latin *fari*, meaning "to speak." See Mary Daly, *Pure Lust: Elemental Feminist Philosophy* (London: The Women's Press, 1984), 95.

41. Catherine Keller, *On the Mystery: Discerning God in Process* (Minneapolis: Fortress Press, 2008), 64.

42. In Kalabari, parents, grandparents, or elders give names to their children to capture their "essences" or the imagined potentialities that need to be actualized. Names are meant to be a well-thought-out title of the life-script of the person.

43. This is the set of possibilities agreed with God before birth.

44. Paul L. Lehman, *Ethics in a Christian Context* (Eugene, OR: Wipf and Stock Publishers, 1998), 23–25.

45. For brilliant analyses of eros as used in the West see Marc Gafni, *The Mystery of Love* (New York: Atria Books, 2003), and Alexander C. Irwin, *Eros Toward the World: Paul Tillich and the Theology of the Erotic* (Philadelphia: Fortress Press, 1991).

46. *Gboloma-a* is the negative form of *gboloma.*

47. See Wariboko, *Depth and Destiny of Work*, chaps. 2, 4; see also Gafni, *Mystery of Love*, xi–xv, 3–77.

48. Sen, *Development as Freedom.*

49. Ernest Bloch, *The Principle of Hope*, vols. 1–3, translated by Neville Plaice, Stephen Plaice, and Paul Knight (Cambridge, MA: MIT Press, 1995). It is my paraphrase of his argument about the essential nature of the future in constituting human beings.

50. Benedict Spinoza, *Ethics*, trans. W. Halle White (London: Oxford University Press, 1927), part IV, prop xxii, 97.

51. Paul Tillich, *The Courage to Be*, 2nd ed. (New Haven: Yale Nota Bene, 2001), 21.

Chapter 5

1. Sen, *Development as Freedom.*

2. Robert Cummings Neville, *Metaphysics of Goodness: Harmony and Form, Beauty and Art, Obligation and Personhood, Flourishing and Civilization* (Albany: State University of New York Press, 2019), 310.

3. For a detailed discussion of excellence as a framework for understanding social ethics and economic development, see Wariboko, *Principle of Excellence.* A good portion of this chapter is culled from this book.

4. Tim Flannery, *The Future Eaters: An Ecological History of the Australasian Land and People* (New York: Grove Press, 1994).

5. Rosi Braidotti, "Posthuman Affirmative Politics," in S. E. Wilmer and Audrone Žukauskaite, *Resisting Biopolitics: Philosophical, Political, and Performative Strategies* (New York: Routledge, 2016), 41.

6. This section is from Wariboko, *Ethics and Society in Nigeria*, 102–115.

7. Jacques Rancière, "In What Time Do We Live?" in *The State of Things*, ed. Marta Kuzma, Pablo Lafuente, and Peter Osborne (London: Koenig Books, 2013), 9–38; quote, 14.

8. Rancière, "In What Time Do We Live?," 11.

9. Rancière, "In What Time Do We Live?," 11, 12.

10. "Portraits are the image of the image in general. A portrait touches, or else it is only an identification photo, a descriptive record, not an image. What touches is something that is borne to the surface out of an intimacy. But here the portrait is only an example. Every image is in some way a 'portrait,' not in that it would reproduce the traits of a person, but in that it pulls and *draws* (this is the semantic and etymological sense of the word), in that it *extracts* something, an intimacy, a force. And, to extract it, it subtracts or removes it from homogeneity, it distracts it from it, distinguishes it, detaches it, and casts it forth. It throws it in front of us, and this throwing [*jet*], this projection, makes its mark, its very trait and its *stigma*: its tracing, its line, its style, its incision, its scar; its signature, all of this at once." Jean-Luc Nancy, *The Ground of the Image*, trans. Jeff Fort (New York: Fordham University Press, 2005), 4; italics and brackets in the original.

11. I wish to thank Ruth Marshall for suggesting that I clarify the distinction between the citizen and the subject.

12. Giorgio Agamben, *The Signature of All Things: On Method*, trans. Luca D'Isanto with Kevin Attell (New York: Zone Books, 2009), 49.

13. Agamben, *Signature of all Things*, 55–57.

14. Franz Kafka, "He: Notes from the Year 1920," 276–277, quoted in Arendt, *Between Past and Future*, 7. Arendt slightly amended the translation from the German.

15. Arendt, *Between Past and Future*, 11.

16. Arendt, *Between Past and Future*, 11.

17. Alain Badiou with Fabien Tarby, *Philosophy and Event*, trans. Louise Burchill (Malden, MA: Polity Press, 2013), 13.

18. Peter Rollins, *Insurrection: To Believe Is Human, to Doubt Is Human* (New York: Howard Books, 2011).

19. Badiou with Tarby, *Philosophy and Event*, 12–13.

20. Badiou with Tarby, *Philosophy and Event*, 146.

21. Badiou with Tarby, *Philosophy and Event*, 147; italics in the original.

22. This section is derived from Wariboko, *Principle of Excellence*, 182–206.

23. Victor Zuckerkandl, *Sound and Symbol*, vol. 1, *Music and the External World*, trans. Willard Trask (Princeton, NJ: Princeton University Press, 1969), 252.

24. Zuckerkandl, *Sound and Symbol*, 252.

25. Zuckerkandl, *Sound and Symbol*, 253.
26. Zuckerkandl, *Sound and Symbol*, 252.
27. Zuckerkandl, *Sound and Symbol*, 12
28. Zuckerkandl, *Sound and Symbol*, 15
29. For the generation of melody and rhythms, this is what Zuckerkandl (*Sound and Symbol*, 248) says:

A tone sounding on uninterruptedly is not yet melody and not yet rhythm. Strictly speaking, melody begins not with the first tone but with the first step from tone to tone. In the same way, rhythm is not born with the first sounding of a tone but with the first interruption and the sounding of a new tone (or the new sounding of the same tone).

30. Here I am writing under the inspiration of Zuckerkandl's analysis of tones. See his *Sound and Symbol*, 20.
31. This is a reversal of Tillich's thought in *Systematic Theology*, vol. 2, 25.
32. Tillich, *Systematic Theology*, vol. 1, 191.
33. Wright, *Nonzero*, 48–51.
34. Robert E. Ulanowicz, "Ecosystem Dynamics: A Natural Middle," *Theology and Science* 2, no. 2 (2004): 231–253; Robert E. Ulanowicz, "Emergence, Naturally!" *Zygon* 42, no. 4 (2007): 945–960; and Robert E. Ulanowicz, "Ecology, a Dialog between the Quick and the Dead," *Emergence* 4, no. 1/2 (2002): 34–52.
35. Fernand Braudel, *Civilization and Capitalism, 15th–18th Century*, vol. 1, *The Structures of Everyday Life* (New York: Harper Row, 1981), 401, quoted in Wright, *Nonzero*, 45.
36. Wright, *Nonzero*, 48.
37. Ulanowicz, "Ecology," 114–115.
38. Tillich, *Systematic Theology*, vol. 1, 241.
39. Wariboko, *Depth and Destiny of Work*, 238–239.
40. See Catherine Keller, *Face of the Deep: A Theology of Becoming* (London: Routledge, 2003), 205–208, 231–232.
41. Keller, *Face of the Deep*, 232; italics in the original.
42. Jürgen Moltmann, *God in Creation: A New Theology of Creation and the Spirit of God* (Minneapolis: Fortress Press, 1993), 266; italics in the original.
43. Michael Hardt and Antonio Negri, *Multitude: War and Democracy in the Age of Empire* (New York: The Penguin Press, 2004), xiv–xv, 197, 225.
44. 45. Hardt and Negri, *Multitude*, 348–351; Michael Hardt and Antonio Negri, *Empire* (Cambridge, MA: Harvard University Press, 2001), 357–359.
46. Ulanowicz, "Emergence, Naturally!" 945–960. The absence of laws should not be taken to mean that there are no orders in social interactions that characterize a society. We need only remove our glance from laws into what biologist Ulanowicz calls *configurative processes*. He defined a process as "an interaction of random events upon a configuration of constraints that result in a nonrandom but indeterminate outcome." See page 950 for quote.

47. In 2008 researchers at Microsoft suggested that there may be a social-connectivity constant for humanity of about seven, precisely 6.6 steps—it takes about seven steps to link everybody up in a community. That is, any two persons are linked by an average of six to seven acquaintances. See Jure Leskovec and Eric Horvitz, "Planetary-Scale View on a Large Instant-Messaging Network," paper presented at International World Wide Web Conference, April 21–25, 2008, Beijing. It should be noted that social connectivity is not identical with a constant for speed of information flow that will be a function of such factors as population size, communication technology, and the freedom of information movement and its related social practices.

48. In a *configuration process* as the clearing that is excellence, one should expect unique and not repeatable events and what might be called "miracles." Any system such as that of a social system or ecosystem having thousands and millions of distinguishable elements will come up with a number of possible combinations that will exceed Walter Elsasser's limit on reality. And thus there will be singular events that are unique, never again to be repeated, though there is an immense number of stochastic events. Mechanical laws or law-like explanations are not usually helpful in these cases, as they are overwhelmed by "variety and combinatorics," to use Ulanowicz's words. "In complex systems so many combinations become possible that a multiplicity of configurations is always available to satisfy any set of parameters in the applicable laws. Laws continue to constrain what can happen, but they become insufficient to determine which configurations eventually prevail." See Ulanowicz, "Emergence, Naturally!" 950.

49. This nature appears akin to life as conceived by Colin E. Gunton, *Father, Son and Holy Spirit: Toward a Fully Trinitarian Theology* (London: T & T Clark, 2003), 134–137. See also Wolfhart Pannenberg, "The God of Hope," in *Basic Questions in Theology: Collected Essays, Vol. 2* (London: SCM Press, 1971), 234–249.

50. Alternatively, one can argue that money's being is not in its becoming. Because it refuses to pass away (when the imagined future arrives, the value of the asset would still be based on expectations of what it would yet be in a further imagined future), its being is in its coming. Value as conceived in valuation techniques of assets is always on the move and coming toward the asset owner. As the coming value, the present and past are set in the light of the future. Value (the present value of assets as calculated by the discounted cash flow method) "flows" out of the future into the present. It has the future in its being, to speak with tongue in cheek. For a theological play on the words "coming" and "becoming" by Jürgen Moltmann, see his *The Coming of God: Christian Eschatology*, trans. Margaret Kohl (Minneapolis: Fortress Press, 1996), 13, 23–24.

51. Philip Goodchild, "Capital and Kingdom: An Eschatological Ontology," in *Theology and the Political: The New Debate*, ed. Creston Davies, John Milbank, and Slavoj Žižek (Durham: Duke University Press: 2005), 143.

52. James Buchan, *Frozen Desire: The Meaning of Money* (New York: Welcome Rain Publishers, 2001), 61.

53. Ernst Bloch, *The Principle of Hope*, vols. 1–3, trans. Neville Plaice, Stephen Plaice, and Paul Knight (Cambridge, MA: MIT Press, 1954–1959), 196–197, 206.

54. Wariboko, *Depth and Destiny of Work*, 4–14, 233–238.

55. I have reworked Albino Barrera's phrasing for my purpose here. See his *God and the Evil of Scarcity: Moral Foundations of Economic Agency* (South Bend, IN: University of Notre Dame Press, 2005), 219.

56. Gibson Winter, *Community and Spiritual Transformation: Religion and Politics in a Communal Age* (New York: Crossroad Publishing Company, 1989), 104.

57. See Nimi Wariboko, *God and Money: A Theology of Money in a Globalizing World* (Lanham: Lexington Books, 2008).

58. My analysis is drawn from Paul Tillich, *Love, Power, and Justice: Ontological Analyses and Ethical Applications* (London: Oxford University Press, 1954), 25–34, 116.

59. See Wariboko, *God and Money*, chapter 4.

60. This is a Tillichian concept that refers to "power," "substance," or "principium vitae." For a discussion of this see Sylvester I. Ihuoma, *Paul Tillich's Theology of Culture in Dialogue with African Theology: A Contextual Analysis* (Munster: LIT, 2004), 63–102.

61. Ihuoma, *Paul Tillich's Theology*, 99–100.

Chapter 6

1. Gabriel Okara, *The Voice* (New York: Africana Publishing Company, 1964).

2. Okara, *Voice*, 127.

3. Thomas Piketty, *Capital and Ideology* (Cambridge, MA: Belknap Press, 2020), 7, inspired these thoughts.

4. Agamben, *Signature of All Things*.

5. Agamben, *Signature of All Things*, 35, 42, 64.

6. Agamben, *Signature of All Things*, 35, 42, 68.

7. Walter Benjamin, *The Arcades Project*, trans. Howard Eiland and Kevin McLaughlin (Cambridge, MA: Belknap Press, 1982), 462–463.

8. Note that it is the forward-moving impulse toward an ideal that we might predict, and not necessarily the ideal.

9. MC Edo Pikin, "MC EDO PIKIN—The Diffrence Betweeen VORTS CARD & PVC," *Mc Edopikin*, February 22, 2019, video, 1:00, www.youtube.com/watch?v= hMJLK4ZcHdc.

10. Moltmann, *Coming of God*, 23–28.

11. MC Edo Pikin, "MC EDO PIKIN—The Difference Between Artistes & Musicians," *Mc Edopikin*, February 19, 2019, video, 1:00, www.youtube.com/watch?v=BZYUkYDdPJc.

12. Webb Keane, *Ethical Life: Its Natural and Social Histories* (Princeton, NJ: Princeton University Press, 2015), 27–32, inspired this thought.

13. MC Edo Pikin, "MC Edo Pikin—The Difference Between Girl & Babe," *Mc Edopikin*, January 25, 2019, video, 0:59, www.youtube.com/watch?v=k45wAxRcHa8.

14. MC Edo Pikin, "Mc Edo Pikin—The Difference Between a Preacher & a Pastor (ft Mc Da Saint)," *Mc Edopikin*, January 28, 2020, video, 2:33, www.youtube.com/watch?v=Ph5ko_4n-Tc.

15. Martha C. Nussbaum, *Love's Knowledge: Essays on Philosophy and Literature* (New York: Oxford University Press, 1990), 380–381.

16. Eviatar Zerubavel, *Hidden Rhythms: Schedules and Calendars in Social Life* (Berkeley: University of California Press, 1981), 1–30.

17. Emergence, as I understand it, reminds me of Paul Tillich's concept of the *kairos* and "the underivable." See his *Systematic Theology*, vol. 3 (Chicago: University of Chicago Press, 1963), 324.

18. Žižek, *Less than Nothing*, 166

19. Žižek, *Less than Nothing*, 166.

20. Tillich, *Love, Power and Justice*, 33, 116.

21. Žižek, *Sublime Object of Ideology*, xx; italics in the original. See also Slavoj Žižek, *For They Know Not What They Do: Enjoyment as a Political Factor* (London: Verso, 2008), 266–267.

22. There is a multidisciplinary methodology to help us retrieve resources from the African past to help us tackle today's pressing social-economic problems. We can retrieve information from scholarly publications, interviewing Africans who have knowledge of the past and the present, observations, conducting ethnographic studies, and doing professional historical analyses of the past. In addition, let me state the methodology the eminent African historian Toyin Falola has developed for precisely dealing with this issue: *ritual archive*. According to Falola, ritual archive represents

> the conglomeration of words as well as texts, ideas, symbols, shrines, images, performances, and indeed objects that document as well as speak to those religious experiences and practices that allow us to understand the African world through various bodies of philosophies, literatures, languages, histories and much more. By implication, ritual archives are huge, unbounded in scale and scope, storing tremendous amounts of data on both natural and supernatural agents, ancestors, gods, good and bad witches, life, death, festivals, and the interactions between the spiritual realms and earth-based human beings. To a large extent, ritual archives constitute and shape knowledge about the

> visible and invisible world (or what I refer to as the "non-world"), coupled with forces that breathe and are breathless, as well as secular and non-secular, with destinies, and within cities, kingships, medicine, environment, sciences, and technologies. Above all, they contain shelves on sacrifices and shrines, names, places, incantations, invocations, and the entire cosmos of all the deities and their living subjects among human and nonhuman species. (Toyin Falola, "Ritual Archives," in *The Palgrave Handbook of African Social Ethics*, edited by Nimi Wariboko and Toyin Falola, 473–497 (Cham, Switzerland, Palgrave Macmillan, 2020); quote, 476)

The use of ritual archives in philosophy necessarily demands transdisciplinarity as it decries the fragmentation of (ritual) knowledge across unnecessary disciplinary boundaries in the study of African societies. I will first turn to Falola to shed more light on the character of the demand. Falola writes,

> Ritual archives tell us that we must review and question our externally derived approaches and the limitations of the methodologies we deploy. Western-derived disciplines (such as Religious Studies, History, and Philosophy as subjects of the Humanities) have carefully fragmented ritual archives, but it is time for all those disciplines to combine to provide an understanding of the centers of indigenous epistemologies, to unify their ontologies, and convert them to theories that will be treated as universal. To take an example of how ritual archives can work, if Ifalogy (studies of Yorùbá divination system) had been created as a discipline and department fifty years ago, it could have enabled hundreds of scholars to learn and work across disciplines, and they probably would have decoded its epistemology by now and used it to create other forms of knowledge. They would have uncovered hidden dimensions of the Yorùbá *endogenius* [local African ideas, perspectives, narratives, and talents], which has sustained and guided the people since their genesis (476).

23. Wariboko, *Mind of African Strategists.*

24. For some of the excellent ideas and entrepreneurial contexts that led to the creation of corporate and business organizational styles, see Nimi Wariboko, "A Theory of the Canoe House Corporation," *African Economic History* 26 (1998): 141–172.

25. Wariboko, *Mind of African Strategists*, 116–117.

26. Chinua Achebe, "Nigeria's Promise, Africa's Hope," Op-ed Essay, *New York Times*, January 15, 2011.

Bibliography

Achebe, Chinua. "Nigeria's Promise, Africa's Hope." Op-ed Essay, *New York Times*, January 15, 2011.

Agamben, Giorgio. *Homo Sacer: Sovereign Power and Bare Life*. Translated by Daniel Heller-Roazen. Stanford, CA: Stanford University Press, 1998.

———. *Infancy and History: On the Destruction of Experience*. London: Verso, 2007.

———. *The Man without Content*. Translated by Georgia Albert. Stanford, CA: Stanford University Press, 1999.

———. *Potentialities: Collected Essays in Philosophy*. Edited and translated by Daniel Heller-Roazen. Stanford: Stanford University Press, 1999.

———. *The Signature of All Things: On Method*. Translated by Luca D'Isanto with Kevin Attell. New York: Zone Books, 2009.

———. *The Use of Bodies*. Translated Adam Kotsko. Stanford, CA: Stanford University Press, 2015.

Arendt, Hannah. *Between Past and Future*. New York: Penguin, 1968.

———. *The Human Condition*. Chicago: University of Chicago Press, 1958.

———. *The Life of the Mind*. Vol. 1, *Thinking*. San Diego: Harcourt, 1978.

———. *The Life of the Mind*. Vol. 2, *Willing*. San Diego: Harcourt, 1978.

Aristotle. *Metaphysics*. Edited by Richard McKeon. New York: Random House, 1941.

Badiou, Alain. *Conditions*. Translated by Steven Corcoran. London: Continuum International Publishing Group, 2008.

———. *Logics of Worlds: Being and Event II*. Translated by Alberto Toscano. London: Continuum International Publishing Group, 2009.

Badiou, Alain, with Fabien Tarby. *Philosophy and Event*. Translated by Louise Burchill. Malden, MA: Polity Press, 2013.

Barrera, Albino. *God and the Evil of Scarcity: Moral Foundations of Economic Agency*. South Bend, IN: University of Notre Dame Press, 2005.

Beiner, Ronald. *Hannah Arendt: Lectures on Kant's Political Philosophy*. Chicago: University of Chicago Press, 1992.

Benjamin, Walter. *The Arcades Project*. Translated by Howard Eiland and Kevin McLaughlin. Cambridge, MA: Belknap Press, 1982.

———. "Notes Toward a Work on the Category of Justice." Translated by Peter Fenves. In Peter Fenves, *The Messianic Reduction: Walter Benjamin and the Shape of Time*, 257. Stanford, CA: Stanford University Press, 2011.

Bloch, Ernst. *The Principle of Hope*, vols. 1–3. Translated by Neville Plaice, Stephen Plaice, and Paul Knight. Cambridge, MA: MIT Press, 1954–1959.

Borges, Jorge Luis. "The Secret Miracle." In *Ficciones*, translated by Anthony Kerrigan. New York: Grove Press, 1962.

Braidotti, Rosi. "Posthuman Affirmative Politics." In *Resisting Biopolitics: Philosophical, Political, and Performative Strategies*, edited by S. E. Wilmer and Audrone Žukauskaite, 30–56. New York: Routledge, 2016.

Braudel, Fernand. *Civilization and Capitalism, 15th–18th Century*. Vol. 1, *The Structures of Everyday Life*. New York: Harper & Row, 1981.

Brennan, Geoffrey, and Philip Pettit. *The Economy of Esteem: An Essay on Civil and Political Society*. Oxford: Oxford University Press, 2004.

Buchan, James. *Frozen Desire: The Meaning of Money*. New York: Welcome Rain Publishers, 2001.

Budziszewki, J. *The Revenge of Conscience: Politics and the Fall of Man*. Dallas: Spence Publishing Company, 1999.

Butler, Judith. *Bodies that Matter: On the Discursive Limits of "Sex."* New York: Routledge, 2011.

Caputo, John D., and Gianni Vattimo. *After the Death of God*. Edited by Jeffrey W. Robbins. New York: Columbia University Press, 2007.

Caputo, John. *The Weakness of God: A Theology of Event*. Bloomington: Indiana University Press, 2006.

Copjec, Joan. *Imagine There's No Woman: Ethics and Sublimation*. Cambridge, MA: MIT Press, 2002.

Csikszentmihalyi, Mihaly. *Flow: The Psychology of Optimal Experience*. New York: HarperCollins, 1990.

Daly, Mary. *Pure Lust: Elemental Feminist Philosophy*. London: The Women's Press, 1984.

Dardot, Pierre, and Christian Laval. *The New Way of the World: On Neoliberal Society*. London: Verso, 2014.

Du Bois, W. E. B. *The Souls of Black Folks*. New York: Penguin, 1989.

Ekeh, Peter. "Colonialism and the Two Publics in Africa: A Theoretical Statement." *Comparative Studies in Society and History* 17, no. 1 (1975): 91–112.

———. "The Public Realm and Public Finance in Africa." In *African Perspectives on Development*, edited by Ulf Himmelstrand, Kabiru Kinyanjui, and Edward Mburugu, 234–258. London: James Currey, 1994.

———. "Social Anthropology and the Two Contrasting Uses of Tribalism in Africa." *Comparative Studies in Society and History* 32, no. 4 (1990): 660–700.

Eliade, Mircea. *The Sacred and the Profane: The Nature of Religion*. New York: Harcourt, 1957.

Eze, Michael Onyebuchi. "What is African Communitarianism? Against Consensus as a Regulative Ideal." *South African Journal of Philosophy* 27, no. 4 (2008): 386–399.

Falola, Toyin. "Ritual Archives." In *The Palgrave Handbook of African Social Ethics*, edited by Nimi Wariboko and Toyin Falola, 473–497. London: Palgrave Macmillan, 2020.

Fanon, Frantz. *The Wretched of the Earth*. New York: Grove, 1968.

Fenn, Richard. "Sociology and Religion: Searching for the Sacred." In *The Oxford Handbook of Religion and Science*, edited by Philip Clayton and Zachary Simpson, 253–270. Oxford: Oxford University Press, 2006.

Fenves, Peter. *The Messianic Reduction: Walter Benjamin and the Shape of Time*. Stanford, CA: Stanford University Press, 2011.

Fink, Bruce. *The Lacanian Subject: Between Language and Jouissance*. Princeton, NJ: Princeton University Press, 1995.

Flannery, Tim. *The Future Eaters: An Ecological History of the Australasian Land and People*. New York: Grove Press, 1994.

Flynn, Sean Masaki. *Economics for Dummies*. Hoboken, NJ: Wiley Publishing, 2005.

Franz, Michael. "Editor's Introduction." In Eric Voegelin, *The Collected Works of Eric Voegelin*. Vol. 17, *Order and History*, vol. 4, *The Ecumenic Age*, 1–28. Columbia: University of Missouri Press, 2000.

Ford, Lewis S. *The Lure of God: A Biblical Background for Process Theism*. Philadelphia: Fotress Press, 1978.

Forell, George W. *Christian Social Teachings: A Reader in Christian Social Ethics from the Bible to the Present*, 2nd ed. Revised and edited by James M. Childs. Minneapolis: Fortress Press, 2013.

Gafni, Marc. *The Mystery of Love*. New York: Atria Books, 2003.

Goodchild, Philip. "Capital and Kingdom: An Eschatological Ontology." In *Theology and the Political: The New Debate*, edited by Creston Davies, John Milbank, and Slavoj Žižek, 127–152. Durham, NC: Duke University Press: 2005.

Gourgouris, Stathis. *Lessons in Secular Criticism*. New York: Fordham University Press, 2013.

Gunton, Colin E. *Father, Son and Holy Spirit: Toward a Fully Trinitarian Theology*. London: T & T Clark, 2003.

Gyekye, Kwame. *An Essay on African Philosophical Thought: The Akan Conceptual Scheme*. Cambridge: Cambridge University Press, 1987.

Hägglund, Martin. *Dying for Time: Proust, Woolf, Nabokov*. Cambridge, MA: Harvard University Press, 2012.

———. *Radical Atheism: Derrida and the Time of Life*. Stanford, CA: Stanford University Press, 2008.

———. *This Life: Secular Faith and Spiritual Faith*. New York: Pantheon Books, 2019.

Hardt, Michael, and Antonio Negri. *Empire*. Cambridge, MA: Harvard University Press, 2001.

———. *Multitude: War and Democracy in the Age of Empire*. New York: The Penguin Press, 2004.

Hodge, Joanna. "Ethics and Time: Levinas between Kant and Husserl." *Diacritics* 32, no. 3-4 (2002): 107–134.

Horton, Robin. "A Hundred Years of Change in Kalabari Religion." In *Black Africa: Its People and Their Cultures Today*, edited by John Middleton, 192–211. New York: Macmillan, 1971.

———. *Kalabari Sculpture*. Lagos: Department of Antiquities, Federal Republic of Nigeria, 1965.

———. "The Kalabari Worldview: An Outline and Interpretation." *Africa* 32, no. 3 (1962): 197–219.

———. "Social Psychologies: African and Western." In *Oedipus and Job in West Africa*, edited by M. Fortes and Robin Horton, 41–82. Cambridge: Cambridge University Press, 1983.

Ihuoma, Sylvester I. *Paul Tillich's Theology of Culture in Dialogue with African Theology: A Contextual Analysis*. Munster: LIT, 2004.

Irwin, Alexander C. *Eros Toward the World: Paul Tillich and the Theology of the Erotic*. Philadelphia: Fortress Press, 1991.

Kafka, Franz. "The City Coat of Arms." In *The Great Wall of China: Stories and Reflections*, translated by Willa Muir and Edwin Muir. New York: Schocken Books, 1946.

———. "He: Notes from the Year 1920." In *The Great Wall of China: Stories and Reflections*, translated by Willa Muir and Edwin Muir. New York: Schocken Books, 1946.

Keane, Webb. *Ethical Life: Its Natural and Social Histories*. Princeton, NJ: Princeton University Press, 2015.

Keller, Catherine. *Face of the Deep: A Theology of Becoming*. London: Routledge, 2003.

———. *On the Mystery: Discerning God in Process*. Minneapolis: Fortress Press, 2008.

Kierkegaard, Søren. *Either/Or*. Translated by H. Hong and E. Hong. Princeton: Princeton University Press, 1987.

Kirkeby, Ole Fogh. *Management Philosophy: A Radical Normative Perspective*. Berlin: Springer, 2000.

Kirkpatrick, Kate. *Sartre on Sin: Between Being and Nothingness*. Oxford: Oxford University Press, 2017.

Lacan, Jacques. *Écrits: A Selection*. Translated by Alan Sheridan. London: Tavistock Publications, 1977.

———. *Seminar II: The Ego in Freud's Theory and in the Technique of Psychoanalysis*. Edited by J. A. Miller, translated by S. Tomaselli. New York: Norton, 1988.

Lehman, Paul L. *Ethics in a Christian Context*. Eugene, OR: Wipf and Stock Publishers, 1998.

Leskovec, Jure, and Eric Horvitz. "Planetary-Scale View on a Large Instant-Messaging Network." Paper presented at International World Wide Web Conference, April 21–25, 2008, Beijing.

Littlechild, Stephen C. "Three Types of Market Process." In *Economic as a Process: Essays in the New Institutional Economics*, 27–39. New York: Cambridge University Press, 1986.

Macintyre, Alasdair. *Ethics in the Conflicts of Modernity: An Essay on Desire, Practical Reasoning, and Narrative*. Cambridge: Cambridge University Press, 2016.

Magesa, Laurenti. *African Religion: The Moral Traditions of Abundant Life*. Maryknoll, NY: Orbis Book, 1997.

Marx, Karl. *Capital: A Critique of Political Economy*, vol. 1. Translated by Ben Fowkes. London: Penguin, 1976.

———. *Capital: A Critique of Political Economy*, vol. 2. Translated by David Fernbach. New York: Penguin, 1981.

———. *Grundrisse*. Translated by Martin Nicolaus. New York: Penguin Classics, 1973.

Mayeda, Graham. *Time, Space and Ethics in the Philosophy of Watsuji Tetsurō, Kuki Shūzō, and Martin Heidegger*. New York: Routledge, 2006.

McGowan, Todd. *Capitalism and Desire: The Psychic Cost of Free Markets*. New York: Columbia University Press, 2016.

Moltmann, Jürgen. *The Coming of God: Christian Eschatology*. Translated by Margaret Kohl. Minneapolis: Fortress Press, 1996.

———. *God in Creation: A New Theology of Creation and the Spirit of God*. Minneapolis: Fortress Press, 1993.

Morrison, Toni. *The Source of Self-Regard: Selected Essays, Speeches, and Meditations*. New York: Alfred A. Knopf, 2019.

Mosès, Stéphane. *The Angel of History: Rosenzweig, Benjamin, and Scholem*. Translated by Barbara Harshav. Stanford, CA: Stanford University Press, 2009.

Moulakis, Athanasios. "Editor's Introduction." In Eric Voegelin, *The Collected Works of Eric Voegelin*. Vol. 15, *Order and History*, vol. 2, *The World of the Polis*, 1–14. Columbia: University of Missouri Press, 2000.

Nancy, Jean-Luc. *The Ground of the Image*. Translated by Jeff Fort. New York: Fordham University Press, 2005.

———. *Inoperative Community*. Translated by Peter Connor, Lisa Garbus, Michael Holland, and Simona Sawhney, foreword by Christopher Fynsk. Minneapolis: University of Minnesota Press, 1991.

Neville, Robert Cummings. *Eternity and Time's Flow*. Albany: State University of New York Press, 1993.

———. *Existence: Philosophical Theology*, vol. 2. Albany: State University of New York Press, 2014.

———. *Metaphysics of Goodness: Harmony and Form, Beauty and Art, Obligation and Personhood, Flourishing and Civilization*. Albany: State University of New York Press, 2019.

———. *Ultimates: Philosophical Theology*, vol. 1. Albany: State University of New York Press, 2013.

Niebuhr, Reinhold. *Love and Justice: Selections from the Shorter Writings of Reinhold Niebuhr.* Edited by D. B. Robertson. Louisville, KY: Westminster/John Knox Press, 1957.

Nishitani, Keiji. *Religion and Nothingness*. Translated with introduction by Jam Van Bragt. Berkeley: University of California Press, 1982.

Nussbaum, Martha C. *Love's Knowledge: Essays on Philosophy and Literature*. New York: Oxford University Press, 1990.

Nussbaum, Martha. *Poetic Justice: The Literary Imagination and Public Life*. Boston: Beacon, 1995.

Nwaezigwe, Nwankwo T. "Ikenga Cultic Symbol and Structural Representation of Igbo Enterprise." *Journal of Tourism and Heritage Studies* 2, no. 1 (2013): 2–13.

Nzegwu, Nkiru. "Art and Community: A Social Conception of Beauty and Individuality." In *A Companion of African Philosophy*, edited by Kwasi Wirendu, 415–424. Malden, MA: Blackwell, 2004.

Ochonu, Moses E. "Introduction: Toward African Entrepreneurship and Business History." In *Entrepreneurship in Africa: A History Approach*, edited by Moses E. Ochonu, 1–28. Bloomington: Indiana University Press, 2018.

Okara, Gabriel. *The Voice*. New York: Africana Publishing Company, 1964.

Pannenberg, Wolfhart. *Basic Questions in Theology: Collected Essays*, vol. 2. London: SCM Press, 1971.

Piketty, Thomas. *Capital and Ideology*. Cambridge, MA: Belknap Press, 2020.

Rancière, Jacques. "In What Time Do We Live?" In *The State of Things*, edited by Marta Kuzma, Pablo Lafuente, and Peter Osborne, 9–38. London: Koenig Books, 2013.

Rollins, Peter. *Insurrection: To Believe Is Human, to Doubt Is Human*. New York: Howard Books, 2011.

Rose, Marika. *A Theology of Failure: Žižek against Christian Innocence*. New York: Fordham University Press, 2019.

Samuelson, Paul. "Proof that Properly Anticipated Prices Fluctuate Randomly." *Industrial Management Review* 6 (Spring 1965): 41–49.

Sandel, Michael J. *Justice: What Is the Right Thing to Do?* New York: Farrar, Straus and Giroux, 2009.

Sartre, Jean-Paul. *Being and Nothingness: A Phenomenological Essay on Ontology*. New York: Washington Square Press, 1943.

Schelling, F. W. J. *Abyss of Freedom/Ages of the World* (Second Draft, 1813). Translated by Judith Norman. Ann Arbor: University of Michigan Press, 1997.

Schmitt, Carl. *The Nomos of the Earth in International Law of the Jus Publicum Europaeum*. New York: Telos Press, 2003.

Sen, Amartya. *Development as Freedom*. New York: Random House, 1999.
Spinoza, Benedict. *Ethics*. Translated by W. Halle White. London: Oxford University Press, 1927.
Stier, Marc. "Reconciling Liberalism and Communitarianism." Paper presented at the Annual Meeting of the American Political Science Association, Washington, DC, August 31–September 3, 2000.
Tasie, G. O. M. *Kali Kulu Kulu Kalika: A Check-List of Kalabari Drum Lore*. Supplement to the *Journal of Niger Delta Studies*. Jos, Nigeria: Ehindero Nig. Ltd., 1999.
Tetsurō, Watsuji. *Climate and Culture: A Philosophical Study*. Translated by Geoffrey Bownas. Tokyo: Monbushō, 1961.
Thurman, Howard. *Essential Writings*. Maryknoll: Orbis Books, 2006.
Tillich, Paul. *The Courage to Be*, 2nd ed. New Haven: Yale Nota Bene, 2001.
———. *Morality and Beyond*. Louisville, KY: Westminster John Knox Press, 1963.
———. *Love, Power and Justice: Ontological Analyses and Ethical Applications*. London: Oxford University Press, 1954.
———. *Systematic Theology*, vol. 1. Chicago: University of Chicago Press, 1951.
———. *Systematic Theology*, vol. 2. Chicago: University of Chicago Press, 1957.
———. *Systematic Theology*, vol. 3. Chicago: University of Chicago Press, 1963.
———. *Theology of Peace*. Edited by Ronald Stone. Louisville: Westminster John Knox Press, 1990.
Tomšič, Samo. *The Capitalist Unconscious: Marx and Lacan*. London: Verso, 2015.
Tutt, Daniel. "The Object of Proximity: The Ethics of Psychoanalysis in Žižek and Santner via Lacan." San Francisco Society for Lacanian Studies. Accessed August 25, 2020, lacan.org/tutt.
Ulanowicz, Robert E. "Ecology, a Dialog between the Quick and the Dead." *Emergence* 4, no. 1/2 (2002): 34–52.
———. "Ecosystem Dynamics: A Natural Middle." *Theology and Science* 2, no. 2 (2004): 231–253.
———. "Emergence, Naturally!" *Zygon* 42, no. 4 (2007): 945–960.
Vedder, Ben. "Heidegger on Desire." *Continental Philosophy Review* 31 (1998): 353–368.
Voegelin, Eric. *The Collected Works of Eric Voegelin*. Vol. 15, *Order and History*, vol. 2, *The World of the Polis*. Columbia: University of Missouri Press, 2000.
———. *The Collected Works of Eric Voegelin*. Vol. 17, *Order and History*, vol. 4, *The Ecumenic Age*. Columbia: University of Missouri Press, 2000.
———. *The Collected Works of Eric Voegelin*. Vol. 18, *Order and History*, vol. 5, *In Search of Order*. Columbia: University of Missouri Press, 2000.
Wariboko, Nimi. "Colonialism, Christianity, and Personhood." In *Blackwell Companion to African History*, edited by Charles Ambler, William A. Worger, and Nwando Achebe, 59–75. Hoboken, NJ: John Wiley and Sons, 2019.
———. *The Depth and Destiny of Work: An African Theological Interpretation*. Trenton, NJ: African World Press, 2008.

———. *Ethics and Society in Nigeria: Identity, History, and Political Theory*. Rochester, NY: University of Rochester Press, 2019.

———. *Ethics and Time: Ethos of Temporal Orientation in Politics and Religion of the Niger Delta*. Lanham, MD: Lexington Books, 2010.

———. *God and Money: A Theology of Money in a Globalizing World*. Lanham, MD: Lexington Books, 2008.

———. "Kalabari: A Study in Synthetic Ideal-Type." *Nordic Journal of African Studies* 8, no. 1 (1999): 80–93.

———. *The Mind of African Strategists: A Study of Kalabari Management Practice*. Madison, NJ: Fairleigh Dickenson University Press, 1997.

———. *The Pentecostal Principle: Ethical Methodology in New Spirit*. Grand Rapids, MI: Eerdmans, 2012.

———. *The Principle of Excellence: A Framework for Social Ethics*. Lanham, MD: Lexington Books, 2009.

———. *The Split Economy: Saint Paul Goes to Wall Street*. Albany: State University of New York Press, 2020.

———. *The Split God: Pentecostalism and Critical Theory*. Albany: State University of New York Press, 2018.

———. "A Theory of the Canoe House Corporation." *African Economic History* 26 (1998): 141–172.

Winter, Gibson. *Community and Spiritual Transformation: Religion and Politics in a Communal Age*. New York: Crossroad Publishing Company, 1989.

Wright, Robert. *Nonzero: The Logic of Human Destiny*. New York: Vintage Books, 2001.

Yannaras, Christos. *Person and Eros*. Translated by Normal Russell. Brookline, MA: Holy Cross Orthodox Press, 2007.

Zerubavel, Eviatar. *Hidden Rhythms: Schedules and Calendars in Social Life*. Berkeley: University of California Press, 1981.

Ziarek, Krzysztof. "The Ethos of History." In *What Happens to History: The Renewal of Ethics in Contemporary Thought*, ed. Howard Marchitello, 67–93. New York: Routledge, 2001.

Žižek, Slavoj. *Event: A Philosophical Journey through a Concept*. London: Penguin Books, 2014.

———. *For They Know Not What They Do: Enjoyment as a Political Factor*. London: Verso, 2008.

———. *Less than Nothing: Hegel and the Shadow of Dialectical Materialism*. London: Verso, 2012.

———. *The Sublime Object of Ideology*. London: Verso, 2008.

Žižek, Slavoj, and John Milbank. *The Monstrosity of Christ: Paradox or Dialectic?* Cambridge, MA: MIT Press, 2009.

Zuckerkandl, Victor. *Sound and Symbol*. Vol. 1, *Music and the External World*. Translated by Willard Trask. Princeton, NJ: Princeton University Press, 1969.

Index

www.ingramcontent.com/pod-product-compliance
Lightning Source LLC
LaVergne TN
LVHW040158080826
844660LV00001B/24

* 9 7 8 1 4 3 8 4 8 9 7 9 7 *